Poised for Partnership

Poised for Partnership

Deepening India–Japan Relations in the Asian Century

edited by
Rohan Mukherjee
and
Anthony Yazaki

OXFORD
UNIVERSITY PRESS

OXFORD
UNIVERSITY PRESS

Oxford University Press is a department of the University of Oxford.
It furthers the University's objective of excellence in research, scholarship,
and education by publishing worldwide. Oxford is a registered trademark of
Oxford University Press in the UK and in certain other countries

Published in India by
Oxford University Press
YMCA Library Building, 1 Jai Singh Road, New Delhi 110 001, India

ISBN-13: 978-0-19-946648-1
ISBN-10: 0-19-946648-3

Typeset in Adobe Garamond Pro 11/13
by The Graphics Solution, New Delhi 110 092
Printed in India by Rakmo Press, New Delhi 110 020

Contents

List of Figures and Tables   vii
Foreword by David M. Malone   ix
Acknowledgements   xiii
List of Abbreviations   xv

Introduction: The Historical Context   1
Rohan Mukherjee and Anthony Yazaki

Part I   ECONOMIC COOPERATION

1. Japan's Economic Recovery and Growing Economic
   Relations with India   35
   Shujiro Urata and Mitsuyo Ando

2. An Economic Partnership for Twenty-first Century Asia   68
   Devesh Kapur and Rohit Lamba

Part II   ENERGY AND CLIMATE CHANGE

3. Towards a Co-beneficial Energy Partnership   101
   Nobuo Tanaka and Anthony Yazaki

4. Energizing India–Japan Cooperation on Clean Energy
   and Climate Change   127
   Shyam Saran and Radhika Khosla

Part III   SECURITY AND DEFENCE

5. Japan–India Security Cooperation: In Pursuit of a
Sound and Pragmatic Partnership   153
Noboru Yamaguchi and Shutaro Sano

6. India–Japan Strategic Partnership: Steady Advance amidst
Enduring Constraints   179
C. Raja Mohan and Rishika Chauhan

Part IV   GLOBAL GOVERNANCE

7. Japan–India Relations from the Perspectives of
Global Governance and International Institutions   209
Shinichi Kitaoka and Naoko Kumagai

8. India and Japan: Partnering to Shape Multilateral
Rules and Institutions?   244
Waheguru Pal Singh Sidhu and Karthik Nachiappan

Conclusion: Overcoming a History of Missed Opportunities   270
Anthony Yazaki and Rohan Mukherjee

Index   289
Notes on Editors and Contributors   303

Figures and Tables

Figures

1.1 Japan's Population: Future Projections 38
1.2 Government Debt Situation in Selected Developed
Countries, 1995–2011 39
1.3 Importance of International Trade for Selected
Countries, 2013 40
1.4 Importance of Foreign Direct Investment for Selected
Countries, 2011 41
1.5 Japan's Exports to India, 1983–2012 42
1.6 Japan's Imports from India, 1980–2012 43
1.7 Japan's FDI in India, 1996–2013 45
1.8 Promising FDI Destinations for Japanese Firms
from 2004–14 (Per Cent of Respondents) 51

2.1 Percentage of Population That is of Working Age
(15–64) in Selected Countries, 1950–2040 72
2.2 Gross Capital Formation (Per Cent of GDP) in
India, China, and South Korea, 1960–2012 73
2.3 Percentage of Population That is of Old Age
(65 and Above) in Selected Countries, 1950–2040 74
2.4 Central Government Debt to GDP Ratio in Japan,
the US, and Germany, 2005–12 75
2.5 Indian Trade with Japan, 2009–10 to 2013–14 76
2.6 FDI by Japan (Assets), 2005–13 77
2.7 Delhi–Mumbai Industrial Corridor: Project Influence
Area 81
2.8 Share of GDP by Sector in India, 1982–3 to 2012–13 83
2.9 Addition to Railway Capacity (Route Km, '000s) in
India and China, 1990–2010 88

2.10 Investment in Railways (Per Cent of GDP) in India and China, 2005–12   88
2.11 Modal Share of Railways (Per Cent) in Domestic Freight for Selected Countries, 2011   89

Tables

1.1 Industry Composition of Japanese FDI Stock (Per Cent) in India at the End of 2013   46
1.2 Number of Affiliates of Japanese Firms in Asia, 2012   49
1.3 Comparison of Infrastructure among Selected Countries, 2013   54

2.1 Most Promising Countries for Overseas Business for Japanese Manufacturing Companies   71
2.2 FDI Inflows to India (Share of Top 10 Sources, Per Cent), 2000–14   78
2.3 Japanese Toshin Fund Exposure to Overseas Assets, 2014   78
2.4 Share of Employment by Sector in India (Per Cent), 1999–2000 to 2009–10   84
2.5 Selected Joint Ventures between Indian and Japanese Firms, 2005–15   93

Foreword

India and Japan have a long and varied history of engagement. Buddhism travelled to Japan from India through China and Korea and the two countries traded with each other directly and indirectly across various Asian seas and oceans. They were allied during the First World War, while they opposed each other during the Second World War, when India was still part of the British Empire. At the same time, an Indian force hostile to the colonial power, the Indian National Army, joined Japan in fighting against British India. Desperate fighting reached into India's north-eastern fringes in Nagaland and Manipur in 1944, with the Japanese defeats at Imphal and Kohima marking the beginning of the Japanese retreat across Asia. I have been privileged to visit war cemeteries there and also a magnificent and well-documented historical museum in Kohima equally sympathetic to the troops of both sides.

Prior to India's independence, Jawaharlal Nehru, later India's first—and still its most influential—Prime Minister, thought and wrote about the foreign policy of a sovereign India (often while sampling the hospitality of the viceroy's jails, which provided plenty of opportunity for reading and writing), which he saw as primarily anti-imperialist and oriented towards Asia. The first policy thrust was carried forward in part through his conception of non-alignment, but the second was largely shelved after the realities of the Cold War intruded on India's international relations. Nevertheless, India and Japan developed cordial relations, with many visits between them, including that of Crown Prince Akihito with Princess Michiko in 1960 and their return engagement in India as emperor and empress in 2013.

Several Indian prime ministers beyond Mr Nehru developed a strong attachment to Japan, including India's most recent Prime

Minister, Manmohan Singh. Like other Asian countries, India was impressed by Japan's stunning economic recovery from the Second World War, although unlike South Korea, Taiwan, and several countries of Southeast Asia, India did not seek to emulate Japan's development track. However, it was open to trade with Japan and increasingly to investment from it, leading to the emergence of several well-known icons of India's industrial world, including the Maruti Suzuki automotive company. Japanese development assistance to India is perceived by Indians to have been particularly effective, addressing as it has the country's infrastructural deficits.

India's testing of nuclear weapons in 1998 proved stressful for Japan—the only victim to date of such armaments at both Hiroshima and Nagasaki—but the two countries overcame their differences in this sphere (which continue to be explicit) to explore further economic engagement with each other.

Nevertheless, the results have proved mixed. As this volume's outstanding set of authors document, both trade and investment have proved underwhelming between India and Japan relative to their potential. Reasons for this relate not so much to geographical distance (although it is considerable), but rather to the very different economic, political, and social values of the two countries, which are nevertheless linked by a strong commitment to democracy. Indians sometimes regard potential Japanese economic partners as cautious and excessively prudent, while their Japanese counterparts quail before India's raucous public and economic life, the forms that corruption can take within its borders, and occasional flare-ups of violence, including in relation to labour disputes. Each has a lot to learn and accept about the other; their mutual comfort level needs to (and, in the view of the authors of this volume, can) rise considerably.

Very helpfully, the current leaders of India and Japan, Prime Ministers Narendra Modi and Shinzo Abe, have provided very strong impetus for a more energetic approach to building up partnerships in all spheres. Tectonic shifts in the geo-strategic dispensation within Asia account for some of these efforts. But so does a personal relationship between the two men significantly predating their current tenures as heads of their respective national governments.

This volume represents the culmination of an in-depth research project on how the bilateral relationship could be strengthened in four major fields, led by two very fine and promising young scholars: Rohan Mukherjee (currently a Stanton Nuclear Security Fellow in the Security Studies Program at the Massachusetts Institute of Technology) and Anthony Yazaki (a former NHK producer in Washington and now a member of the United Nations University's Centre for Policy Research). The project has been generously supported and helpfully shaped at times by the Sasakawa Peace Foundation (SPF). The United Nations University (UNU) has been proud to host it, with excellent support in Delhi from the University of Pennsylvania Institute for the Advanced Study of India (UPIASI).

In their introduction, the co-editors of this volume explain how the project was structured not just to pull in some of the most respected academics and practitioners from Japan and India but also to introduce new, younger voices into the debate.

As an occasional author on India, and as a very happy resident of Japan, I am doubly delighted to be associated with their work.

David M. Malone
Tokyo, August 2015
Rector, UN University and
Under-Secretary-General of the UN

Acknowledgements

This volume would not have been possible without the generous financial support of the Sasakawa Peace Foundation (SPF). Both its chairman, Jiro Hanyu, and executive director, Junko Chano, believed in the importance of the Japan–India partnership and supported the project from the outset, while Miko Maekawa, Iwao Matsuoka, and Mariko Hayashi oversaw the grant that supported our work with their characteristic patience, grace, and flexibility.

Equally vital was the institutional support and home provided us by the United Nations University (UNU) in Tokyo, whose rector David Malone helped conceive the volume and resolutely backed its editors. We can confidently say that such an outstanding set of contributors would have been impossible to assemble without David's goodwill and stature in the worlds of academia and diplomacy. Of course, a leader owes much to his team, and UNU's outstanding staff cannot be thanked enough for putting up with our habit of overlooking details and asking unnecessary questions—David Passarelli, Max Bond, and Francois d'Artagnan on administration and finance; Mari Yamamoto, Miho Kimura, Misako Takano, and Kaori Masuda on accounting and logistics; Francesco Foghetti on legal matters; and Sebastian von Einsiedel, director of the UNU Centre for Policy Research, the university's exciting new in-house think tank, which took our project under its wing.

In the early stages of planning this volume, Tsuneo Watanabe of the Tokyo Foundation, Daniel Kliman of the German Marshall Fund (GMF), and Junichi Koyanagi of SPF provided critical guidance on potential themes and contributors especially in the Japanese context. Sharon Stirling-Woolsey of GMF gave us a sense of what it would take to host our first authors' meeting in Tokyo in October 2014. At this meeting, we had the honour of being addressed by India's ambassador to Japan, Deepa Gopalan Wadhwa; Japan's former ambassador to India, Hiroshi Hirabayashi; and the director-general of the Southeast and Southwest Asian Affairs Department at the Japanese Ministry of Foreign Affairs, Takio Yamada. In their roles as discussants at this meeting, Harsha Vardhana Singh, Ken Koyama, Toshiya Hoshino, and Sanjaya Baru provided the authors with valuable feedback on their chapters. Chantal Doran was a most able and reliable rapporteur.

For the second authors' meeting and book launch in New Delhi in January 2016, we are grateful to E. Sridharan and his team at the University of Pennsylvania Institute for the Advanced Study of India (UPIASI) for their administrative and logistical support. Devesh Kapur, board member of UPIASI and contributor to this volume, was a deeply thoughtful and engaged mentor for this project from beginning to end. C. Raja Mohan, Srinath Raghavan, and Dick Samuels took time out to help us think through the organization and substance of our second meeting.

To our editors at Oxford University Press, we owe thanks for believing in the volume and investing much time and energy in its success.

Needless to say, we are indebted to the volume's contributors, who were enthusiastic about our suggestion of inter-generational co-authorship for each chapter and eventually produced a remarkable body of work that will undoubtedly impact the trajectory of India–Japan relations going forward.

Finally, a few notes of personal thanks. To Junko Yazaki, Toyu Yazaki, and Liina Lind for their love and support. And to Utpala Mukherjee, Utsa Mukherjee, and Shailey Hingorani, whose powerful examples of brilliance, discernment, and equanimity made this volume better in subtle and fundamental ways.

Abbreviations

ADB	Asian Development Bank
ADIZ	Air Defense Identification Zone
ADMM	ASEAN Defence Ministers Meeting
AIIB	Asian Infrastructure Investment Bank
APEC	Asia-Pacific Economic Cooperation
ARF	ASEAN Regional Forum
ASEAN	Association of Southeast Asian Nations
BASIC	Brazil, South Africa, India, China
BEE	Bureau of Energy Efficiency (India)
BHEL	Bharat Heavy Electricals Limited
BJP	Bharatiya Janata Party (India)
BLF	Business Leaders' Forum (India–Japan)
BRIC	Brazil, Russia, India, and China
BRICS	Brazil, Russia, India, China, and South Africa
C-10	Committee of Ten
C-34	Committee of Thirty-Four (or Special Committee on Peacekeeping Operations)
CBDR	common but differentiated responsibilities
CBDR-RC	common but differentiated responsibilities and respective capabilities
CBIC	Chennai–Bangalore Industrial Corridor
CCS	carbon capture and storage
CDM	clean development mechanism
CEPA	Comprehensive Economic Partnership Agreement
CII	Confederation of Indian Industry
CoC	code of conduct
CoO	certificate of origin
CoP	Conference of Parties
CSM	Champions for Societal Manufacturing
CTBT	Comprehensive Nuclear-Test-Ban Treaty

DAC	Development Assistance Committee
DFC	dedicated freight corridor
DIPP	Department of Industrial Policy and Promotion (India)
DMIC	Delhi–Mumbai Industrial Corridor
DOTS	direction of trade statistics
DPJ	Democratic Party of Japan
EU	European Union
FDI	foreign direct investment
FICCI	Federation of Indian Chambers of Commerce and Industry
FMCT	Fissile Material Cut-off Treaty
FTA	free trade agreement
FTAAP	Free Trade Area of the Asia Pacific
G-2	Group of Two
G-4	Group of Four
G-20	Group of Twenty
G-77	Group of Seventy-Seven
GAIL	Gas Authority of India Limited
GATS	General Agreement on Trade in Services
GATT	General Agreement on Tariffs and Trade
GDP	gross domestic product
GMF	German Marshall Fund
GoJ	Government of Japan
GTAP	Global Trade Analysis Project
GW	gigawatt
HADR	humanitarian assistance and disaster relief
HLP	High-Level Panel
IAEA	International Atomic Energy Agency
IBSA	India, Brazil, and South Africa
IEA	International Energy Agency
IFI	international financial institution
IFR	integral fast reactor
IGCAR	Indira Gandhi Centre for Atomic Research (India)
IGCC	integrated gasification combined cycle
IISS	International Institute for Strategic Studies (UK)
IMF	International Monetary Fund
INS	Indian Naval Ship
IORA	Indian Ocean Rim Association

IPR	intellectual property rights
ISDS	investor–state dispute settlement
ISI	import-substitution industrialization
ISIS	Islamic State of Iraq and Syria (or Islamic State of Iraq and the Levant)
ISRO	Indian Space Research Organisation
IT	information technology
JASDF	Japan Air Self-Defense Force
JAXA	Japan Aerospace Exploration Agency
JBIC	Japan Bank for International Cooperation
JCCII	Japan Chamber of Commerce and Industry in India
JCM	Joint Crediting Mechanism
JCOAL	Japan Coal Energy Centre
JETRO	Japan External Trade Organization
JGSDF	Japan Ground Self-Defense Force
JICA	Japan International Cooperation Agency
JIMEX	Japan–India Maritime Exercise
JMSDF	Japan Maritime Self-Defense Force
JPC	Japan Peacekeeping Training and Research Center
JSDF	Japan Self-Defense Forces
LDP	Liberal Democratic Party (Japan)
LNG	liquefied natural gas
LWR	light water reactor
MEA	Ministry of External Affairs (India)
METI	Ministry of Economy, Trade and Industry (Japan)
MoCI	Ministry of Commerce and Industry (India)
MoD	Ministry of Defense (Japan)
MoFA	Ministry of Foreign Affairs (Japan)
MoU	memorandum of understanding
MTCR	Missile Technology Control Regime
NAM	Non-Aligned Movement
NAPCC	National Action Plan for Climate Change (India)
NCR	National Capital Region (India)
NDA	National Democratic Alliance (India)
NDB	New Development Bank
NDPG	National Defense Program Guidelines (Japan)
NEDO	New Energy and Industrial Technology Development Organization (Japan)
NEXI	Nippon Export and Investment Insurance (Japan)

NGO	non-governmental organization
NITI	National Institution for Transforming India (or NITI Ayog)
NPT	Non-Proliferation Treaty (or Treaty on the Non-Proliferation of Nuclear Weapons)
NSDC	National Skill Development Corporation (India)
NSG	Nuclear Suppliers Group
NSS	National Security Strategy (Japan)
NTPC	National Thermal Power Corporation (India)
ODA	official development assistance
OECD	Organisation for Economic Co-operation and Development
P5	permanent five members of the UNSC
P5+1	permanent five members of the UNSC and Germany
PCRA	Petroleum Conservation Research Association (India)
PKO	peacekeeping operations
PPP	public–private partnership
PSI	Proliferation Security Initiative
R&D	research and development
R2P	responsibility to protect
RBI	Reserve Bank of India
RCEP	Regional Comprehensive Economic Partnership
RIETI	Research Institute of Economy, Trade and Industry (Japan)
RWP	responsibility while protecting
S5	Small Five Group
SAARC	South Asian Association for Regional Cooperation
SCO	Shanghai Cooperation Organization
SIPRI	Stockholm International Peace Research Institute
SLOC	sea lines of communication
SME	small and medium-sized enterprises
SPF	Sasakawa Peace Foundation
SPS	sanitary and phytosanitary measures
START	Strategic Arms Reduction Treaty
TBT	technical barriers to trade
TPP	Trans-Pacific Partnership
TTIP	Transatlantic Trade and Investment Partnership
UfC	Uniting for Consensus

UK	United Kingdom
UN	United Nations
UNCLOS	United Nations Convention on the Law of the Sea
UNCTAD	United Nations Conference on Trade and Development
UNFCCC	United Nations Framework Convention on Climate Change
UNGA	United Nations General Assembly
Unpkos	United Nations Peacekeeping Operations
UNSC	United Nations Security Council
UNU	United Nations University
UPA	United Progressive Alliance (India)
UPIASI	University of Pennsylvania Institute for the Advanced Study of India
US	United States (of America)
VLFM	Visionary Leaders for Manufacturing
WTO	World Trade Organization

Introduction

The Historical Context

Rohan Mukherjee and Anthony Yazaki

The growing partnership between India and Japan is one of the most keenly observed developments of the Asian Century. This chapter studies the six decades of diplomacy that preceded this strategic embrace and examines three potential explanations for it—a changing security environment, the logic of economics, and a congruence of political values. Starting in the late 1940s, the chapter traces the relationship from its initial warmth to the estrangement of the Cold War, the rupture caused by India's nuclear tests of 1998, and the current phase of new found intimacy. While the pressures of a changing security environment have played a vital role, India and Japan have become closer primarily through what Prime Minister Shinzo Abe has termed 'value-oriented diplomacy', or the shared democratic ideals that create a foundation for mutual understanding.

In the summer of 1916, Indian poet and Nobel laureate Rabindranath Tagore spent four months in Japan. During his stay, he delivered a lecture at Keio University in which he marvelled at his host country's greatness and warmth towards him. 'I have come to the conclusion,' he said, 'that the welcome which flowed towards me, with such outburst of sincerity, was owing to the fact that Japan felt the nearness of India to herself, and realised that her own heart has room to expand beyond her boundaries and the boundaries of modern time.'[1] Almost a hundred years later, Indian Prime Minister Narendra Modi echoed this sentiment during his first official visit to Tokyo in September 2014: 'I am ... touched by the warmth and enthusiasm that I have experienced in meeting a wide cross-section of people here,' he said. 'I am excited about the boundless possibilities for our cooperation.'[2] The warmth in India–Japan relations has been evident in the century that has passed since Tagore's visit. As two of the world's largest economies with democratic political systems, no historical disputes, and a long history of societal contacts grounded in the emergence and spread of Buddhism, India and Japan have been poised for partnership since 1947, the year when India gained independence from British colonial rule and Japan enacted a new constitution that would help it step out of the dark shadows of the Second World War.

Despite this congruence of interests and identities, India and Japan's mutual appreciation has been confined largely to the societal and cultural domain. Looking back on the relationship at the end of the twentieth century, a former Indian envoy to Japan concluded, '[T] he absence of problems in itself did not automatically contribute to adding substance to [India–Japan] ties. On the contrary, a friction free but non substantive relationship actually suffered from want of attention.'[3] Even today, the desire for deeper relations tends to overshadow any serious discussion of the ways in which such deepening might unfold. In the words of one observer, '[T]here are numerous strategic perspectives in both Japan and India in favour of such a relationship... . However, there is not yet any clear understanding between Japan and India as to what substance the relationship will have.'[4]

The academic record reflects this ambiguity. On the Indian side, while numerous analysts have authored articles since the 1960s on the importance of Japan to India, few have focused on any concrete steps the two countries might take to deepen their partnership (a possibility that in any case did not become real until the end of the Cold War). In terms of book-length studies, barring a handful of edited volumes published by foundations and think tanks, rigorous policy-relevant scholarship on the India–Japan relationship is virtually absent.[5] The record on the Japanese side is much thinner. As a frequent Indian commentator on Japan has noted, 'Scholarship by Japan's multitude of observers interested in Japan-Asia relations generally registers only passing attention to relations with India or fails to acknowledge them at all.'[6] While various Indian scholars have focused their energies on Japan, the first doctoral thesis on India's military strategy was completed in Japan only in 2010, at Gakushuin University.[7]

Despite the lack of scholarly attention, developments in India–Japan relations at the highest political levels have continued apace in the twenty-first century. After decades of speaking the language of cooperation, Asia's two democratic giants are finally edging closer in a strategic embrace. How they should proceed is the subject of this volume. In the chapters that follow, some of India's and Japan's top scholars, practitioners, and analysts—both established and emerging—chart a course for the bilateral relationship from the shallow waters of lofty rhetoric into the open sea of concrete action and boundless possibility. This chapter will contribute a broad overview of India and Japan's diplomatic relations since 1947, followed by an analysis of the factors driving the two countries closer together in the twenty-first century. It will conclude with a brief discussion of the book's structure and approach.

Historical Overview

The late 1940s were a fundamentally transformative period for both India and Japan. The former emerged as a newly independent republic after a long period of British colonization, the latter from a period of imperialist ambition and conquest that culminated in the devastation of the Second World War and occupation by the United States of America. Indian elites had long admired Japan's industriousness and rise to great power status at the turn of the twentieth century, and Japan for its part had made an abortive attempt during the Second World War to aid a militant faction of India's freedom movement in overthrowing British rule.

Initial Warmth

Their remarkably different experiences of the war notwithstanding, both nations emerged deeply concerned with the need for racial equality between the West and East, and both espoused ideas of Asian solidarity. As a member of the Far Eastern Commission formed by the Allied powers to oversee Japan's terms of surrender, India pushed for an early end to the occupation of Japan. Concurrently, the Indian justice Radhabinod Pal became the only judge in the International Military Tribunal for the Far East—designed by the Allies to pros- ecute Japanese war criminals—to argue that none of the defendants should be convicted.[8] Although the organizers of the 1948 Summer Olympics in London had denied Japan permission to participate, India invited a still-occupied Japan to participate in the 1951 Asian Games in New Delhi (where Japan won the highest number of gold and total medals).[9] Later that year, India refused to participate in the conference that led to the Treaty of San Francisco, which officially ended the occupation of Japan, on the grounds that the agreement did not take into account the wishes of the Japanese people.[10] In 1952, India signed its own peace treaty with Japan, which did not require Japan to pay any war reparations.

Despite this initial warmth, Japan's reliance on the United States—formalized in a mutual defence agreement in 1954—and India's turn towards a foreign policy of non-alignment with any of the world's great powers began to create a wedge between the two countries. Japan followed what came to be known as the Yoshida Doctrine, formulated in the early 1950s by Prime Minister Shigeru Yoshida, which relied on three pillars: pacifism, the security alliance with the US, and a focus on external economic engagement for postwar reconstruction.[11] This doctrine left little room for coop- eration with a country such as India that was at odds with the US and lacked the purchasing power to be a strong trading partner. Nonetheless, India, as an influential actor among Third World countries, advocated for Japan's presence at the first major confer- ence of African and Asian nations held in Bandung, Indonesia, in 1955. The following year, the two countries signed an agreement to deepen their cultural links through academic exchange, cultural institutes, scholarships, and other means. In May 1957, Nobusuke Kishi became the first Japanese premier to visit India, and Prime Minister Jawaharlal Nehru reciprocated five months later. Shortly thereafter, India became the recipient of the very first yen loan issued by Japan's nascent foreign aid programme, and both countries signed an agreement on commerce granting each other most favoured nation status.

Gradually, however, the creeping freeze of the Cold War began to catch up with India–Japan relations. Visits by the Japanese crown prince and princess in 1960 and Prime Minister Hayato Ikeda in 1961 did little to contain the drift as Delhi formally co-launched the Non-Aligned Movement (NAM) and Tokyo moved more firmly towards the Western bloc. To India's disappointment, Japan maintained a strictly neutral (but by no means uncommon) stance during India's war with China in 1962 and with Pakistan in 1965. Nonetheless, the Japanese government held up its end of a prior agreement to hold annual consultative meetings with the Indian government, the first meeting taking place in New Delhi in March 1966 (the initiative lost momentum over the next four years).[12] The India–Japan Business Cooperation Committee, an organization that is active even today, was formed in the same year, and a round table conference on the economic development of Japan and India was held in 1968. In her first tenure as prime minister, Indira Gandhi visited Japan in 1969, around which time the Japanese government began funding the first university course on Japanese language and culture in India, at the University of Delhi.[13] The flurry of economic and cultural activities led one observer at the time to conclude that 'India-Japan relations seem to have entered a new stage.'[14]

Cold War Drift

The international politics of the Cold War ensured that Japan's approach to India stayed in step with that of the United States. The nadir in Japan–India relations came, therefore, in the early 1970s through three sets of events. The first was the admission of the People's Republic of China as a permanent member of the United Nations Security Council (UNSC) in place of the Republic of China (that is, Taiwan), which had held the seat at the behest of the Western bloc since 1945. In October 1971, the United Nations General Assembly (UNGA) voted in favour of Taiwan's seat being given to China, a move that India supported and Japan (and the United States) opposed. An Indian analyst noted at the time that Japan, on the path to becoming an economic superpower, could afford to alienate China, whereas

India, facing a mounting crisis in East Pakistan, could not.[15] The second set of events that pushed India and Japan further apart was the genocide in East Pakistan itself. India made strenuous diplomatic efforts to convince other countries to pressure Pakistan into halting its brutal crackdown and thus alleviating the flow of millions of refugees into Indian territory. However, most countries were unwilling to publicly condemn Pakistan, especially when it had the support of both the United States and China. Japan was no different: an Indian envoy who visited Tokyo reported that 'Japan's government agreed that an independent Bangladesh was inevitable, but dared not say so in public.'[16] The third and final nail in the coffin was India's first nuclear test, conducted in 1974, which was roundly condemned by the Japanese public and government, the latter being concerned not just about proliferation but about the lessons domestic nationalists might draw from India's defiance of the global regime for the control of nuclear weapons.[17] In each of these three cases, Japanese policy hewed to the Western line, and India maintained the rhetoric of non-alignment while growing ever closer to the Soviet Union.

The remainder of the 1970s was a quiet period in India–Japan relations. Although Prime Minister Takeo Fukuda announced in 1977 that Japan would seek closer ties with Asian countries—a policy known as the Fukuda Doctrine—Tokyo's focus did not extend as far as South Asia. In 1978, the US and Japan adopted formal guidelines for defence cooperation that laid out the roles and responsibilities of both countries in the event of an imminent threat to or attack on Japan. The same year, India and Japan held their first talks at the level of foreign ministers and began consultations on ways to improve their overall trade and investment relationship. Indian elites were impressed by Japan's economic achievements. Writing in the 1970s, an Indian observer noted that India's attitude towards Japan consisted of 'a tremendous admiration for Japan's economic and technological success, and … a feeling of "if one Asian country can breakthrough to affluence, then why not India?"'[18] Some Indian observers drew important geopolitical conclusions from Japan's success. K.R. Narayanan, a career diplomat who would later become president of India, noted: 'Hitherto Indo-Japanese relations have been somewhat muffled largely because of Japan's preoccupation with the United States and the tendency to follow the US line… . Now that Japan is coming out into the open politically in Asia and India has improved her own image … both New Delhi and Tokyo might experience a greater degree of mutuality of interests.'[19]

Although this prediction would require another three decades to come true, the focus on economics in India–Japan relations paid off in the early 1980s with the signing of the first joint venture between an Indian company and a Japanese company. The result, Maruti Suzuki, became India's top automobile company and remains so to this day, with a market share of approximately 45 per cent in 2014.[20] The company's flagship car, the Maruti 800, was released in 1983, a few months before Prime Minister Yasuhiro Nakasone made the first visit to India by a Japanese premier in over two decades. Nakasone's visit heralded an increase in Japanese investment and aid to India, and the following year Prime Minister Rajiv Gandhi reciprocated the visit as India and Japan signed an agreement on cooperation in science and technology. Gandhi visited Japan again in 1987, a year in which the Indian government held 'Japan Month' in four major Indian cities. Gandhi returned to Tokyo in 1988 to attend the first ever Festival of India organized by the Japanese government.[21] Thus, although India and Japan did not see eye to eye on security issues, cooperation on economic and cultural fronts continued apace through the 1980s.

The Lost Decade

The 1990s were a tumultuous decade for the world. The end of the Cold War fundamentally altered the global balance of power and caught a number of countries off guard as they struggled to recalibrate their worldviews and foreign policies to take into account the demise of the Soviet Union, the advent of American primacy in world politics, and the unfreezing of numerous regional and bilateral rivalries from Cold War stasis. In retrospect, the 1990s have been characterized as 'the lost decade' for Japanese foreign policy and for the India–Japan relationship.[22] Long accustomed to a global geopolitical stalemate that allowed it to prosper by dint of its economic diplomacy, Japan was rapidly thrown into the deep end by the Gulf War of 1990–1. When called upon by the United States to contribute troops to the war effort, the Diet dithered and eventually failed to oblige. Instead, Japan belatedly contributed a large sum of money (US$13 billion) to the war effort, earning America's disapproval for 'chequebook diplomacy'.[23]

The Gulf War turned out to be just the beginning of Japan's woes. In May 1993, North Korea fired a medium-range ballistic missile into the Sea of Japan, the first of a number of missile and nuclear tests in years to come. Two years later, over a span of three months, China conducted two nuclear tests and began missile tests in the Taiwan Strait in response to the US granting a visa to Taiwan's pro-independence prime minister, Lee Teng-hui. The crisis ended the following year, but not before a tense military stand-off between Washington and Beijing in the Taiwan Strait. No sooner was the military crisis resolved than East Asia was plunged into an unprecedented financial crisis. Japan's economy had already slowed down considerably since the beginning of the decade, and the crisis exacerbated the situation by hurting Japanese exports to the region. In 1998, to round off Japan's lost decade, India and Pakistan conducted nuclear tests within days of each other in May, and North Korea tested an intermediate-range ballistic missile (the Taepodong-1) as a space launch vehicle in August.

India's nuclear tests came towards the end of what could have been its own lost decade were it not for domestic economic changes. Threatened by a major balance of payments crisis in 1991, India undertook a raft of reforms to reduce the state's control over various sectors of the economy. As a result, India's economy grew at a compounded annual rate of 5.5 per cent through the 1990s, compared to 0.8 per cent for the Japanese economy.[24] On the security front, India's challenges were comparable to Japan's. Newly enriched by the vast amounts of money and materiel poured into the anti-Soviet war effort in Afghanistan during the 1980s, Pakistan turned its attention to the Kashmir valley. Starting in the early 1990s, increasing numbers of mujahideen flowed from Afghanistan to Kashmir and formed the backbone of a deadly insurgency against the Indian state in the region. Beijing's continued support for Islamabad further rankled the Indian establishment, so much so that Prime Minister Atal Bihari Vajpayee explained in a letter to US president Bill Clinton that India's decision to conduct nuclear tests in May 1998—labelled Pokhran-II after their location in the Rajasthan desert—was partly motivated by the fact that China had 'materially helped another neighbour of ours to become a covert nuclear weapons state'.[25]

Two years prior to Pokhran-II, a prominent anti-nuclear activist and scholar in India had noted, 'In no country in the world is popular sentiment against nuclear weapons and weaponization as deep and widespread as it is in Japan.'[26] As expected, Japan's reaction to the tests was visceral. In contrast to China's earlier nuclear tests, which resulted in the suspension of grants from Tokyo—a small component of the overall Japan–China relationship—Japan suspended all new yen loans and grant assistance to India, with the exception of humanitarian and grassroots aid.[27] S. Jaishankar, India's deputy chief of mission in Tokyo at the time, later characterized Japan's reaction as 'surprisingly swift and exceptionally harsh'.[28] In addition to economic sanctions, Tokyo imposed strict controls on technology transfers, temporarily recalled the Japanese ambassador to India, cancelled a number of official dialogues, co-sponsored a UNSC resolution condemning India's and Pakistan's tests, applied pressure on other international forums such as the G-8 to condemn India, and—worst of all from Delhi's perspective—publicly identified the Kashmir issue as the root cause of South Asia going overtly nuclear.[29] Some Indians alleged that in order to prevent a Pakistani nuclear test, in discussions with Islamabad, Tokyo had offered to use its temporary membership at the UNSC to raise the Kashmir issue in the council, an event that India had consistently sought to preclude since the 1950s.[30]

Until 1998, India–Japan relations had remained tepid at best. Japan provided economic assistance to India during the latter's balance of payments crisis of 1991 and, in keeping with India's newly launched Look East policy, Prime Minister Narasimha Rao visited Tokyo in 1992 with the intention of forging a new type of post–Cold War partnership. Although Japan's subsequent economic malaise precluded this development, Tokyo adequately signalled its future intentions—the Japan Foundation opened its first India office in New Delhi in 1994, and 1995 witnessed the first ever visit of a minister of international trade and industry, Ryutaro Hashimoto. India's nuclear tests, however, erased these gains, and Delhi's disenchantment with Tokyo grew further during the Kargil War with Pakistan in 1999. The conflict began with Pakistan's violation of the de facto border (the Line of Control) in Kashmir; while the rest of the G-8 countries sought to pressure Pakistan into undoing this act of aggression, Japan remained obstinately neutral and—to India's chagrin—refused to entertain any discussion of how the conflict began.[31] The lost decade of the 1990s thus ended with the prospect of even further estrangement. Writing in early 2000, an Indian observer bemoaned Delhi's lacklustre Asia policy: 'Despite its best efforts India has not made any substantial breakthroughs in its relationship with Japan, China or even ASEAN,' he wrote. 'Are we missing the Asian bus?'[32] Fortunately for India and Japan, a number of changes were in the making that would prove otherwise.

Newfound Intimacy

In March 2000, President Clinton made a historic visit to New Delhi, during which he addressed the Indian Parliament. The visit ended a two-year period of American sanctions following India's nuclear tests and signalled the beginning of an India–US rapprochement. After decades of Cold War estrangement, the two countries had begun to set aside their differences, largely driven by the increasing involvement of the American private sector in India's liberalizing economy. Prime Minister Yoshiro Mori of Japan, who came to office the following month, was quick to sense the changing winds.[33] He visited India just five months after Clinton and called for a 'global partnership' between India and Japan.[34] Until then, Japan had used this term only in the context of relations with the US.[35] By October 2001, Japan had waived all economic sanctions against India. Prime Minister Vajpayee visited Tokyo in December; Japan soon resumed yen loans to India, and both countries held their first comprehensive security dialogue.

These events heralded a new era in Japan–India relations, described by one scholar as a period of 'newfound intimacy'.[36] In 2004, the Japanese and Indian navies in coordination with other countries conducted joint relief efforts following the tsunami in the Indian Ocean. In April 2005, Prime Minister Junichiro Koizumi visited India and both countries unveiled an 'eight-fold initiative' focused on enhancing all aspects of the relationship: economy, security, culture, science and technology, regional cooperation, and global governance. Significantly, both countries decided to institutionalize annual meetings between their prime ministers. A major outcome of Koizumi's visit was Japan's support for India's membership in the first East Asia Summit held in 2005. The following year, against the backdrop of North Korea's first nuclear test and its abortive test of the Taepodong-2 ballistic missile, Prime Minister Manmohan Singh visited Tokyo and became the first Indian premier to receive the rare honour of addressing a joint session of the Diet.[37] In his address, Singh sought Japan's support for India's imminent agreement with the US on civil nuclear cooperation, which had been in the works since July 2005. Given the strong public opposition to nuclear weapons in Japan and based on Tokyo's reaction to India's earlier nuclear tests, India was keen to ensure that Japan would not oppose the deal when it came up for approval at the Nuclear Suppliers Group (NSG) and other forums that controlled the global movement of nuclear materials and technology.

Koizumi's and Singh's respective visits accelerated their countries' strategic embrace, but the most perceptible changes occurred during and after Shinzo Abe's year-long tenure as prime minister in 2006–7. Abe, the grandson of Nobusuke Kishi, the first Japanese prime minister to visit India (in 1957), was—like Koizumi—ideologically neoconservative on the Japanese political spectrum, and an ardent advocate of more robust relations with India as part of a broader attempt at making Japan's security policy more proactive.[38] Early in 2007, he proposed a quadrilateral security dialogue between the US, Japan, Australia, and India. The four countries met in Manila in May, shortly after India, the US, and Japan conducted naval exercises in the South China Sea and Australia became the second country (after the US) to sign a declaration on security cooperation with Japan.[39] In August, during his first visit to India, in an unapologetic acknowledgement of Japan and India's close ties during and after the Second World War, Abe visited the former home of Subhas Chandra Bose— who had sought Japanese military assistance to overthrow British rule in India during the Second World War—and met with the son of Radhabinod Pal. A month later, the annual India–US Malabar naval exercises took place in the Bay of Bengal and included Japan, Australia, and Singapore. Although Abe's quadrilateral initiative did not last long due to strong diplomatic protests by China, he had in a very short period of time made significant strides in bolstering Japan's security profile in Asia and improving ties with India.

Abe's successors from his party—the Liberal Democratic Party (LDP)—maintained a focus on India that was not as enthusiastic as his but made significant advances nonetheless. Of particular note were Japan's assent to the India–US nuclear agreement in the NSG under Prime Minister Yasuo Fukuda in September 2008, and the signing of a joint declaration on security cooperation between India and Japan in October 2008 under Prime Minister Taro Aso, a close ally of Abe. This declaration, which described a formal framework of cooperation and dialogue at multiple bureaucratic levels for both governments, was described by one analyst as 'a truly epoch-making development'.[40] At a time of domestic political instability, when Japan had a new prime minister roughly every 12 months, Aso's successors from the opposition Democratic Party of Japan (DPJ) maintained the momentum of India–Japan relations.[41] Prime Minister Yukio Hatoyama visited India in 2009 and concluded an action plan to advance the security declaration of the previous year. In 2010, Prime Minister Naoto Kan began his tenure by launching a dialogue with India on civil nuclear cooperation despite controversy on the subject within Japan.[42]

Around this time, Japan and India also concluded a Comprehensive Economic Partnership Agreement (CEPA), originally recommended in 2006 by a joint study group of government officials and experts from both countries. The CEPA, which came into effect in August 2011, was India's third such agreement after Singapore and South Korea. It eventually aimed to cover 90 per cent of the trade between Japan and India, in addition to services, investment, customs, and other bilateral economic issues. In a significant gesture, Japan agreed to immediately eliminate tariffs on 87 per cent of its product lines, while India agreed to immediately eliminate tariffs on only 17.4 per cent of its product lines (with another 66.3 per cent to be eliminated over a ten-year period).[43]

In June 2012, India and Japan conducted their first bilateral naval exercises off the coast of Japan. While the exercises were a basic step in developing familiarity and interoperability between the two navies, they signalled a further deepening of security cooperation between the two nations. Abe's return as prime minister in

December 2012 promised further improvements in India–Japan relations, though he was quickly preoccupied with regional tensions in 2013 as North Korea conducted its third nuclear test and China announced an Air Defense Identification Zone (ADIZ) in the East China Sea that covered the disputed Senkaku/Diaoyu Islands, which both Tokyo and Beijing claim. Nonetheless, in a historic first, the Japanese emperor and empress visited India towards the end of 2013, 53 years after their first official visit as crown prince and princess. In January 2014, Abe became the first Japanese prime minister to attend India's annual Republic Day parade as chief guest (an honour that was extended to US president Barack Obama only in 2015). Later that year, India's new prime minister, Narendra Modi, visited Tokyo and the two nations upgraded their relationship to a Special Strategic and Global Partnership. For the first time in the history of India–Japan relations, the Indian prime minister made a reference to Chinese expansionism in his public remarks in Tokyo.[44] The continued warmth in India–Japan relations has been in no small measure due to the personal friendship shared by Abe and Modi. As chief minister of the Indian state of Gujarat, Modi had travelled to Delhi especially to meet with Abe during the latter's official visit in 2007. In 2012, Modi (still chief minister) had visited Japan, and Abe—then out of power—had met with him again. Enjoying a comfortable majority in the lower house of the Indian Parliament since coming to power in mid-2014, Modi will remain in office at least until 2019. Abe himself was re-elected prime minister for a four-year term following an early election called in December 2014. In many ways, there could not be a more opportune moment for India and Japan to convert their ambitious rhetoric of the last decade into concrete policies and actions.

Explaining the Strategic Embrace

India and Japan have evidently come a very long way since the initial cordialities of the 1940s, the subsequent freeze of the Cold War, and the lost decade of the 1990s. What explains the increasing warmth of this relationship in the twenty-first century? A number of potential factors seem to have played a role, and they can be divided into three categories: security, economics, and values.

Securing Japan and Realigning India

The rise of China as a major world power is the most commonly cited reason for rapprochement between India and Japan. As early as the 1970s, Indian diplomat K.R. Narayanan had noted, 'Japan and India are immense and obstinate factors [in Asia] which China must take into account as they must perforce take China into account.'[45] China's economy and military have grown by leaps and bounds since then. In the years following the end of the Cold War, Japan was cautiously optimistic about China's rise, but Beijing's subsequent nuclear tests, its policies towards Taiwan, its support for North Korea, its burgeoning defence expenditure, and its creeping maritime territorial claims gradually altered this perception to the point where Japan's foreign minister in 2005, Taro Aso, unprecedentedly declared publicly that China was 'starting to become a considerable threat'.[46] Since 2008, China's behaviour towards Japan and other nations in East and Southeast Asia has grown more assertive, with a steady rise in maritime incidents involving Chinese fishing vessels, coastguard ships, and patrol boats crossing paths with vessels from other nations in disputed waters.[47] Although economic relations between China and Japan have grown considerably over the last two decades, Japan remains exceedingly wary of potential Chinese belligerence or coercion, particularly over the disputed Senkaku/Diaoyu Islands. India remains equally wary of Chinese activity along the shared Himalayan border disputed by both countries since the 1950s. Although the Indian military itself has grown in size and sophistication over time, India's defeat in the Sino-Indian War of 1962 over the border issue remains a potent reminder of Chinese military power and Beijing's willingness to wield it. In the maritime domain, Indian strategists have frequently decried China's so-called 'string of pearls' strategy of sponsoring commercial ports in countries surrounding India such as Pakistan, Bangladesh, Sri Lanka, and the Maldives. The consistent assistance that China has provided Pakistan since the 1960s in terms of money, equipment, and even nuclear technology remains a major source of threat to India's security.

It is hardly surprising then that Japan and India might have found common cause out of their respective anxieties regarding China's rise. A Japanese analyst summarizes the underlying strategic logic: 'If

China needs to spend money against both Japan and India, its military budget gets dispersed on two fronts which is beneficial for both Japan and India.'[48] However, the picture remains incomplete without a consideration of the US role in Asia. A security alliance with the US has allowed Tokyo to sustain an essentially pacifist and mercantile foreign policy for almost seven decades. However, the alliance has never been tested, and consequently many Japanese elites tend to harbour a lingering fear of abandonment by their superpower ally. As one commentator has observed in the case of the Senkaku/Diaoyu Islands dispute, '[T]he United States government assures Japan of its commitment to Japanese security in principle, but it maintains a policy of not taking sides when a territorial sovereignty issue is involved.'[49] Japan's fear of abandonment was not an overriding concern as long as China was a manageable threat. Such was the thinking behind what observers have labelled Tokyo's 'double hedging' strategy, whereby Japan relied on the US as a hedge against military threats and on China (and other countries) as a hedge against economic dangers.[50] It was only when Sino-Japanese relations worsened and the Senkaku/Diaoyu dispute intensified with Japan claiming formal control over the islands in 2005 that the dual hedge began to falter. Tokyo soon realized that a crisis could arise in which the very things that it relied on the US and China for—military and economic security, respectively—would no longer be forthcoming.[51]

Japan has addressed its security predicament in two ways. The first is internal—since the early 1990s, Japan has steadily augmented its military capabilities and modified its laws and institutions in order to take a more proactive stance on regional security issues.[52] Japan has maintained Self-Defense Forces (JSDF) since 1954 and has spent considerable sums to keep its troops well equipped and well trained. Measured in constant US dollars, in 2013 Japan had the sixth largest military budget in the world (whereas India had the ninth largest budget).[53] In 2015, Japan announced its largest ever defence budget of US$42 billion.[54] On the legal front, since 1992 Japan has steadily increased the JSDF's scope of operations to include peacekeeping, anti-terrorism, and most recently collective security. These measures have required ever more creative interpretations of Article 9 of Japan's constitution, which renounces war and the threat of force in perpetuity and precludes Japan from maintaining any military forces that might be used in war. In 2007, Japan created its first ministry of defence since the end of the Second World War by enhancing the resources, role, and status of what was until then the Japanese Defense Agency (JDA). In keeping with these measures, Tokyo and Washington have gradually modified the terms of their alliance—through a declaration in 1996, revised guidelines in 1997, and another revision in 2015—to give Japan a more expansive and equal role in providing for its own security.

Japan's second strategy for ensuring its security is external—Tokyo has cultivated new strategic partners and invested in regional multilateral security institutions that might enmesh China in a web of rules and obligations.[55] Japan's new strategic partners include the members of the Association of Southeast Asian Nations (ASEAN), Australia, and India. Bilateral security cooperation with ASEAN countries has mainly involved the transfer of non-combat equipment (such as surveillance systems and patrol boats), know-how, and training by Japan.[56] Security cooperation with Australia and India is of a higher order, involving formal security declarations and institutionalized comprehensive dialogues on regional and global issues.

With regard to India, it is worth noting that the two initial turning points in India–Japan relations—the visits of Yoshiro Mori in 2000 and Junichiro Koizumi in 2005—coincided with major shifts in US–India relations, namely, President Bill Clinton's and President George W. Bush's respective visits to Delhi. Put bluntly, the deepening of India–US relations facilitated the development of India–Japan relations.[57] This was especially true in the nuclear domain, where Washington's strong support for India's de facto inclusion in the nuclear club helped Tokyo overcome its vehement opposition to the same.[58]

India's foreign policy focus at the end of the Cold War was also on securing its interests within its region and beyond, and the degree of policy adjustment required was similar to Japan's. During the Cold War, India had pursued a non-aligned foreign policy that sought to remain independent of both superpower blocs. In reality, for a variety of reasons, India grew closer over time to the Soviet Union and relied on the latter for the bulk of its defence procurement. In 1991, with a full-blown economic crisis at home and the severe diminution of its superpower patron abroad, Delhi struggled to come to terms with the United States' newfound hegemony.[59] Moreover, as discussed earlier, a rising internal rebellion sponsored by Pakistan coupled with an external threat from China added considerably to India's security challenges. Like Tokyo, Delhi's response also took place along internal and external dimensions. Internally, as India's economy grew, the government invested increasing amounts in defence. Measured in constant US dollars between 1991 and 2000, India's defence budget grew at a compound annual rate of 4.6 per cent per year.[60] In the following decade, it accelerated to 5.4 per cent per year.[61] In 2010, as China began spending more resources on domestic defence production, India became the world's largest arms importer.[62] In 2015, India increased its defence budget by 11 per cent to US$40 billion and sought to reduce its dependence on imported equipment and rely more on domestic manufactures.[63]

On the external front, India rapidly shed the ideological moorings of non-alignment and began developing so-called strategic partnerships with a host of countries over time, including Russia, China, Indonesia, Australia, Singapore, Vietnam, South Korea, Iran, Israel, and, most importantly for this volume, Japan and the US. While India continued to prize its autonomy very highly for historical and cultural reasons, these strategic partnerships served as a helpful modus vivendi between India's traditional worldview and the demands of the post–Cold War world.[64] India especially renewed its focus on East Asia, becoming a full dialogue partner of ASEAN in 1994 and joining the ASEAN Regional Forum (ARF) in 1996. For Delhi, closer relations with Japan were a natural corollary to these policies and, barring the brief interregnum following the 1998 nuclear tests, India remained optimistic about the relationship. On the security front, therefore, Japan and India's growing strategic embrace was the result of both countries seeking to diversify security relationships in order to better manage new regional and global challenges after the end of the Cold War.

Economic Complementarities

It is commonly assumed that economics played a major role in the strategic diversifications undertaken by Japan and India, respectively, in the 1990s and later. While this is certainly true for India's relationships with China and the United States, and for Japan's relationships with China and the ASEAN countries, it is less the case with the India–Japan relationship itself. While trade in goods between the two countries certainly increased in absolute terms, it remained small as a share of each country's overall goods trade with the world. In fact, Japan's share of India's total goods trade through the 1980s, an annual average of 9.3 per cent, was significantly higher than its share in the 1990s (6.7 per cent) and 2000s (2.9 per cent).[65] India's share of Japan's total goods trade, meagre to begin with, declined from an annual average of 0.7 per cent in the 1980s to 0.6 per cent in the 1990s and 2000s.[66] In 2013, Japan's share of India's total goods trade was 2.2 per cent, and India's share of Japan's goods trade was 1.1 per cent,[67] the latter being higher than previous years likely due to the 2010 CEPA, which was weighted in India's favour for an initial period of 10 years.

The lack of more substantial economic relations between India and Japan is 'surprising given the complementarities between the two countries', as one observer has noted.[68] Indeed, there is much that a capital-intensive, high-technology economy such as Japan and a labour-intensive economy specializing in primary and intermediate goods such as India might trade. Yet India's trade with Southeast Asian countries rose more rapidly than its trade with Japan in the 1990s.[69] At the bilateral level, India consistently undervalued Japan as a trade partner. Their bilateral trade intensity index—which measures whether the value of a country's trade with another is greater or smaller than would be expected based on the latter's importance in world trade—went from 1.0 (the optimal level) in 1991 to 0.5 in 2013, suggesting that by 2013, India was trading 50 per cent less with Japan than Japan's importance in world trade would predict.[70] In 1973, at the height of their Cold War difficulties, this index was at 2.0.[71]

When it came to foreign direct investment (FDI), the picture was considerably better. At current prices, Japan's annual FDI flows to India went from US$262 million in 1996 to a peak of US$5.6 billion in 2008 before dropping back down to US$2.2 billion in 2013, the most recent year for which data are available.[72] Data from the Reserve Bank of India (RBI), which include only FDI requiring government approval (as opposed to automatic routes and reinvested earnings), show that in this category, from 2001 to 2009 Japan's average annual share in India's total FDI was 3.3 per cent,[73] which is only 0.2 percentage points lower than the cumulative share of FDI flows from Japan to India between 1991 and 2009.[74] In the period 2010–13, Japan's average annual share jumped to 9 per cent.[75] In terms of FDI intensity, an index similar to the trade intensity index for the period 2001–13 based on RBI data shows an FDI intensity of 0.9 per year on average.[76] In other words, given India's relative importance as a destination for FDI, Japan's investment flows into India were very close to what we would expect them to be (1.0 being the optimal level).

While the data paint a positive picture, the growth of Japanese FDI in India was more a symptom than a cause of better relations. This is evident from the fact that the major spike in FDI inflows occurred in 2007, once diplomatic relations were already on a firmly upward trajectory. Prior to this period, Japanese companies were generally reluctant to invest in India, which they considered a promising but extremely difficult business environment. This reluctance was in sharp contrast to the success of Korean enterprises in India.[77] Even as FDI began pouring into India from Japan, the objections of Japanese companies did not change substantially. The 2013 edition of the annual list of suggestions to the Government of India submitted by the Japan Chamber of Commerce and Industry in India (JCCII) ran into 35 pages detailing obstacles related to the tax system, banking, insurance, logistics, intellectual property rights, and infrastructure (the last item alone occupying 12 pages).[78] The types of problems listed did not substantially differ from the types of problems listed by Japanese companies engaged in technology transfers with Indian firms in the 1980s, which included 'delays in decision-making, lack of inter-departmental coordination, inordinate bargaining on licensing fees, and complicated procedures'.[79] Although things have certainly improved in the Indian business environment over the last three decades, Japanese firms have continued to struggle.

Official development assistance (ODA) constitutes the one continuous bright spot in India–Japan economic relations. Being the first recipient of a yen loan in 1958, India by 2008 had received a total of US$28 billion in development assistance loans from Japan.[80] In 2003, India became the largest recipient of ODA from Japan, and in 2013 alone, Japan committed US$2.32 billion in loans for infrastructure development in India.[81] On this front, therefore, Japan has always maintained ties with India and recent years have witnessed a significant increase in the quantum of funding. As with FDI, ODA does not constitute a major cause of the growing closeness between Japan and India. Arguably, it contributed to creating a basis for goodwill between the two nations that allowed their rapprochement to proceed, but this is the most that can be said about the role of foreign aid as a potential driver of deeper bilateral relations.

Value-Oriented Diplomacy

As the preceding discussion demonstrates, India and Japan were driven closer together by structural factors such as the rise of China and regional security concerns such as the nuclear programmes of Pakistan and North Korea, respectively. Unlike India–US relations, strong and growing economic ties did not form the bedrock of the new relationship. However, security alone is insufficient as an explanation for the post–Cold War rapprochement. After all, neither country was the sole strategic option for the other. So why then did Japan focus on India and vice versa, to the extent that Abe wrote in his 2007 book, 'It will not be a surprise if in another decade, Japan–India relations overtake Japan–US and Japan–China ties'.[82]

The answer lies in the fact that domestic political change in post–Cold War Japan brought leaders such as Koizumi and Abe to the fore, who wanted Japan to play a more proactive security role in Asia and believed that, by virtue of their shared democratic ideals, Japan and India could be close partners. It is now widely accepted that since the 1990s, Japan has witnessed a gradual shift towards realpolitik in its strategic thought, at both the societal and the leadership levels. In 1996, two American analysts argued that in its relations with China, Japan was transitioning 'from commercial liberalism to reluctant realism'.[83] This shift was mirrored in Japan's overall strategic outlook as well, and eventually in its relations with India.[84] In 2002, another set of analysts observed, '[A]lthough pacifism remains a central part of Japanese political discourse, public antimilitary sentiment has declined drastically over the years.'[85] A wide-ranging study of public and elite attitudes in 2006 confirmed Japan's 'creeping realism'.[86]

A Japanese scholar noted with regard to the JSDF's involvement in Afghanistan:

Only a decade ago, the notion of engaging the JSDF abroad had aroused fury in Japan. But photographs of JSDF ships operating in the Indian Ocean have evoked the feeling among the Japanese that Japan has come a long way, not toward the resumption of militarism, as the pacifists warned, but toward a closer working relationship with other likeminded countries in their fight against terrorism.[87]

Although this shift in attitudes was driven by changes in the external security environment, it still did not preordain a strategic embrace between India and Japan. The latter occurred due to the domestic political consequences of Japan's reluctant path to realpolitik. In particular, the election of nationalist neoconservative figures such as Koizumi and Abe led to a more values-based and less mercantile approach to foreign policy. In a major speech in November 2006, then foreign minister Taro Aso announced Japan's plans to pursue 'value-oriented diplomacy' and to establish an 'arc of freedom and prosperity' along the outer rim of the Eurasian continent.[88] In the neoconservative vein, the specific values Japan sought to promote through its diplomacy were '"universal values" such as democracy, freedom, human rights, the rule of law, and the market economy'.[89] Japanese leaders such as Abe and Aso considered India 'a natural partner to help promote these values'.[90] The idea of a quadrilateral initiative in 2007 stemmed from such thinking. As one observer noted, 'Abe and Aso, encouraged by the growing strength of US–Japan and US–Australia alliance ties in the wake of the "war on terror", and by India's seeming flirtation with US alignment, envisaged that these four powers could form a "concert of democracies" to counter or even contain Chinese power.'[91] A Japanese analyst was more straightforward: '[F]reedom of expression helps build confidence between countries.'[92]

India, while proud of its democratic credentials, has since the end of the Cold War been reluctant to promote democracy or any other values through its foreign policy.[93] Thus, while Japan's leaders from Koizumi onwards have tended to view India through the lens of a democratic partner, India's interest has primarily been in the security externalities and economic potential of deeper relations with Japan. This disconnect is by no means fatal to the India–Japan relationship so long as both countries are able to create the military and economic glue required to bind them together in times of crisis. Japan's tendency to hedge in all possible directions, India's preference for strategic autonomy, and the relative weakness of their economic ties compared to their respective ties with China and the US are all likely to get in the way of deeper cooperation. It therefore becomes imperative for Prime Ministers Modi and Abe to firmly institutionalize the bilateral relationship and ground it in lasting mutual interest while exercising leadership to overcome obstacles in the short and long terms. Only by doing so can the current phase of newfound intimacy between India and Japan outlast the leaders—Koizumi, Singh, Abe, and Modi, among others—that have made it possible.

Structure and Approach of the Book

This volume stands out from existing work on India–Japan relations in a number of ways. First, it brings together scholars and analysts who are preeminent experts in specific sectors—economics, energy, security, and global governance—rather than experts in India–Japan relations per se. A vital objective of the volume is to look at the bilateral relationship from a perspective that mirrors the sectorally specialized knowledge that both countries now need in order to truly deepen their ties. Second, each chapter is co-authored by one established and one emerging scholar from the respective countries. This format pairs insight and experience on the one hand with cutting-edge skills and fresh thinking on the other to make each chapter comprehensive, insightful, and accessible to a wide cross-section of readers. The inclusion of new and younger voices in the conversation between India and Japan is vital not only for generating new insights but also for the longevity of the current bilateral trajectory. Third, the volume is both an academic work of foreign policy analysis and grand strategy, as well as a roadmap for statesmen and government officials in both countries. In addition to analysing their country's interests and strategies in a particular area, the authors have been invited to think ambitiously and for the long term so that the volume may have a long shelf life. Finally, the volume's chapters focus not just on the potential for cooperation but on the very real pitfalls and obstacles in the way of deeper India–Japan cooperation. This unacknowledged underbelly of the bilateral relationship, as it were, is virtually absent from existing literature on the subject.

Within each focus area, the volume contains one chapter from the Indian perspective and one from the Japanese perspective. All authors work within a common framework of inquiry, which requires them to answer the following four sets of questions. First, what are their country's primary interests in a particular area and what strategies has it adopted so far to achieve these objectives? Second, how successful has their country been in securing its interests or achieving its objectives in this area? Third, what is the scope of cooperation with the other country on these issues? What is the current state of cooperation? What challenges and opportunities do the two countries face in trying to improve cooperation? Finally, what are the major policy recommendations for leaders on both sides?

In keeping with this framework, Chapter 1, by Shujiro Urata and Mitsuyo Ando, examines the current state of Japan's economy, which is gradually emerging from a long slump. It discusses the particular demographic and macroeconomic challenges facing Japan, and the various ways in which Tokyo and Delhi might enhance their economic cooperation such as creating a better climate for FDI in India. In Chapter 2, Devesh Kapur and Rohit Lamba consider the problem from the Indian perspective, focusing on issues of trade, investment, production networks, and demographics with the aim of fully leveraging the complementarities that exist between the two economies. The authors argue for greater Japanese investment in Indian manufacturing and the latter's integration into the global supply chains of Japanese firms on the one hand, and Indian firms' developing trade in services with Japan on the other.

Chapter 3, by Nobuo Tanaka and Anthony Yazaki, highlights Japan's dependence on energy imports—which has worsened following the Fukushima Daiichi nuclear disaster—and explores various ways in which Japan and India might cooperate in order to secure access to cheaper natural resources, promote energy efficiency, and jointly develop better civil nuclear technologies. In order to achieve these goals, they suggest short-term initiatives such as the re-indexation of natural gas prices in Asia and long-term goals such as the creation of a regional energy security forum. In Chapter 4, Shyam Saran and Radhika Khosla study the common vulnerabilities that India and Japan share in terms of energy import dependence and threats from climate change, as well as the disconnect between the bilateral and multilateral positions taken by India and Japan on energy and climate change issues. Ultimately, they argue for enhancing mutual benefits by focusing on energy efficiency, solar energy, and clean coal technologies.

Chapter 5, by Noboru Yamaguchi and Shutaro Sano, discusses various potential obstacles that India and Japan face in deepening their security cooperation, including India's nuclear programme, the impact of aid to Afghanistan on Pakistan–India relations, and the security dilemma with China. In light of these obstacles, the authors argue for focusing on less risky areas of cooperation where real gains can be achieved such as peacekeeping and humanitarian assistance and disaster relief (HADR). In Chapter 6, C. Raja Mohan and Rishika Chauhan analyse the constraints that limit the pace and scope of the India–Japan strategic partnership. These include resistance in national security bureaucracies in both capitals to new ways of thinking about the bilateral relationship; the persistent sentiments of military isolationism in India and pacifism in Japan; and the residual legacy of non-alignment in Delhi and the primacy of the US alliance in Tokyo's calculus. The authors suggest various measures both capitals can take to overcome these constraints.

Chapters 7 and 8 focus on a relatively under-studied area of potential cooperation between India and Japan: global governance. In Chapter 7, Shinichi Kitaoka and Naoko Kumagai zero in on nuclear security, UNSC reform, international trade, and international finance as potential areas of cooperation. Like the authors of Chapter 5, they recommend that India and Japan choose pragmatism over idealism and focus on manageable issues such as semi-permanent UNSC seats, nuclear terrorism, food security, and complementarity between new international institutions and the existing global governance architecture. In Chapter 8, Waheguru Pal Singh Sidhu and Karthik Nachiappan argue that India has extensive economic, normative, and security interests across the global governance landscape, but has not had a stellar record in achieving its interests. Despite this, they suggest ways in which Japan and India can enhance their cooperation in areas such as international development cooperation, maritime security, civil nuclear issues, UN peacekeeping, and in reforming the UNSC and international financial institutions (IFIs).

Finally, the Conclusion provides thoughts from the editors of the volume. It ties together the broad themes that emerge from the preceding chapters and the lessons that both India and Japan can learn from the in-depth sectoral analyses contained therein. To reiterate, the volume is intended both as a comprehensive work of foreign policy analysis and a ready handbook for practitioners on both sides of the relationship who might seek a deeper understanding of its opportunities and challenges. There is no more opportune time than the present to firmly institutionalize the gains of the last decade. If India and Japan are sensitive to the analysis and insights presented in this volume, they can proceed to build a truly lasting partnership for the twenty-first century, which can rightly be called the Asian Century.

Notes

1. R. Tagore, *The Spirit of Japan*, Tokyo: Indo-Japanese Association, 1916, p. 5.
2. Press Information Bureau, Government of India, 'Remarks by Prime Minister at the Joint Press Briefing with Prime Minister Shinzo Abe of Japan', 2014, retrieved from http://www.pib.nic.in/NEWSITE/PrintRelease.aspx?relid=109222 on 31 August 2015.
3. S. Jaishankar, 'India-Japan Relations after Pokhran II', *Seminar*, 487, 2000, retrieved from http://www.india-seminar.com/2000/487/487%20jaishankar.htm on 31 August 2015.
4. D. Brewster, 'The India-Japan Security Relationship: An Enduring Security Partnership?', *Asian Security*, 6(2), 2010, p. 95.
5. Exceptions include: H. Takenori and L. Varma (eds), *India–Japan Relations in Emerging Asia*, New Delhi: Manohar Books, 2013; R. Panda, Y. Fukazawa, and K.K. Kokusai (eds), *India and Japan: In Search of Global Roles*, New Delhi: Promilla and Co., 2007; N.S. Sisodia and G.V.C. Naidu (eds), *India–Japan Relations: Partnership for Peace and Security in Asia*, New Delhi: Promilla and Co., 2006; M.D. Dharamdasani (ed.), *Indo-Japan Relations: Challenges and Opportunities*, New Delhi: Kanishka Publishers, 2004; U.S. Bajpai (ed.), *India and Japan: A New Relationship?* New Delhi: Lancer Books, 1988; and P.A.

N. Murthy, *India and Japan: Dimensions of Their Relationship, Historical and Political*, New Delhi: ABC Publishing House, 1986.

6. P. Jain, 'Japan–India Relations: Peaks and Troughs', *Round Table*, 99(409), 2010, p. 410.

7. The thesis in question was written by Satoru Nagao, who in 2015 was an associate at the Tokyo Foundation and a lecturer at Gakushuin University.

8. Jain, 'Japan–India Relations', p. 404.

9. 'The Asian Games, 1951–2002: Medal and Gold Medal Table', *Sport in Society: Cultures, Commerce, Media, Politics*, 8(3), 2005, p. 522.

10. K.V. Kesavan, 'India and Japan: Changing Dimensions of Partnership in the post-Cold War Period', Occasional paper #14, Observer Research Foundation, New Delhi, 2010.

11. H. Laurence, 'Japan's Proactive Foreign Policy and the Rise of the BRICS', *Asian Perspective*, 31(4), 2007, p. 179.

12. A. Panda, 'Asia's Democratic Bulwark: A Theoretical Analysis of Strategic Convergence between India and Japan in the Early 21st Century', Unpublished undergraduate thesis, Princeton University, Princeton, New Jersey, 2013.

13. P.A.N. Murthy, 'India and Japan: A New Stage in Bilateral Relations', *China Report*, 5(2), 1969, p. 7.

14. Murthy, 'India and Japan'.

15. Dhananjoy, 'China, India and Japan', *Economic and Political Weekly*, 6(46), 1971, pp. 2298–9.

16. G. Bass, *The Blood Telegram: Nixon, Kissinger, and a Forgotten Genocide*, New York: Alfred A. Knopf, 2013, pp. 138–9.

17. F.C. Langdon, 'Japanese Reactions to India's Nuclear Explosions', *Pacific Affairs*, 48(2), 1975, pp. 173–80.

18. A.K.N. Reddy, 'Basis of the Japanese "Miracle": Lessons for India', *Economic and Political Weekly*, 7(26), 1972, pp. 1241–2.

19. K.R. Narayanan, 'Towards a New Equilibrium in Asia', *Economic and Political Weekly*, 7(5–7), 1972, p. 224.

20. R. Bhattacharya, 'Maruti to Launch 3 Models, Upgrade 6 Others This Year', *Business Standard*, 29 January 2015.

21. Ministry of Foreign Affairs, Government of Japan, 'Japan and India', n.d., retrieved from http://www.mofa.go.jp/region/asia-paci/india/relation/relation.html on 31 August 2015.

22. Y. Funabashi, 'Japan's Moment of Truth', *Survival*, 42(4), 2000, pp. 73–84; V. Pinto, 'Making Up for the Lost Decade', *Economic and Political Weekly*, 41(25), 2006, pp. 2518–20.

23. K. Ishizuka, 'Japan and UN Peace Operations', *Japanese Journal of Political Science*, 5(1), 2004, p. 139.

24. Authors' calculations from the World Bank's world development indicators, retrieved from http://databank.worldbank.org/data/views/variableSelection/selectvariables.aspx?source=world-development-indicators on 31 August 2015.

25. 'Nuclear Anxiety; Indian's Letter to Clinton on the Nuclear Testing', *New York Times*, 13 May 1998.

26. A. Vanaik, 'Nuclear/CTBT Debate: Japan and India', *Economic and Political Weekly*, 31(34), 1996, p. 2275.

27. K. Togo, *Japan's Foreign Policy, 1945–2003: The Quest for a Proactive Policy*, Leiden: Brill, 2005, p. 219.

28. Jaishankar, 'India-Japan Relations after Pokhran II'.

29. Jaishankar, 'India-Japan Relations after Pokhran II'.

30. S. Joshi, 'Prospects for Security Cooperation between India and Japan', *Strategic Analysis*, 25(2), 2001, p. 188.

31. Jaishankar, 'India-Japan Relations after Pokhran II'.

32. Y.R. Rahman, 'Sino-Japan Relations and India', *Seminar*, 487, 2000, retrieved from http://www.india-seminar.com/2000/487/487%20rahman.htm on 31 August 2015.

33. M. Ghosh, 'India and Japan's Growing Synergy: From a Political to a Strategic Focus', *Asian Survey*, 48(2), 2008, p. 285.

34. G.V.C. Naidu, 'India-Japan Relations: Towards a Strategic Partnership', *China Report*, 41(3), 2005, pp. 327–30.

35. Ghosh, 'India and Japan's Growing Synergy', p. 283.

36. H.V. Pant, 'India in the Asia–Pacific: Rising Ambitions with an Eye on China', *Asia-Pacific Review*, 14(1), 2007, p. 65.

37. V. Pinto, 'A Strategic Partnership between India and Japan?', *Economic and Political Weekly*, 41(52), 2006, pp. 5299–301.

38. On Koizumi and Abe's place in Japanese politics, see R.J. Samuels, 'Securing Japan: The Current Discourse', *Journal of Japanese Studies*, 33(1), 2007, pp. 125–52. On Abe's support for India, see G.V.C. Naidu, 'New Dimensions to the India-Japan Strategic Partnership: Shinzo Abe's Visit', *Strategic Analysis*, 31(6), 2007, pp. 965–71.

39. H.V. Pant, 'The Emerging Balance of Power in the Asia Pacific', *RUSI Journal*, 152(3), 2007, p. 50.

40. Kesavan, 'India and Japan', p. 14.

41. C.W. Hughes, 'The Democratic Party of Japan's New (but Failing) Grand Security Strategy: From "Reluctant Realism" to "Resentful Realism"?', *Journal of Japanese Studies*, 38(1), 2012, p. 134.

42. C.R. Mohan, 'Japan and India: Towards Nuclear and Security Cooperation', RSIS Commentaries, Nanyang Technological University, Singapore, 2010.

43. Press Information Bureau, Government of India, 'India-Japan CEPA Comes into Force, Commerce Secretary Calls It a Major Step for a Larger East Asian Partnership', 2011, retrieved from http://pib.nic.in/newsite/erelease.aspx?relid=73596 on 31 August 2015.

44. See R. Lakshmi, 'Modi Goes to Japan, Takes an Indirect Swipe at China', *Washington Post*, 1 September 2014.

45. Narayanan, 'Towards a New Equilibrium in Asia', p. 221.

46. Laurence, 'Japan's Proactive Foreign Policy', p. 190.

47. For a timeline of such events, see Center for New American Security, 'Flashpoints: Security in the East and South China Seas', n.d., retrieved from http://www.cnas.org/flashpoints/timeline on 31 August 2015.

48. S. Nagao, 'Japan-India Military Partnership: India Is the New Hope for Asia', *CLAWS Journal*, Winter 2013, p. 72.

49. T. Inoguchi, 'Japanese Ideas of Asian Regionalism', *Japanese Journal of Political Science*, 12(2), 2011, p. 238.

50. E. Heginbotham and R.J. Samuels, 'Japan's Dual Hedge', *Foreign Affairs*, 81(5), 2002, pp. 110–21.

51. C.J. Wallace, 'Japan's Strategic Pivot South: Diversifying the Dual Hedge', *International Relations of the Asia-Pacific*, 13, 2013, pp. 479–517.

52. T. Wilkins, 'Japan's Alliance Diversification: A Comparative Analysis of the Indian and Australian Strategic Partnerships', *International Relations of the Asia Pacific*, 11(1), 2010, pp. 115–55.

53. Authors' calculation from the Stockholm International Peace Research Institute (SIPRI) military expenditure database, retrieved from http://www.sipri.org/research/armaments/milex/milex_database on 31 August 2015.

54. J. McCurry, 'Japan Reveals Record Defence Budget as Tensions with China Grow', *Guardian*, 14 January 2015.

55. On the latter strategy, see R. Sahashi, 'The Rise of China and the Changing Regional Security Architecture', US-Japan papers, Japan Center for International Exchange, Tokyo and New York, 2011.

56. Wallace, 'Japan's Strategic Pivot South', p. 491.

57. P.G. Rajamohan, D.B. Rahut, and J.T. Jacob, 'Changing Paradigm of Indo-Japan Relations: Opportunities and Challenges', Working paper no. 212, Indian Council for Research on International Economic Relations, New Delhi, p. 15.

58. S. Koizumi, 'The U.S.-India Nuclear Agreement Tests Japan's Proactive Diplomacy', Japan Chair Platform, Center for Strategic and International Studies, Washington, D.C., 2006. On Japan's commercial incentives, see J. Nandakumar and V. Kumar, 'India-Japan Relations: Are There Prospects for Civil Nuclear Cooperation?', *Strategic Analysis*, 31(6), 2007, pp. 973–84.

59. C.R. Mohan, *Crossing the Rubicon: The Shaping of India's New Foreign Policy*, New Delhi: Viking Books, 2003.

60. Authors' calculation from the SIPRI military expenditure database.

61. Authors' calculation from the SIPRI military expenditure database.

62. 'India Is World's "Largest Importer" of Arms, Says Study, *BBC News South Asia*, 14 March 2011.

63. F. Gady, 'Is India's Defense Budget Adequate?', *Diplomat*, 3 March 2015.

64. A. Panda, 'Why Does India Have So Many "Strategic Partners" and No Allies?', *Diplomat*, 23 November 2013.

65. Authors' calculation from the International Monetary Fund's (IMF's) direction of trade statistics (DOTS) database, retrieved from http://elibrary-data.imf.org/DataExplorer.aspx on 31 August 2015.

66. Authors' calculation from the IMF's DOTS database.

67. Ibid.

68. Laurence, 'Japan's Proactive Foreign Policy', p. 195.

69. M.G. Asher and R. Sen, 'India-East Asia Integration: A Win-Win for Asia', *Economic and Political Weekly*, 40(36), 2005, pp. 3932–40.

70. Authors' calculation from the IMF's DOTS data. For an explanation of the trade intensity index, see http://wits.worldbank.org/wits/wits/witshelp/Content/Utilities/e1.trade_indicators.htm retrieved on 31 August 2015.

71. Authors' calculation from the IMF's DOTS data.

72. Japan External Trade Organization, 'Japanese Trade and Investment Statistics', n.d., retrieved from http://www.jetro.go.jp/en/reports/statistics/ on 1 September 2015.

73. Authors' calculation based on United Nations Conference on Trade and Development (UNCTAD), 'Bilateral FDI Statistics', 2014, retrieved from http://unctad.org/en/pages/diae/fdi%20statistics/fdi-statistics-bilateral.aspx on 1 September 2015; and RBI, 'Appendix Table 8', *Annual Report 2013–14*, retrieved from http://www.rbi.org.in/scripts/AnnualReportPublications.aspx on 1 September 2015.

74. Parliament of India, Lok Sabha unstarred question no. 3899, 14 December 2009, in Indiastat.com, *Country-wise FDI Inflows in India*,

2009, retrieved from http://www.indiastat.com/table/industries/18/countrywiseforeigndirectinvestment19912012/449567/466262/data.aspx on 1 September 2015.

75. Parliament of India, Lok Sabha unstarred question no. 3899.
76. Authors' calculation based on UNCTAD and RBI data, as well as UNCTAD, 'Annex Table 02', *World Investment Report 2014*, retrieved from http://unctad.org/en/pages/PublicationWebflyer.aspx?publicationid=937 on 1 September 2015.
77. G. Nataraj, 'India-Japan Investment Relations: Trends and Prospects', Working paper no. 245, Indian Council for Research on International Economic Relations, New Delhi, p. 14.
78. Japan Chamber of Commerce and Industry in India (JCCII), 'Suggestions for the Government of India by JCCII 2013', retrieved from http://jccii.in/Docs/20130321_13_suggestions_koukai.pdf on 1 September 2015.
79. S. Ito, 'Technology Transfer from Japanese to Indian Firms', *Economic and Political Weekly*, 20(45–47), 1985, p. 2039.
80. Kesavan, 'India and Japan', p. 19.
81. Press Trust of India, 'Japan to Grant India $2.32 Bln Aid', *Hindu*, 27 March 2013.
82. D. Brewster, *India as an Asia Pacific Power*, New York: Routledge, 2012, p. 178, fn 33.
83. M.J. Green and B.L. Self, 'Japan's Changing China Policy: From Commercial Liberalism to Reluctant Realism', *Survival*, 38(2), 1996, pp. 35–58.
84. R.S. Yadav, 'Changing India-Japan Relations in the Post-Cold War Era', *India Quarterly*, 58(2), 2002, pp. 191–212.
85. Heginbotham and Samuels, 'Japan's Dual Hedge', p. 112.
86. D. Kliman, *Japan's Security Strategy in the Post-9/11 World: Embracing a New Realpolitik*, Westport: Praeger, 2006.
87. Y. Kawashima, *Japanese Foreign Policy at the Crossroads: Challenges and Options for the Twenty-First Century*, Washington, D.C.: Brookings Institution Press, 2005, p. 42.
88. Ministry of Foreign Affairs, Government of Japan, Speech by Mr. Taro Aso, Minister for Foreign Affairs, on the occasion of the Japan Institute of International Affairs seminar 'Arc of Freedom and Prosperity: Japan's Expanding Diplomatic Horizons', 30 November 2006, retrieved from http://www.mofa.go.jp/announce/fm/aso/speech0611.html on 1 September 2015.
89. Speech by Mr. Taro Aso, Minister for Foreign Affairs, 30 November 2006.

90. Koizumi, 'The US-India Nuclear Agreement', p. 1.
91. C.W. Hughes, 'Japan's Response to China's Rise: Regional Engagement, Global Containment, Dangers of Collision', *International Affairs*, 85(4), 2009, p. 850.
92. S. Nagao, 'The Emerging India Is Not a Threat, Why? An Assessment from Japan', *Asia Pacific Journal of Social Sciences*, 3(2), 2011, p. 99.
93. C.R. Mohan, 'Balancing Interests and Values: India's Struggle with Democracy Promotion', *Washington Quarterly*, 30(3), 2007, pp. 99–115.

Part I

ECONOMIC COOPERATION

1

Japan's Economic Recovery and Growing Economic Relations with India

Shujiro Urata and Mitsuyo Ando

The Japanese economy is faced with structural problems such as a declining and ageing population and a closed market, making it difficult to achieve growth. By contrast, the Indian economy is registering high growth, but it has the potential to achieve even higher growth by overcoming problems such as poor infrastructure. Given the complementary relationship between the two countries in terms of their levels of economic development, natural resource endowments, and sectoral specializations, both Japan and India can benefit substantially by expanding their economic relations—which have been very limited—through foreign trade, foreign direct investment, and economic cooperation. To achieve these objectives, Japan and India need to have close collaboration and cooperation at government as well as private sector levels. They should use existing frameworks such as the Japan–India Comprehensive Economic Partnership Agreement and the Japan–India Business Leaders Forum in addition to other official and private dialogues and cooperation programmes.

Since Shinzo Abe returned to the prime minister's office in December 2012, the Japanese economy has shown signs of recovery after two decades of slow economic growth. Prime Minister Abe formulated a three-arrow strategy, the so-called 'Abenomics', which consists of an aggressive monetary policy (the first arrow), a flexible fiscal policy (the second arrow), and a growth strategy (the third arrow), in order to recover from a long recession and to regain economic dynamism. The first two arrows have been shot, and they seemed to have achieved the expected impacts of lifting the Japanese economy from its long recession (although it may be too early to present a final verdict on this issue). Unlike the first two arrows, the third arrow has been quite slow. Indeed, the growth strategy, which is aimed at tackling structural problems such as demographic change, is considered to be of crucial importance for the Japanese economy to get back on a growth trajectory, which would result in the improvement of Japan's economic welfare.

While Japan was struggling to deal with a long recession, the international economic landscape surrounding Japan changed dramatically. Many developing countries, particularly those in East Asia, achieved high economic growth. Among the rising economies, Brazil, Russia, India, and China, or the BRIC countries, which are large in terms of population, economic size, and geographical area, have received attention from business, policy makers, and mass media as their future economic prospects seem bright (with the possible exception of Russia), and they may dominate the world economy in a few decades. Among the BRIC countries, India has been at the centre of attention since Narendra Modi became prime minister in May 2014, as he is expected to implement policy reforms in order to achieve high and sustained economic growth. Modi is particularly popular among Japanese politicians and business people, as he appears to be keen on having close ties with Japan and Japanese businesses.

Another new development in the global economy is the rapid expansion of regionalism, particularly in the form of free trade agreements (FTAs), which eliminate trade barriers such as tariffs and non-tariff barriers between FTA members while maintaining existing barriers with non-FTA members. The discriminatory nature of these agreements has resulted in an explosion of FTAs, because those countries excluded from them have hurried to either join existing agreements or establish new ones. The wave of FTAs struck Europe and the Americas in the late 1980s and early 1990s. Asia was slow in catching up with the rest of the world in this race, but it caught up quickly in the twenty-first century. Against this background, both Japan and India became active in formulating their own agreements, and they enacted the Japan–India FTA (formally named the Japan–India Comprehensive Economic Partnership Agreement, or CEPA) in August 2011. Currently, two mega FTAs are under negotiation involving Asian countries: the Trans-Pacific Partnership (TPP) and the Regional Comprehensive Economic Partnership (RCEP). Japan is participating in both negotiations, while India is participating only in the RCEP negotiations.

In light of these recent developments in the Japanese economy and the changing international and regional economic landscape, this chapter discusses the economic policies that would contribute to Japan's achieving optimistic economic prospects in the future. Recognizing India's huge economic potential, the analysis focuses on Japan's economic relations with India. The analysis finds that Japan and India have much to gain from enhancing their bilateral economic relationship, as their economic relations are complementary.

The chapter proceeds in five parts. First, it discusses Japan's structural problems that have prevented its economy from achieving reasonable economic growth. Second, it analyses Japan's economic relations with India by focusing on international trade, foreign direct investment (FDI), and production networks. Third, it examines the Japan–India FTA and its possible economic impacts. Fourth, it discusses economic cooperation between Japan and India. Finally, it concludes by providing recommendations to the Japanese and Indian governments for achieving mutual economic benefits.

Japan's Structural Economic Problems

Signs of economic recovery have now been detected, but the future prospects for the Japanese economy are still quite pessimistic. This is because the Japanese economy is faced with a number of structural problems, the most serious of which is an ageing and shrinking population. Economic growth is achieved through the interaction of supply and demand factors, but this demographic problem has negative impacts on both. On the supply side, to achieve economic growth it is necessary to increase labour inputs, increase capital inputs, or raise productivity, but the ageing and shrinking population is making it hard to increase labour and capital. The Japanese population fell in 2005, and although it temporarily rose in 2006, it has been falling continuously since 2007 (Figure 1.1). According to the estimates of the National Institute of Population and Social Security Research, the current population of over 120 million people is projected to drop below 100 million in 2046, and will become as low as 90 million in 2055.[1] Meanwhile, the labour force has been shrinking since 1997,[2] and is predicted to continue to fall in the future as well.[3] If this population decline cannot be reversed, it will be difficult to increase labour inputs without increasing labour by women and the elderly or without receiving foreign workers.

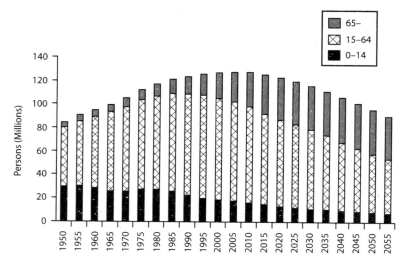

Figure 1.1   Japan's Population: Future Projections
Source: Ministry of Internal Affairs and Communications, Statistical Bureau, *Jinko no suii to shorai jinko* (Past population trend and future projections), retrieved from http://www.stat.go.jp/data/nihon/02.htm on 1 September 2015; and National Institute of Population and Social Security Research, *Nihon no shorai suikei jinko (Heisei 18 nen 12 gatsu suikei) chui suikei* (Japan's future projected population [December 2006 projection] central projection), retrieved from http://www.ipss.go.jp/syoushika/tohkei/suikei07/suikei.html#chapt1-1 on 1 September 2015.

To increase capital inputs, domestic saving or investment from abroad is necessary, but Japanese domestic saving is decreasing partly due to the ageing population, and the inflow of foreign capital has been limited due to uncertainty in the future of the Japanese economy. The overall domestic savings rate was 29.5 per cent in 1995—a high figure even among developed countries—but has steadily dropped, reaching 18.3 per cent in 2013.[4] A large part of this is due to a declining household savings rate, which dropped from 9.6 per cent in 1995 to minus 1.3 per cent in 2013,[5] and due to declining government savings or an increasing government deficit, which will be discussed below.

Economic growth cannot be expected from the demand side either. Due to decline and a low economic growth rate, consumption is not growing; and because future consumption is not likely to increase, it is expected that investment by companies will stagnate. Also, the government is saddled with enormous debt exceeding double the gross domestic product (GDP) (Figure 1.2), therefore it is difficult to

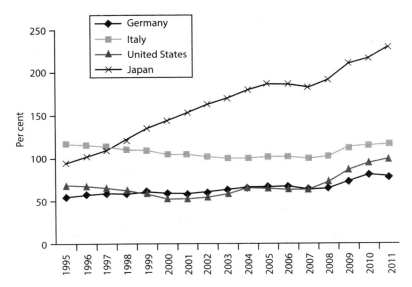

Figure 1.2 Government Debt Situation in Selected Developed Countries, 1995–2011 (Government Debt to GDP Ratios)
Source: The Annual Macroeconomic Database (AMECO) of the European Commission's Directorate General for Economic and Financial Affairs, retrieved from http://ec.europa.eu/economy_finance/db_indicators/ameco/ on 1 September 2015.

expand spending in a manner that would lead to real demand. Since it is expected that public spending on social security and health care will increase due to the rapid ageing of the population, if the integrated reform of social security and taxes currently being debated is not implemented, the fiscal situation will worsen, and the likelihood of economic growth will become ever smaller.

Moreover, due to the relatively closed nature of its market and society, Japan remains unable to take advantage of the opportunities provided by globalization for mutual exchanges with other countries of important factors for increased economic activity, including goods, people, capital, and information. This observation can be supported by the fact that the proportion of trade and direct investment as a share of GDP is lower in Japan than in other countries. Specifically, the trade (exports and imports) to GDP ratios for Japan in 2013 were 14.5 per cent for the exports to GDP ratio and 16.9 per cent for the imports to GDP ratio, respectively (Figure 1.3). These figures are somewhat comparable to those for India, while they are smaller compared to China and Indonesia and significantly smaller compared to South Korea and Germany. Turning to FDI, one finds a notably low inward FDI stock to GDP ratio for Japan in Figure 1.4. Indeed, the

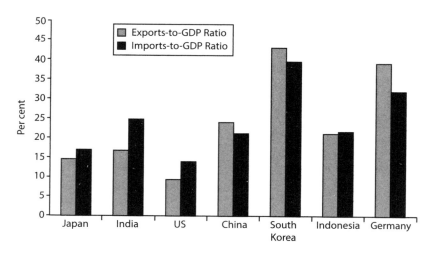

Figure 1.3　Importance of International Trade for Selected Countries, 2013
Source: World Bank's World Development Indicators.

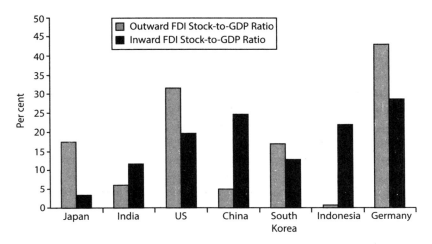

Figure 1.4   Importance of Foreign Direct Investment for Selected Countries, 2011
Note: Figures for India and Indonesia are for 2010.
Source: UNCTAD's FDI database (FDI stock) and the World Bank's World Development Indicators (GDP).

ratio for Japan is 3.4 per cent, the lowest among the countries in this figure. The second lowest is India at 11.6 per cent. The figures for the US, China, Indonesia, and Germany are at around 20 per cent or higher.

The circumstances in which the Japanese economy is placed are quite severe, and it is understood that just maintaining the status quo would create a pessimistic view of its future. To escape from this situation and achieve economic prosperity in the future, it is necessary to revitalize economic activity and increase productivity by furthering structural reforms and opening the market. It would also be effective to intensify economic exchanges with Asian countries including China, India, and members of the Association of Southeast Asian Nations (ASEAN), where high growth is expected in the future. One important policy to achieve these objectives is participating in mega FTAs including the TPP, RCEP, and the Japan–EU FTA.

Japan's Economic Relations with India: Trade, FDI, and Production Networks

International Trade

Japan's trade with India began increasing notably in the twenty-first century. The magnitude of Japan's exports to India remained more or less at around US$1–2 billion a year until the early 2000s (Figure 1.5).[6] It began to increase in the early 2000s, exceeding $3 billion in 2004, and then it increased sharply to reach $10 billion in 2011. Japan's imports from India also began to rise in the twenty-first century (Figure 1.6). However, compared to Japan's exports to India, the rate of increase of Japan's imports from India was not as high, at around $2 billion until the early 2000s. It then increased to over $3 billion in 2005 and continued to increase, reaching almost $7 billion in 2012.

Despite the relatively rapid expansion of Japan's trade with India, India's share in Japan's overall trade is still very low. The shares of India in Japan's total exports and imports were 1.4 and 0.8 per cent, respectively, in 2012. These shares appear small considering

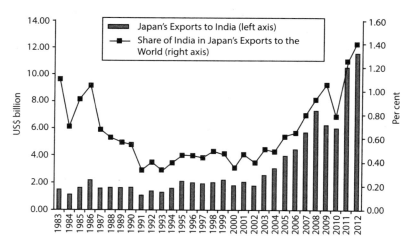

Figure 1.5   Japan's Exports to India, 1983–2012

Source: Research Institute of Economy, Trade and Industry (RIETI), retrieved from http://www.rieti-tid.com/ on 2 September 2015.

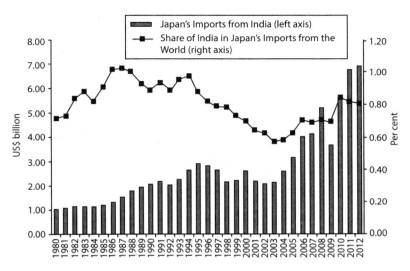

Figure 1.6   Japan's Imports from India, 1980–2012
Source: RIETI, retrieved from http://www.rieti-tid.com/ on 2 September 2015.

the magnitude of India's imports and exports in world trade, which accounted for 2.8 and 1.4 per cent, respectively, in 2012.[7] This assessment is very rough, as the magnitude of bilateral trade is affected by not only the magnitude of their overall trade but also geographical, cultural, and historical distances, trade policies, and other factors.[8] It should be noted that the bilateral trade balance between Japan and India changed from a surplus for India in the 1990s to a surplus for Japan in the twenty-first century. This shift largely reflects the differences in economic growth performance between the two countries. In the 1990–2012 period, Japan's economic growth remained quite low while India's economic growth rose sharply in the twenty-first century, resulting in a trade surplus for Japan.

It is worth noting that the product structure of bilateral trade is very different on both sides. Japan's exports to India consist mainly of machinery products, while Japan's imports from India are mainly natural resource–based products. In general, Japan's major export products and their shares in its total exports are general machinery (24.3 per cent), iron and steel (15.1 per cent), transportation machinery including auto parts (12.8 per cent), electronic machinery (8.0 per cent), and precision machinery (4.3 per cent), whereas India's major export items and their shares are petroleum products such as naphtha (42.0 per cent), agricultural and fishery products (13.1 per cent), machine tools (5.7 per cent), gems and jewellery (4.9 per cent), and alloy iron (3.9 per cent).[9] These findings appear to indicate that the trade structures of Japan and India are complementary, reflecting differences in their respective levels of economic development and natural endowments.

Considering that the income elasticity of demand for natural resource-based products is low, and that Japan's prospects of future economic growth are rather low, one cannot expect that India's exports to Japan will grow significantly unless India is successful in exporting manufactured products, particularly machinery products. The current Indian government's focus on 'Make in India' is therefore a timely initiative that might have beneficial impacts for India–Japan trade in the future. In contrast, Japan's exports to India are likely to increase because they consist of manufactured products with high income elasticity and because India's economic growth rate is expected to be high. These observations indicate the increasing importance of India's high economic growth for Japanese firms, as it would provide them with an increasingly attractive market.

Foreign Direct Investment (FDI)[10]

Japan's FDI in India increased sharply in the mid-2000s (Figure 1.7).[11] The magnitude of Japan's FDI in India remained below US$500 million annually until 2004. In 2005 it reached $512 million, and then it started to increase sharply in 2007 and reached a peak at $5.6 billion in 2008. It then declined notably to reach a trough at $2.3 billion in 2011. Since then, the magnitude of Japan's FDI in India has continued to be around $2–3 billion. With a rapid expansion of Japan's FDI to India, the share of India in Japan's total outward FDI increased from less than 1 per cent in the first half of the 2000s to 4–5 per cent in the 2008–10 period before declining to approximately 2 per cent in 2011–13. The importance of India for Japan is greater in terms of FDI compared to the case of foreign trade, which was examined in the previous section. One reason for this is the limited importance of geographical distance in the case of FDI, whereas geographical distance is an important factor determining the magnitude of international trade.

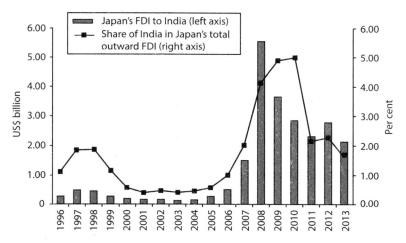

Figure 1.7   Japan's FDI in India, 1996–2013
Source: The JETRO database, retrieved from http://www.jetro.go.jp/world/japan/
stats/fdi.html on 2 September 2015.

India has been one of the major destinations of Japanese FDI in recent years. In 2008, when Japan's FDI to India recorded a peak, India was the second largest recipient of Japanese FDI in the developing world after China. But India lost the second position after 2009, as Japan's FDI to India declined. At the end of 2013, India was ranked eighth among developing countries in terms FDI stock by Japanese firms at ¥1.4 trillion, or roughly US$13.5 billion, behind China (¥10.3 trillion), Thailand (¥4.7 trillion), Singapore (¥3.9 trillion), Brazil (¥3.5 trillion), South Korea (¥3.1 trillion), Hong Kong (¥2.1 trillion), and Indonesia (¥2.1 trillion).[12] India accounted for 1.9 per cent of Japan's overall outward FDI stock at the end of 2013. Since the share of India in world inward FDI stock at the end of 2013 was 0.8 per cent, Japan's FDI is found to be more concentrated in India compared to that of other countries investing in India.[13]

The rising interest of Japanese firms in India as an FDI destination is reflected in information on Japanese firms operating in India released by the Embassy of Japan in India.[14] According to an investigation conducted by the Embassy of Japan and the Japan External Trade Organization (JETRO) office in India, the number of Japanese firms operating in India in October 2014 was 1,209, an increase of

13 per cent from 2013.[15] The number of affiliates of Japanese firms in India was 3,961, an increase of 56 per cent from 2013. The composition of Japan's FDI in India is rather uneven across sectors. Manufacturing and non-manufacturing accounted for 72 and 28 per cent, respectively, of Japan's total FDI stock in India at the end of 2013 (Table 1.1). Among the manufacturing sectors, transportation equipment makes up approximately half of Japanese FDI stock in Indian manufacturing, or 36 per cent of total Japanese FDI stock in India. Other manufacturing sectors with sizeable shares include electric machinery (9.7 per cent of total), chemicals and pharmaceuticals (8.7 per cent), and general machinery (8.1 per cent). Among non-manufacturing sectors, finance and insurance have a dominant share, accounting for 76 per cent of Japanese FDI stock in Indian non-manufacturing sectors, or 21 per cent of total Japanese FDI stock in India.

Table 1.1 Industry Composition of Japanese FDI Stock (Per Cent) in India at the End of 2013

Manufacturing	72.21	Non-manufacturing	27.79
Food	na	Farming and forestry	0.00
Textiles	0.35	Fishery and marine products	0.00
Wood and pulp	0.81	Mining	0.00
Chemicals and pharmaceuticals	8.66	Construction	0.44
Petroleum	0.00	Transportation	1.25
Rubber and leather	1.59	Communications	0.40
Glass and ceramics	1.52	Wholesale and retail	2.69
Iron, non-ferrous metals	3.61	Finance and insurance	21.13
General machinery	8.12	Real estate	na
Electric machinery	9.69	Services	1.17
Transportation equipment	35.53	Other non-manufacturing	na
Precision machinery	1.11		
Other manufacturing	na		

Source: Bank of Japan, Balance of Payments Statistics, Direct Investment Position, retrieved from https://www.boj.or.jp/statistics/br/bop/iip.htm/ on 2 September 2015.
Note: The components of Manufacturing and Non-manufacturing sum to 98.07 per cent. The remaining 1.93 per cent is attributed to components labelled 'na', which are not disclosed by the Bank of Japan.

Various motives may be found behind Japanese firms' FDI in India. First, a large and growing Indian market is very attractive for Japanese firms. India had a population of approximately 1.3 billion in 2014, behind China's 1.4 billion, and population growth was around 1.4 per cent per annum between 2000 and 2014, significantly faster compared to China, where the corresponding value was 0.5 per cent.[16] At this rate, India's population will surpass China's by 2023. One of the important characteristics of India's population is a large proportion of young people. Indeed, as much as 46 per cent of the population is 25 years old or younger.[17] These observations indicate that India's domestic market is already huge, and it is likely to grow further if economic growth continues.

Second, the availability of low-wage labour is another attractive element of India as an FDI destination. According to a survey conducted by JETRO, the average monthly wage of a factory worker in Mumbai in October–November 2012 was US$188, which is lower compared to the average in many Asian cities including Shenzhen ($329), Guangzhou ($395), Jakarta ($239), and Bangkok ($345), while it is higher compared to cities in Vietnam such as Hanoi ($145) and Ho Chi Minh City ($148).[18] In addition to these factors, there are Japanese firms that are interested in setting up a base in India from which they would like to conduct business in the Middle East and Africa. Finally, the liberalization of trade and FDI policies as well as deregulation which have been pursued by the Indian government since the early 1990s have contributed to the expansion of Japanese FDI by improving the FDI environment.

International Production Networks in East Asia and India

One of the important factors that contributed to the rapid economic growth of East Asian developing countries is their involvement in international production/distribution networks, which have been constructed through FDI by foreign firms, especially those from Japan.[19] Taking advantage of wide differences in wages (reflecting the different levels of economic development among East Asian developing countries), foreign firms fragmented their production processes into a number of sub-processes and located these sub-processes in countries where they could be conducted most efficiently or at least cost. Firms connected these sub-processes through distribution networks, resulting in active transaction of parts and components that are produced from sub-processes, before assembling them to produce final products. Formed in this way, international production networks have been constructed in industries such as machinery, in which many parts and components are used for production.

Involvement in international production networks contributed to rapid economic growth in participating countries, as it enabled them not only to expand production, exports, and employment, but also to improve productivity by obtaining and assimilating foreign technology and know-how. In addition to diversity in wages among the developing countries in East Asia, as discussed earlier, the liberalization of trade and FDI policies pursued by East Asian developing countries contributed to the formation of production networks as they reduced transaction costs.

These networks have been expanding rapidly in East Asia as new countries as well as new foreign and local firms become involved. One useful indicator of the level of involvement or engagement in international production networks is the magnitude of international trade in parts and components. The evidence shows that the share of parts and components of the machinery sector in total trade (exports and imports) rose rapidly in many East Asian developing countries from the 1990s to 2010, indicating an expansion of international production networks.[20] For example, the share of parts and components exports in total exports for the Philippines in 2010 was as high as 50 per cent. The corresponding shares for other East Asian countries were lower, ranging between 20 and 40 per cent. Compared to East Asian developing countries, the extent of India's involvement in international production networks has been limited. This observation can be supported by the low share of parts and components trade in total trade in India. In 2010, the shares of parts and components in total exports and imports for India were 6.6 and 9.0 per cent, respectively.

Japanese firms are major players in these production networks in East Asia. In this region, not only large firms but also small and medium-sized enterprises (SMEs) are active investors and are playing an important role in forming networks. Table 1.2 shows the number of Japanese affiliates in Asia in 2012. This table clearly demonstrates

Table 1.2   Number of Affiliates of Japanese Firms in Asia, 2012

	World	Asia	India	China	ASEAN6	NIEs3
Total	23,351	15,234	410	6,479	5,360	2,852
Manufacturing	10,425	7,962	197	3,879	2,868	960
Food and beverage	508	344	5	185	123	31
Textile	554	504	3	353	113	27
Wood, pulp, paper	155	120	-	64	51	5
Chemicals	1,213	837	27	328	317	157
Petroleum and coal	52	37	1	15	16	4
Ceramic, stone, and clay	269	207	4	102	67	31
Iron and steel	297	227	10	102	101	13
Non-ferrous metals	316	264	2	127	107	27
Metal products	528	456	5	226	171	52
General-purpose machinery	347	252	8	132	72	39
Production machinery	674	536	11	286	168	69
Business-oriented machinery	381	263	5	127	79	50
Electrical machinery	667	535	13	306	153	61
IC electronics equipment	1,095	905	5	397	330	170
Transport equipment	1,950	1,310	83	530	583	102
Other manufacturing	1,419	1,165	15	599	417	122
Non-manufacturing	12,926	7,272	213	2,600	2,492	1,892
Information and communication	s 786	514	19	278	141	67
Transport	1,322	684	18	250	286	120

(*Cont'd*)

Table 1.2   (Cont'd)

	World	Asia	India	China	ASEAN6	NIEs3
Wholesale	6,381	3,825	112	1,308	1,173	1,223
Retail trade	705	430	5	179	119	123
Services	1,918	1,027	38	395	350	232
Other non-manufacturing	1,814	792	21	190	423	127

Source: Ministry of Economy, Trade, and Industry (METI), Survey of Overseas Business Activities, No. 43, retrieved from http://www.meti.go.jp/statistics/tyo/kaigaizi/result/result_43.html on 2 September 2015.

Note: The number is based on the affiliates (with operation) of Japanese firms that returned the questionnaire. ASEAN6 are Indonesia, Malaysia, Philippines, Singapore, Thailand, and Vietnam. NIEs3 are Hong Kong, Korea, and Taiwan.

that Japanese firms are active in investing in manufacturing sectors, particularly machinery, in East Asian countries such as China, the ASEAN6, and NIEs3 (Newly Industrialized Economies). Table 1.2 also indicates that the number of Japanese manufacturing affiliates in India is much smaller compared with other Asian countries. A large portion of Japanese manufacturing affiliates in India are concentrated in the transport equipment sector, probably without deeper involvement in electrical machinery and integrated circuit electronics equipment sectors, unlike the case of East Asian countries. This evidence seems to confirm that India is not deeply and widely involved in the production networks of Japanese firms.

Future Business Prospects in India for Japanese Firms

Although the level of Japan's FDI in India declined after reaching a peak in 2008, it still remains at a much higher level compared to the level before the twenty-first century. This section investigates the future prospects of India as an FDI destination for Japanese firms.

The Japan Bank for International Cooperation (JBIC) has conducted annual surveys of Japanese firms operating in foreign countries since 1989. One of the questions in the survey is about firms' views on promising countries for their future investments. According to the survey conducted in July 2014, India was chosen as the most promising country for investment for the next three years.[21] Specifically, 45.9 per cent of the 617 respondents indicated that India is a very promising FDI destination (Figure 1.8). India was followed closely by Indonesia (45.7 per cent) and China (43.7 per cent). Although India had been ranked very highly for many years from the early 2000s, the 2014 survey was the first time that India was ranked first. India's popularity rose sharply in the latter half of the 2000s, while China's popularity declined sharply. Among the four manufacturing sectors surveyed—chemicals, automobiles, electric and electronic machinery, and general machinery—India was ranked first in chemicals and electric and electronic machinery, while it was ranked second in automobiles and general machinery.

A similarly optimistic view of the future prospect of the Indian market by Japanese firms can be obtained from a survey conducted by

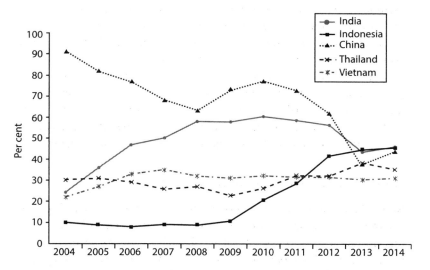

Figure 1.8   Promising FDI Destinations for Japanese Firms from 2004–14 (Per Cent of Respondents)

Source: JBIC, *Wagakuni seizogyo kigyo no kaigai jigyo tenkai ni kansuru chosa hokoku: 2014 nendo kaigai chokusetsu toshi anketo kekka* (no. 26) (Report of the research on overseas activities of Japanese manufacturing firms: Results of questionnaire survey on FDI in 2014 [no. 26]).

Note: The figures indicate the percentage of respondents indicating that the country in question is a promising investment location in approximately the next three years.

JETRO in 2014, which indicated that 78.2 per cent of 417 Japanese firms operating in India that responded to the questionnaire planned to expand their operations in India, while 20.9 per cent planned to maintain more or less the same level of operations.[22] Only 0.9 per cent indicated that they would either diminish or terminate their operations. The survey, which covered the non-manufacturing sector as well as the manufacturing sector showed that as many as 83 per cent of 106 Japanese firms in wholesale and retail services have plans to expand their operations.

Among the reasons for India being a promising FDI destination, the future growth potential of the local market was indicated as the most important factor by 85 per cent of the respondent firms that chose India as a promising destination in the JBIC survey.[23] Availability of low-wage labour was the second most important reason as it received 33.6 per cent of the responses. Other reasons included the current size of the local market (31.8 per cent), the supply base for assembly operations (20.9 per cent), and the availability of capable human resources (13.6 per cent). The JETRO survey also identified the rapid increase of local sales and the future growth potential of the local market as the most important factors behind Japanese firms' plans for expanding their operations.[24] It should be noted that in the JBIC survey, 93.3 per cent of the Japanese firms that showed strong interest in India indicated that they considered the economic policy of the new government as an important factor.

Obstacles to Conducting Business in India

Many Japanese firms have shown strong interest in investing and expanding their operations in India. However, they identify various obstacles in doing so. If these obstacles were to be reduced or removed, FDI by Japanese firms would likely increase rapidly and substantially. This section examines the obstacles Japanese firms have faced regarding their operations in India.

The 2014 JBIC survey mentioned earlier listed six obstacles that received substantial reporting from Japanese firms: underdevelopment of infrastructure (51.6 per cent of respondents), harsh competition with other firms (36.7 per cent), lack of transparency in the implementation of the legal system (35.1 per cent), complicated tax system (28.2 per cent), labour issues (24.5 per cent), and social instability and insecurity (24.5 per cent).[25] The problem of underdeveloped infrastructure has been pointed out by Japanese and other foreign investors in India for many years.[26] Infrastructure covers a wide range of items including both hard (physical) infrastructure such as transportation and communication services and soft (systemic) infrastructure including legal and educational systems. The main hard infrastructure problems that Japanese firms identify are limited and unreliable transportation and communication systems as well as insufficient and unreliable supply of electricity.

Table 1.3 provides some evidence to support the Japanese firms' claims. It shows the level of electric power consumption per capita and the number of internet users in India, Indonesia, China, Thailand, and Vietnam. These countries have been chosen because previous analysis of Japanese firms' perceptions of potential investment destinations in Asia suggests that they are considered to be competitors. Regarding electricity supply capacity, India and Indonesia are found to be ranked very low compared to other countries. The level of electric power consumption per capita for India is one-fifth of China's and one-third of Thailand's. Similar findings can be obtained from the ranking on accessing electricity in the World Bank's Ease of Doing Business Index. Among 189 countries in the survey, India is ranked 137th, the lowest among the five countries in the table. Turning to the number of internet users per 100 people, which reflects the level of communication networks, one finds that India is the lowest among the countries at 15.1, which is approximately one-third of the number in China or Vietnam.

A lack of transparency in the implementation of Indian laws and a complicated tax system, which are indicated as problems by Japanese firms in the JBIC survey and may be considered as issues with soft infrastructure, are also reflected in India's Ease of Doing Business ranking. For 'enforcing contracts' and 'paying taxes', India is ranked very low at 186 and 156, respectively. Indeed, India's low overall ranking at 142 in the Ease of Doing Business Index indicates the difficulties foreign firms face in establishing affiliates through FDI in India.

Table 1.3 Comparison of Infrastructure among Selected Countries, 2013

Country	Electric Power Consumption (kWh per capita)	Internet Users (per 100 people)	Ease of Doing Business Ranking (189 Countries)										
			Overall	Starting a Business	Dealing with Construction Permits	Getting Electricity	Registering Property	Getting Credit	Protecting Minority Investors	Paying Taxes	Trading Across Borders	Enforcing Contracts	Resolving Insolvency
India	684.1	15.1	142	158	184	137	121	36	7	156	126	186	137
Indonesia	679.7	15.8	114	155	153	78	117	71	43	160	62	172	75
China	3298.0	45.8	90	128	179	124	37	71	132	120	98	35	53
Thailand	2316.0	28.9	26	75	6	12	28	89	25	62	36	25	45
Vietnam	1073.3	43.9	78	125	22	135	33	36	117	173	75	47	104

(Cont'd)

Table 1.3 *(Cont'd)*

Logistics Peformance Index (168 Countries)

Country	Overall	Customs	Infrastructure	International Shipments	Logistics Competence	Tracking and Tracing	Timeliness
India	54	65	58	44	52	57	51
Indonesia	53	55	56	74	41	58	50
China	28	38	23	22	35	29	36
Thailand	35	36	30	39	38	33	29
Vietnam	48	61	44	42	49	48	56

Sources: World Bank, World Development Indicators (electric power in 2011 and internet usage in 2013), Ease of Doing Business Rankings, retrieved from http://www.doingbusiness.org/rankings, and Logistics Performance Index, retrieved from http://lpi.worldbank.org/ on 2 September 2015.

The 2014 JETRO survey discussed in the previous section reveals the problems relating to customs administration. The Japanese firms that reported problems of long waiting times and complicated procedures at customs amounted to 61.0 and 60.8 per cent of respondents, respectively, both of which are higher compared to the previous year, at 56.8 per cent and 55.9 per cent, respectively.[27] These observations corroborate the findings from the World Bank's Global Logistics Performance Index. Among the five countries listed in Table 1.3, India is ranked lowest at 65th in the 'customs' category. Having noted this, it may be worth mentioning that the Asian countries listed in the table including India are ranked rather high compared to developing countries in other regions in the Global Logistics Performance Index. Overall, these findings indicate that service link costs are rather high for India, making it difficult for India to be involved in international production networks.

The analysis in this section suggests that India needs to improve its hard and soft infrastructure in order to attract more FDI from Japan and other countries. To look at this problem differently, one can argue that India has great potential because it has been successful in raising its attractiveness as an FDI destination despite these serious problems. In order to deal effectively with these problems by improving infrastructure, the Indian government needs to formulate appropriate policies and implement them effectively not only by itself, but with economic cooperation extended by international organizations and foreign countries including Japan.

The Japan–India CEPA

Japan began to discuss FTAs towards the end of the 1990s, when it was approached by several countries including Mexico, Singapore, and South Korea. At the time, many countries that were interested in expanding exports became interested in forming FTAs with like-minded countries, as multilateral trade negotiations for trade liberalization under the General Agreement on Tariffs and Trade (GATT) became increasingly difficult due to differences in views towards agricultural trade policies between the US, the EU, and Japan. The difficulty in making progress in multilateral trade liberalization continued even after the World Trade Organization (WTO) was established in 1995 to succeed the GATT with a strengthened foundation as an international organization.

In light of the new global trading environment, where the number of FTAs was rapidly increasing, Japan decided to participate in these agreements in order to avoid negative impacts caused by discrimination. An FTA is a discriminatory trade policy, where a member provides preferential market access with reduced or eliminated tariffs to another member. As such, non-FTA members suffer from reduced export opportunities. Japan, China, and South Korea were among the few countries that did not join the global FTA race until the end of 1990s, as these countries thought that they should continue relying on the multilateral trade system, which provided them with ample export opportunities, contributing to their rapid economic growth.

Japan enacted its first FTA with Singapore in November 2002, which was followed by FTAs with Mexico and Malaysia in 2005. The Japan–India FTA, also known as the Comprehensive Economic Partnership Agreement,[28] enacted in August 2011, was Japan's 10th such agreement. Similar to Japan's earlier FTAs, the Japan–India FTA focuses comprehensively on trade in goods and services, customs procedures, rules of origin, investment, movement of natural persons, technical barriers to trade (TBT), sanitary and phytosanitary (SPS) measures, government procurement, intellectual property rights, and competition policy.

The areas that Japanese firms are seen to be most interested in are goods and services trade, and investment liberalization and facilitation. India imposes high tariffs on many imported manufactured products from Japan: 10 per cent on many auto parts and electric and electronic products, 7.5 per cent on general machinery, and 5 per cent on iron and steel products.[29] With the enactment of the Japan–India FTA, a large proportion of these tariffs on manufactured products will be reduced or eliminated in 10 years.[30] With the reduction and elimination of high tariffs, Japanese firms expect not only to expand their exports to India, but also to enable their affiliates and subsidiaries in India to procure parts and components freely in order to achieve efficient operation. In the area of trade in services, India agreed to extend its commitments, which are higher compared to its commitments made in the General Agreement on Trade in Services

(GATS) under the WTO. One of the important commitments for Japan that India accepted is liberalization of FDI in retail services for a single-brand firm and a single-brand franchise.

Under the Japan–India FTA, in addition to investment protection—which includes fair and equitable treatment, appropriate compensation in the case of expropriation, protection from strife, and investor–state dispute settlement (ISDS)—Japan gained substantially in the area of investment liberalization. India agreed to provide Japanese firms national treatment before and after the establishment of foreign investment. In other words, Japanese firms will not face discrimination in their investments in India vis-à-vis Indian firms. In addition, India agreed to prohibit performance requirements in many areas—including export requirements, export restrictions, local content requirements, export and import balance requirements, domestic sale restriction requirements, and officers' nationality requirements—as conditions for approving Japanese FDI. India also agreed to adopt the negative-list approach for indicating the sectors open for investment, which is considered more liberal compared to the positive-list approach.

In the Japan–India FTA, a framework and measures for improving the business environment for firms from both countries in their partner countries have been set up.[31] To achieve this objective, a sub-committee on improvement of business environment was established. The functions of this sub-committee include: (*a*) to supervise the activities of consultative groups set up in India and Japan to collect complaints from firms; (*b*) to address and resolve issues, taking into account the findings reported by consultative groups; and (*c*) to report the findings and make recommendations to the countries concerned. This framework was first adopted in the Japan–Mexico FTA, and it has proved effective in improving the business environment in Mexico, which in turn contributed to the expansion of Japanese FDI to Mexico.

Finally, Japan and India agreed to promote cooperation for their mutual benefit in various fields that are related to the contents of their FTA. One of these fields is trade and investment promotion.[32] Specific measures of cooperation for trade and investment promotion include human resource development and capacity building.

Before closing this section on the Japan–India FTA, let us make an assessment of the agreement. Based on a general equilibrium simulation analysis using the Global Trade Analysis Project (GTAP) model, one scholar reported that the Japan–India FTA would increase the GDPs of Japan and India by 0.05 and 0.99 per cent, respectively.[33] These figures can be considered as a lower bound because the simulation only considers tariff elimination on imported goods and does not consider other elements such as trade in services or investment, which are important parts of the Japan–India FTA.

One important indicator that shows the impact of the Japan–India FTA is the use of preferential tariff schemes by firms. In order to use preferential tariff schemes under this FTA, Japanese firms have to obtain a certificate of origin (CoO) by satisfying the rules of origin that certify that a product is made in Japan and thus is qualified for preferential treatment. In Japan, the Chamber of Commerce issues the CoOs. The number of CoOs issued increased notably in the first two years after the enactment of the Japan–India FTA. The number of CoOs issued in August 2011, the first month of the enactment of the FTA, was 439.[34] The number increased rapidly to over 1,000 in January 2012 and then continued to increase, reaching 2,000 in March 2013. The number has stabilized around 2,600–2,700 after the middle of 2014, but it began to rise again in 2015. Among 12 FTAs for which information on the number of issued CoOs is available for May 2015, India ranked third at 3,254 after Thailand (6,951) and Indonesia (3,519). Considering that Japan's exports to India for December 2014 were approximately 28 and 65 per cent of those to Thailand and Indonesia, respectively,[35] one could say that roughly speaking, the use of the Japan–India FTA by Japanese exporters was rather high, indicating that the FTA contributed to an increase in Japan's exports to India.[36] One possible way to further increase the use of the Japan–India FTA by Japanese firms is to relax the conditions for obtaining the CoOs. India imposes two conditions—local value added content and change in tariff classifications—for the use of the FTA, while many FTAs impose only one condition.

Economic Cooperation

Economic cooperation with India has been extended by the Japanese government as well as by the Japanese private sector. In this section, we first look at economic cooperation provided by the Japanese government and then turn to economic cooperation by the private sector involving Japanese and Indian firms.

For the Japanese government, India has been one of the oldest and most important partners in economic cooperation.[37] India was the first country to which Japan provided a yen loan in 1958. Since then, the yen loan has been a major method of economic cooperation by the Japanese government. Although the amount of official development assistance (ODA) provided by the Japanese government has varied widely among recipient countries over time, India has been the largest recipient of Japan's ODA in recent years. For a period of seven years from 2007 to 2013, India was the largest recipient of Japanese ODA, receiving 9.1 per cent of Japan's cumulative ODA over that period.[38] Myanmar was the second largest with a 5.9 per cent share. For India, Japan is the largest donor of ODA. For the period of five years from 2009 to 2013, Japan provided 39.8 per cent of cumulative bilateral ODA to India by Development Assistance Committee (DAC) countries.[39]

The Japanese government has identified three major areas for economic cooperation with India: promotion of economic development, alleviation of poverty and environmental problems, and human resource development. For the promotion of economic development, construction and improvement of infrastructure such as transportation networks, electricity generation, and industrial parks have been major programmes. Specific important programmes include the Delhi–Mumbai Industrial Corridor (DMIC) project and the Chennai–Bangalore Industrial Corridor (CBIC) project. These infrastructure projects will contribute to the economic development of India not only by themselves but also by attracting FDI. It should be stressed that the alleviation of poverty and environmental problems as well as the development of human resources would also contribute to the economic development of India by increasing its attractiveness to FDI. In other words, these ODA projects would benefit not only India but also Japanese and other foreign firms.

The Japanese government contributes to the expansion of FDI by Japanese firms by providing financial assistance through JBIC and Nippon Export and Investment Insurance (NEXI). While JBIC provides financial resources to Japanese firms, NEXI provides insurance on exports and investment by Japanese firms. In addition to providing financial resources directly to Japanese firms for investment, JBIC contributes to the expansion of Japanese firms' FDI by providing financial resources for the construction of infrastructure, which would improve the FDI climate of recipient countries.

The importance of economic cooperation through ODA and other means is not only to provide financial resources but also to induce financial resources from the private sector. Indeed, government assistance is considered to play a supplementary role to private sector activities. The private sector sees the role of the government as being to provide financial resources to reduce the risk of projects. As such, the private sector would be more willing to participate in projects with government involvement.

Cooperation by the Japanese and Indian business sectors can contribute to the economic growth of both countries, although firms in the business sector are often competitors. There are several ways that cooperation by the business sector can contribute to the promotion of mutual economic growth. One is to initiate and increase business ties such as joint research and development (R&D) involving Japanese and Indian firms. For this type of cooperation, complementarity between the firms is necessary.

Another type of cooperation that would contribute to economic growth is to provide advice and recommendations to the governments, which would contribute to the expansion of business activities. There are several frameworks that have been set up for this purpose. One example is the establishment of the India–Japan Business Leaders' Forum (BLF), for which major business organizations such as the Confederation of Indian Industry (CII) and the Keidanren (Japan Business Federation) are serving secretariat roles for India and Japan, respectively. The establishment of the BLF was announced in 2006, and its first meeting was held in 2007. Since then, several meetings have been held and joint reports of the meetings released, containing a number of recommendations to the governments. Some of the recommendations from the forum held in September 2014 included the following: improving the business environment through effective use of the Japan–India CEPA, the importance of infrastructure development, cooperation in strategic areas, and global cooperation.[40] Under these broad headings, specific recommendations were presented. Some of the recommendations to the Indian government included simplification of land acquisition, early implementation of a goods and services tax, and resolution of inconsistencies in tax collection between central and state governments, which would contribute to the expansion of FDI by Japanese firms. Close collaboration and cooperation between the private sector and the government through various channels is essential in dealing with the obstacles that prevent the private sector from expanding and improving its operations.

Recommendations: Exploiting Complementary Bilateral Relations

This chapter began with a discussion of the structural problems that have made it difficult for the Japanese economy to achieve growth. The analysis indicated the need for implementing structural reforms and opening markets, which would promote economic growth by increasing productivity. Furthermore, the analysis showed the importance of increasing economic interaction with rapidly growing Asian countries such as China and India. Considering these findings and discussions, in this section we explore ways for Japan and India to benefit from increasing bilateral economic relations.

Japan and India have been expanding their economic relationship through foreign trade and FDI since the beginning of the 1990s. However, the level of bilateral economic exchanges appears to be much lower than their potential. Japan and India can obtain substantial economic gains by expanding their economic relations. Such gains can be enormous once one realizes that the economic relationship is contrasting and complementary in many respects. Japan is a developed, high-income country with very low economic growth, while India is a developing, middle-income country with high economic growth. Their respective demographic situations, which have huge impacts on economic activities, are also very contrasting. Japan's population is relatively small, declining, and rapidly ageing, while India's population is large, growing, and very young.

For Japanese firms, which are faced with a saturated domestic market, India provides ample business opportunities with its huge and growing population. Japanese firms can serve the large and growing market through exports and/or FDI. Japanese firms are particularly keen on investing in India so that they can serve the Indian market effectively. For Japanese firms, using their financial and managerial resources by employing human resources in India would be very efficient and beneficial. Indeed, many Japanese firms are trying to adopt a strategy under which they make profits in overseas markets, which are recycled back to their parent firms in Japan. These repatriated earnings are then used for R&D activities for the development of new technologies and products, which in turn would become their competence.

India can benefit by hosting Japanese firms, as the latter can bring technology and managerial know-how that can be transferred to local firms. Local firms with improved technology and skills can contribute to India's economic growth, as they can grow by expanding sales in local as well as foreign markets. Indeed, the expansion and improvement of the manufacturing sector would contribute to the 'Make in India' initiative promoted by Prime Minister Modi. Indian firms can participate in international production networks to gain various benefits such as higher sales and skills as well as technology upgrading, once they are able to satisfy requirements such as high quality requested by Japanese firms.

Now that we have presented a picture for obtaining mutual economic benefits, we present specific recommendations to attain the expected and desired outcome. The preceding analysis and discussions revealed that one of the most important challenges is to improve the investment environment in India, as attracting FDI and acquiring benefits from hosting FDI play very important roles benefiting both India and Japan. For the improvement of the FDI environment, several important challenges have to be dealt with. They include: (*a*) establishment of an open, transparent, stable, fair, and non-discriminatory policy environment; (*b*) development of well-functioning soft and hard infrastructure; and (*c*) development of capable and competent human resources. It is important to recognize that dealing with these challenges effectively would benefit both Japan and India. To illustrate this point, building infrastructure contributes to the economic development of India, while it is likely to benefit Japanese firms if they are able to export infrastructure. Indeed, exporting infrastructure such as railway systems is one of the important foreign economic policy agendas for the Abe government.

To meet these challenges, various strategies, policies, and measures have already been formulated and some of them have been implemented. Given the situation, what needs to be done is not to reinvent the wheel, but to formulate effective policies by evaluating past policies and by introducing new ones. Japan and India need to have close collaboration and cooperation at government as well as private sector levels. They can use existing frameworks such as the Japan–India FTA and the Japan–India Business Leaders' Forum, in addition to other official and private dialogues and cooperation programmes. In this regard, Japan and India should contribute to the speedy conclusion of the RCEP negotiation, as this agreement would contribute to the establishment of an FDI-friendly business environment involving 10 ASEAN countries and the six countries that have FTAs with ASEAN (Australia, China, India, Japan, New Zealand, and South Korea). The need for strong commitment by leaders has to be emphasized to make these strategies and policies successful.

Finally, although somewhat disconnected from the preceding discussions, it is important to emphasize the need to increase human exchange between Japan and India at various levels, ranging from students and researchers to business persons, politicians, and ordinary people, in order to obtain the potential economic gains discussed here. Without deep mutual understanding, the establishment of a reliable and trusting relationship, which is essential for business engagement, cannot be constructed. According to the statistics compiled by the Japan Student Service Organization, the number of Indian students studying in Japan was 727 in 2014, accounting for 0.4 per cent of all foreign students studying in Japan.[41] This number is very small compared to the numbers of Chinese (94,399), Vietnamese (26,439), and Nepali (10,448) students. In order to increase student exchanges, the relaxation of visa policies is effective, but it is also very important for Indians to be exposed to Japanese culture, society, and history, and for Japanese nationals to be exposed to Indian culture, society, and history as well.

Notes

1. National Institute of Population and Social Security Research, *Nihon no shorai suikei jinko (Heisei 18 nen 12 gatsu suikei) chui suikei* (Japan's Future Projected Population [December 2006 Projection] Central

Projection), December 2006, retrieved from http://www.ipss.go.jp/syoushika/tohkei/suikei07/suikei.html#chapt1-1 on 1 September 2015.

2. Ministry of Internal Affairs and Communication, *Survey on Labor Force* (Long-Term Series Data), n.d., retrieved from http://www.stat.go.jp/data/roudou/longtime/03roudou.htm on 1 September 2015.

3. Cabinet Office, Government of Japan, *Rodoryoku jinko to kongono keizaiseicho nitsuite* (Labor Force and Economic Growth in the Future), March 2015.

4. World Bank, World Development Indicators, n.d., retrieved from http://databank.worldbank.org/data/reports.aspx?source=world-development-indicators# on 1 September 2015.

5. Cabinet Office, Government of Japan, *Heisei 25 nendo kokumin keizai keisan kakuho* (National Account Statistics), 2013, retrieved from http://www.esri.cao.go.jp/jp/sna/data/data_list/kakuhou/files/h25/sankou/pdf/point20141225.pdf on 1 September 2015.

6. Unless otherwise noted, the values are expressed in US dollars.

7. Source is same as the source of Figures 1.5 and 1.6.

8. One needs to undertake more rigorous analysis such as gravity model analysis to examine if the bilateral trade relationship is more or less than what is expected.

9. The figures are for 2013 and taken from Japan External Trade Organization (JETRO), *Sekai boeki toshi hokoku* (Report on World Trade and Investment), 2014.

10. Foreign direct investment is generally measured in terms of flow and stock. In this chapter, FDI is measured in flows unless indicated otherwise.

11. JETRO, FDI Database, n.d., retrieved from http://www.jetro.go.jp/world/japan/stats/fdi.html on 2 September 2015.

12. Bank of Japan, *Balance of Payments Statistics, Direct Investment Position*, n.d., retrieved from https://www.boj.or.jp/statistics/br/bop/iip.htm/ on 2 September 2015.

13. Computed from the United Nations Conference on Trade and Development (UNCTAD) FDI database, retrieved from http://unctadstat.unctad.org/wds/ReportFolders/reportFolders.aspx on 2 September 2015.

14. Embassy of Japan in India, *Japanese Companies in India*, January 2015, retrieved from http://www.in.emb-japan.go.jp/Japanese/20150105_j_co_list_j(rev).pdf on 2 September 2015.

15. Embassy of Japan in India, *Japanese Companies in India*.

16. World Bank, World Development Indicators.

17. Central Intelligence Agency, 'Age Structure (Country Comparison to the World)', *The World Factbook*, n.d., retrieved from https://www.

cia.gov/library/publications/the-world-factbook/fields/2010.html on 2 September 2015.

18. JETRO, *Ajia Oceania shuyo toshi chiiki no toshi kanren cost hikaku* no. 23 (Comparison of Investment Related Cost in Cities in Asia and Oceania [no. 23]), 2013.

19. For the development of international production and distribution networks in East Asia, see M. Ando, 'Fragmentation and Vertical Intra-industry Trade in East Asia', *North American Journal of Economics and Finance*, 17(3), 2006, pp. 257–81; and M. Ando and F. Kimura, 'Production Linkage of Asia and Europe via Central and Eastern Europe', *Journal of Economic Integration*, 28(2), 2013, pp. 204–40.

20. Ibid.

21. JBIC, *Wagakuni seizogyo kigyo no kaigai jigyo tenkai ni kansuru chosa hokoku: 2014 nendo kaigai chokusetsu toshi anketo kekka* (no. 26) (Report of the Research on Overseas Activities of Japanese Manufacturing Firms: Results of Questionnaire Survey on FDI in 2014 [no. 26]), 2014.

22. JETRO, *Zai Ajia Oceania nikkei kigyo jittai chosa: 2014 nendo chosa* (Survey of Affiliates of Japanese Firms Operating in Asia and Oceania in 2014), 2014.

23. JBIC survey no. 26.

24. JETRO, *Sekai boeki toshi hokoku* (Report on World Trade and Investment), 2014.

25. JBIC survey no. 26.

26. According to the *Global Competitiveness Report 2014–15*, which reports the opinions of foreign investors, India is ranked 87th out of 144 countries in the area of infrastructure, while China, Indonesia, and Vietnam are ranked 46th, 56th, and 81st, respectively. See K. Schwab, *The Global Competitiveness Report 2014–15*, Geneva: World Economic Forum, 2014, pp. 16–19.

27. JETRO Survey of Affiliates.

28. Formally, the Japan–India FTA is named the Comprehensive Economic Partnership Agreement (CEPA) between Japan and the Republic of India. In this chapter, we call it the Japan–India FTA, as the expression 'FTA' is more commonly used than CEPA.

29. METI, *Fukosei boeki hokokusho 2014* (Report on Compliance by Major Trading Partners with Trade Agreements: WTO, FTA/EPA and BIT), 2014.

30. In terms of import value, India committed to eliminate tariffs on 90.3 per cent of its imports from Japan within 10 years, while the corresponding commitment level for Japan is 97.5 per cent. See METI, Report on Compliance.

31. Chapter 12 in the Japan–India FTA, on 'Improvement of Business Environment', is included for this purpose.
32. Cooperation is included in chapter 13 of the FTA. Other fields of cooperation are environment, infrastructure, information and communications technology, science and technology, energy, tourism, textiles, SMEs, health, entertainment and information, metallurgy, and other fields to be mutually agreed upon by the parties.
33. K. Kawasaki, 'Determining Priority among EPAs: Which Trading Partner Has the Greatest Economic Impact?', *RIETI Column 218*, retrieved from http://www.rieti.go.jp/en/columns/a01_0318.html on 2 September 2015.
34. METI, *Daiisshu tokutei gensanchi shomeisho no hakkyu jokyo* (The Number of Issuance of Certificates of Origin), n.d., retrieved from http://www.meti.go.jp/policy/external_economy/trade_control/boeki-kanri/download/gensanchi/coissuance.pdf on 19 September 2015.
35. Ministry of Finance of Japan, Trade Statistics, Monthly Statistics by Country, n.d., retrieved from http://www.customs.go.jp/toukei/shinbun/trade-st/2015/201505e.xml#pg2 on 2 September 2015.
36. The proportion of CoOs issued for Japan's exports to India to those issued for its exports to Thailand and Indonesia are 47 and 75 per cent, respectively.
37. Ministry of Foreign Affairs of Japan (MoFA), ODA home page, n.d., retrieved from http://www.mofa.go.jp/mofaj/gaiko/oda/shiryo/kuni/13_databook/pdfs/02-01.pdf on 2 September 2015.
38. The figures are in terms of net ODA disbursement and have been taken from Organisation for Economic Co-operation and Development (OECD), 'Geographical Distribution of Financial Flows to Developing Countries 2015', 2015, retrieved from http://www.oecd-ilibrary.org/development/geographical-distribution-of-financial-flows-to-developing-countries_20743149 on 2 September 2015.
39. OECD, 'Geographical Distribution of Financial Flows'.
40. Keidanren, 'Joint Report of the India-Japan Business Leaders Forum 2014', 1 September 2014, retrieved from http://www.keidanren.or.jp/en/policy/2014/072.html on 2 September 2015.
41. Japan Student Service Organization, 'Result of an Annual Survey of International Students in Japan 2014', 27 February 2015, retrieved from http://www.jasso.go.jp/statistics/intl_student/data14_e.html#no3 on 2 September 2015.

2

An Economic Partnership for Twenty-first Century Asia

Devesh Kapur and Rohit Lamba

As the two largest democratic Asian countries with economies that are complementary, Japan and India's economic engagement has been relatively limited. In this chapter, we first discuss the principal dimensions of their economic relationship, focusing on trade, aid, investment, and financial flows. We then analyse why Japanese foreign direct investment (FDI) in India has been modest. Subsequently we examine areas in which the economic relationship has the greatest potential—FDI in urban infrastructure and railways, trade, labour, capital flows, and education. Finally, we examine how Japanese investment and aid can address India's infrastructural weaknesses to pave the way for Japanese firms to make India a manufacturing hub for their operations, and how Indian firms can leverage their comparative advantage in information technology (IT) services to serve customers in Japan, and more broadly how the two countries can collaborate to better develop India's human capital in order to address the needs of both countries.

There are few major economies in the world with as little historical baggage between them as India and Japan. The spread of Buddhism in Japan led the land of its origin to be christened Tenjiku, an ancient name for the Indian subcontinent defined as the land far away where dharma was first preached and practised.[1] But, reeling under colonial rule, India could not gain much from the rapid strides made by Japan under the Meiji restoration of the late nineteenth century. Following India's independence in 1947, its import-substitution industrialization (ISI) economic model meant that trade and foreign investment played little role in the country's development, which further limited economic engagement with Japan.

Instead, for more than half a century, foreign aid played a key role in Japan's engagement with India. Japanese aid to India commenced in 1958 and has been mainly in the form of yen loans (95 per cent of Japan's official development assistance [ODA] to India is in yen loans).[2] However, the lack of strategic convergence and growing Japanese interest in Southeast Asia from the 1970s and in China from the 1980s resulted in weak economic and diplomatic relations between the two countries. The nadir was in 1998 when, following India's nuclear tests, Japan suspended its aid programme. However, matters began to change considerably from the early 2000s, and since 2003 India has been the largest recipient of Japanese ODA, which averaged about US$2.6 billion annually between 2008 and 2012.[3]

Commercially, while there were a number of joint ventures between Japanese and Indian firms, it was not until the early 1980s, when Suzuki invested in a joint venture with the Indian government in what would become India's largest automobile company (Maruti Suzuki)—unlocking the car ownership aspirations of India's middle class—that an iconic Japanese investment took root in India. Unforeseen cultural links formed as well, such as Tamil movie star Rajinikanth's popularity in Japan and children in India growing up watching dubbed versions of Japanese animated series. Nonetheless, the economic relationship between the two countries continued to be anaemic. In the 2000s, even as South Korean firms invested heavily in India's white goods sector, risk-averse Japanese firms stayed away, ceding ground to the competition.

The modest economic links are striking both on economic logic and political grounds. Japan is a capital-rich country with an ageing and declining population. India is a capital-poor country poised to reap a major demographic dividend in the next few decades. Japan has long had a comparative advantage in manufacturing while India has developed a comparative advantage in services. However, as Japanese companies looked for newer pastures to graze their manufacturing aspirations, their destinations were inevitably in East Asia (especially China and South Korea) and Southeast Asia (particularly Indonesia and Thailand).

Additionally, unlike other East and Southeast Asian countries, Japan has no historical baggage with India. The legacies of Japanese colonialism and WWII are bitterly contested, especially in China and South Korea, and periodically erupt in tensions between those countries and Japan. Indeed, rather than waning, if anything this historical legacy has become a bigger issue over time. In contrast, there is no such historical baggage between Japan and India and few major countries enjoy as much consensus across the Indian political spectrum as Japan.

The good news, however, is that despite the lost decades, these favourable fundamentals still exist. A growing rapport between the national leaderships of the two countries and, especially, changes in the strategic environment in Asia are adding impetus to a deeper economic relationship between the two countries. In a survey of overseas business operations of Japanese manufacturing companies done by the Japan Bank for International Cooperation (JBIC) in 2014, India was ranked second on the list of promising countries/regions for the medium term and ranked first for the long term (Table 2.1).[4]

In this chapter, we first lay out the complementary nature of the two economies, characterized by demography and capital. Next, the chapter discusses the recent history of economic interaction between Japan and India, a history marked by missed opportunities. After that, the chapter switches gear and examines the way forward, focusing on a series of sectors that present opportunities for the two countries to deepen their economic engagement, particularly urban infrastructure and railways in India and labour mobility for Indian workers—especially in services—to work in Japan. We then report on the experience of Japan Plus, a team set up by the Government of India exclusively to attract and facilitate Japanese investments. We conclude by examining some other key features of the 2014 Tokyo Declaration between Prime Ministers Narendra Modi and Shinzo

Table 2.1   Most Promising Countries for Overseas Business for Japanese Manufacturing Companies

	Medium Term	Long Term
1	Indonesia	**India**
2	**India**	China
3	Thailand	Indonesia
4	China	Brazil
5	Vietnam	Thailand
6	Brazil	Vietnam
7	Mexico	Myanmar
8	Myanmar	Russia

Source: JBIC, 'Survey Report on Overseas Business Operations by Japanese Manufacturing Companies', 2014, retrieved from https://www.jbic.go.jp/wp-content/uploads/press_en/2014/11/32994/20141128English1.pdf on 2 September 2015.

Abe, as well as the salience of the Japan–India economic relationship against the backdrop of a changing geopolitical environment.

Complementary Economies

With regard to factors of production, India and Japan have complementary strengths that provide a strong basis for an economic partnership. Most Asian countries that grew rapidly after the Second World War were aided by favourable demographics, namely, a declining dependency ratio—the ratio of the number of people not in the labour force to the number of people in the labour force—and an expanding and young labour force that underpinned the big push towards industrialization. Figure 2.1 illustrates this trend. The 'take-off period' for South Korea (1970) and for China (1980) was also when this 'demographic dividend' started to kick in. Today, India is the anvil of a similarly favourable demographic moment.

Since investment is a key driver of economic growth, gross capital formation—which delineates the fraction of new value added directed towards investment rather than consumption—is a good indicator of future growth. Figure 2.2 illustrates how India has

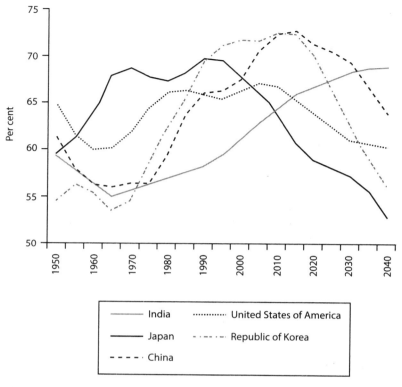

Figure 2.1   Percentage of Population That is of Working Age (15–64) in Selected Countries, 1950–2040
Source: UN Statistics Division Demographic Yearbooks (http://unstats.un.org/unsd/demographic/) and authors' estimates.

lagged behind China and South Korea over the last half-century. Note that the figure does not capture the fact that this difference is compounded annually. But this also means that there is considerable room for ramping up capital formation in India.

India requires large amounts of capital investment to strengthen infrastructure, reinvigorate manufacturing, and sustain its burgeoning urbanization. The erstwhile Planning Commission of India—until recently in charge of setting economic priorities for the Indian government through centralized plans every five years—had set a target of close to 40 per cent gross capital formation for the Twelfth

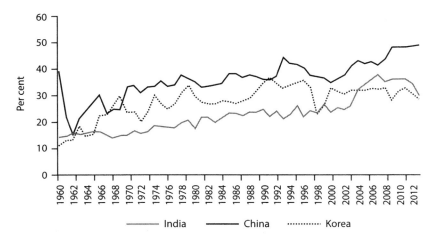

Figure 2.2   Gross Capital Formation (Per Cent of GDP) in India, China, and South Korea, 1960–2012
Source: World Bank database (http://data.worldbank.org/).

Five Year Plan (2012–17).[5] For India to achieve this target, it will need to increase savings (both public and private) as well as attract large capital inflows from overseas.

Japan is a capital-rich country whose high labour costs have led Japanese firms to look towards China, South Korea, Indonesia, and other Association of Southeast Asian Nations (ASEAN) countries for the labour-intensive parts of their supply chains. The success of South Korea and China has meant that while the former has long crossed the low-cost manufacturing frontier, China is getting close to the low-cost frontier even as India is still quite far from it.

Japan faces two singular economic challenges in the first half of the twenty-first century: an ageing population (Figure 2.3) and high and rising government debt (Figure 2.4). Both are, of course, interconnected. While fertility rates invariably decline as per capita incomes rise, in Japan the effect has been particularly pronounced, in part because of the lack of immigration into Japan, in contrast to many European countries or the United States. Japan's public debt has mounted due to sharp increases in government spending to stimulate the economy to counter the economic stagnation of the

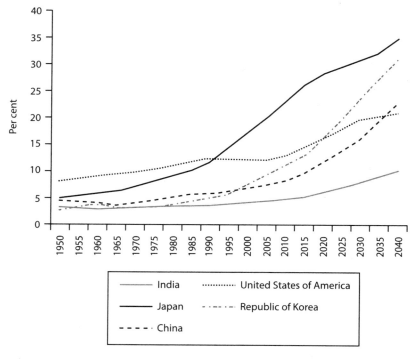

Figure 2.3   Percentage of Population That is of Old Age (65 and Above) in Selected Countries, 1950–2040

Source: UN Statistics Division, Demographic Yearbooks (http://unstats.un.org/unsd/demographic/) and authors' estimates.

1990s. By 2013, the gross debt to gross domestic product (GDP) ratio stood at 240 per cent. Even after cancelling cross-ownership of this debt within the government, the figure stood at 135 per cent.[6] The only way such high levels of debt have been sustainable is that the debt is largely domestically owned.

Managing public expenditures for an ageing population and keeping public debt within reasonable limits simultaneously is going to be a major challenge for Japan. Raising taxes will be politically unpopular (and may further stymie growth), and printing more money can be dangerous. The solutions lie (at least partly) in some combination

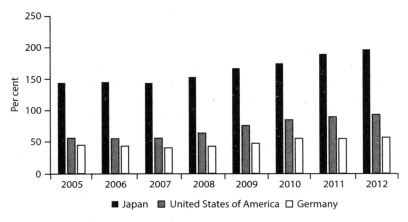

Figure 2.4   Central Government Debt to GDP Ratio in Japan, the US, and Germany, 2005–12

Source: World Bank database (http://data.worldbank.org/).

of: (*a*) seeking growth in emerging markets; (*b*) investing capital and pensions smartly; and (*c*) hiring cheap services.

Enter India.

A History of Missed Opportunities: Trade, Foreign Direct Investment (FDI), and Capital Markets

The weakness of trade and investment between India and Japan poses a puzzle in political economy. While Japan's massive investments in the United States are understandable in the geopolitical scenario of the second half of the twentieth century, the breadth and depth of Japan's investments in China, a country with whom it has a heavy historical burden, were driven by strategic and commercial factors. The marriage between Japanese firms and Chinese labour and access to the world's fastest-growing market was a seemingly natural partnership, and its mutual benefits were meant to soothe the painful memories of the past. But instead of mutual reinforcement, the strategic and commercial goals have undermined each other, as the cumulative effect of the thousands of investment decisions has been to nurture Japan's most formidable strategic competitor in the twenty-first century.

In contrast, trade and investment between India and Japan has been quite low (Figure 2.5). Total trade between the two countries (exports and imports) forms around 2 per cent of India's total trade and less than 1 per cent of Japan's.

Overseas FDI has become an important part of the Japanese economy since the early 1990s. In 2013, Japan was the second largest source of global outward FDI (investing US$138 billion), with large investments in the automotive sector, followed closely by machinery, metals, electronics, and financial services.[7]

Despite a big investment by Suzuki during the 1980s, from a global perspective Japanese investment in India has been modest (Figure 2.6). There are several reasons for this prolonged hiatus. An annual survey conducted over the last few years by JBIC amongst Japanese firms has repeatedly pointed out underdeveloped infrastructure, an unclear legal system, labour problems, and a complicated tax system as some of the major hurdles of doing business in India. These concerns are shared by most overseas investors and indeed by Indian business as well.

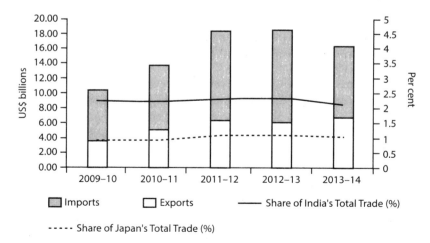

Figure 2.5   Indian Trade with Japan, 2009–10 to 2013–14

Source: Ministry of Commerce and Industry (MoCI), India (Export and Import Databank), and the World Trade Organization database (http://stat.wto.org/).

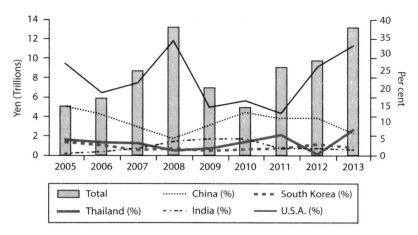

Figure 2.6   FDI by Japan (Assets), 2005–13
Source: Ministry of Finance, Government of Japan (http://www.mof.go.jp/english/statistics).

A closer look at the Indian side of the data reveals that Japan has actually been doing fairly well compared to other FDI source countries (see Table 2.2), which suggests that the constraints inhibiting direct investment for Japan are the general ones faced by most countries with respect to investing in India. (However, a caveat is in order since many US and European firms reroute their investments through Mauritius for tax reasons.)

It is important to note that the same is not true for trade, which, as pointed out earlier, has been modest from the perspective of both countries. As a correlation exercise, this seems to be driven by Japanese trade patterns: in comparison to India, for Japan the main propeller is intra-firm trade, and it is highest amongst the countries where Japan has substantial direct investments of assets.

Capital markets in India are relatively underdeveloped in comparison to the US, UK, and Hong Kong, where Japanese funds have been much more active. Japanese overseas investments have traditionally been more focused on the bond market. Table 2.3 lists the top 10 destinations for Japanese funds in terms of investment in equities. It is interesting to note that Japanese investments in Indian capital

Table 2.2   FDI Inflows to India (Share of Top 10 Sources, Per Cent), 2000–14

Rank for the period 2000–14	Country	1991–2000	2000–March 2014
1	Mauritius	31.51	36.09
2	Singapore	2.76	11.69
3	United Kingdom	5.44	9.54
4	Japan	7.41	7.48
5	USA	20.10	5.48
6	Netherlands	5.19	5.16
7	Cyprus	0.20	3.42
8	Germany	5.61	3.00
9	France	2.59	1.78
10	UAE	0.08	1.24

Sources: Department of Industrial Policy and Promotion, Government of India; S. Ray, 'Impact of Foreign Direct Investment on Economic Growth in India: A Co-integration Analysis', *Advances in Information Technology and Management*, 2(1), 2012, pp. 187–201.

Table 2.3   Japanese Toshin Fund Exposure to Overseas Assets, 2014

Country	Allocation to Equity (Rank)	Allocation to Bonds (Rank)	Bond/Equity Ratio
USA	1	1	2.32
Euro	2	3	4.46
Hong Kong	3	23	0.01
United Kingdom	4	6	2.69
Brazil	5	4	5.35
India	6	21	0.06
Switzerland	7	22	0.05
Australia	8	2	22.29
Canada	9	5	10.35
Taiwan	10	25	0.03
Top 26 Total			3.02

Source: Nomura Global Markets Research, 'Abenomics × Modinomics = Greater Opportunities for Japan and India', Anchor Report, 2014, p. 30. Reprinted with permission of the Nomura Group.

markets have favoured equities rather than bonds (unlike Brazil but very much like Hong Kong).

Despite complementary factors of production and a rapidly growing Indian market relative to anaemic economic growth in Japan, the India–Japan economic partnership has not really been able to take off. However, a rapidly changing strategic environment in Asia, a greater recognition within India of the need to address the concerns of investors, and strong political commitment at the highest levels of government in both countries now offer a rare opportunity to build a robust economic partnership. India has a range of options as it seeks to build a robust economic partnership with Japan. While many of the constraints are in the general area of 'ease of doing business'— essentially issues of cutting red tape that India needs to address in the coming years—it is also important to look at specific sectors.

Supply Chains and Industrial Clusters

Industrial clusters have been empirically proven to enhance productivity and efficiency—the underlying economic force is often referred to as the agglomeration effect, or localization economies.[8] With a large and cheap labour force, India needs to work with Japan to build industrial clusters that offer a common but high-quality infrastructure catering to specific sectors. Three examples come to mind.

First, adding to the existing three major supply chain networks (which have also been major export-driven success stories) in the Indian automobile sector—the Mumbai–Pune corridor, the Chennai–Bengaluru corridor, and the National Capital Region (NCR)—and linking them to the global supply chains of Japanese auto firms.

Second, creating completely new clusters around the proposed Delhi–Mumbai and Mumbai–Bengaluru industrial corridors. The Delhi–Mumbai Industrial Corridor (DMIC), an ambitious infrastructure project with rail-cum-highway trunk corridors along with manufacturing zones and new urban centres, is being partially funded by the Government of Japan. A Japanese industrial cluster is taking shape in Vithalpur in Gujarat. The governance models of these new urban centres and industrial clusters are still evolving. One possible model they could draw from is the industrial city of Jamshedpur, a private firm-dominated governance model that has successfully provided better public services than most Indian cities.

Third, developing an infrastructure (transportation and energy) corridor connecting eastern India–Bangladesh–Myanmar with Southeast Asia and piggybacking new supply chains on this corridor. This is especially important for India since the eastern wing of the country has so far been unable to partake in much of the twenty-first century growth story.

The industrial clusters can be organized around five sectors where Japanese firms are acknowledged leaders: automotive; railways, public transportation, and people-moving systems for urban India; shipbuilding; heavy industry for energy (low-emission, high-efficiency power plants); and consumer electronics and chips.

Delhi–Mumbai Industrial Corridor

The *Economic Survey of India 2012–13* states that '[T]he Delhi-Mumbai Industrial Corridor (DMIC) is being developed by the Government of India with a view to using the high capacity western Dedicated Freight Corridor as a backbone for creating a global manufacturing and investment destination.'[9] The master plan has a vision for 24 cities, each linked to a manufacturing zone. General manufacturing, information technology (IT)-enabled services, electronics, agricultural and food processing, heavy engineering, pharmaceuticals, biotechnology, and services are some of the sectors being actively promoted in the proposed industrial clusters. Investment is pegged at US$90 billion. The DMIC was conceived by the Ministry of Economy, Trade and Industry (METI) of Japan and the Ministry of Commerce and Industry (MoCI) of India.

By 2014, US$4.5 billion worth of investment was already under implementation in the first stage of the DMIC through the Japan International Cooperation Agency (JICA) and JBIC. They hold a combined 26 per cent stake in the project. Of the seven cities being developed in the first phase of the DMIC project, master planning for six is complete (Figure 2.7).

The DMIC project's influence area of 436,486 square kilometres is about 13.8 per cent of India's geographical area. It extends over seven states and two union territories, namely, Delhi, Uttar Pradesh, Haryana, Rajasthan, Madhya Pradesh, Gujarat, Maharashtra, Diu and Daman, and Dadra and Nagar Haveli. The population influenced would be around 17 per cent of the country's total population.

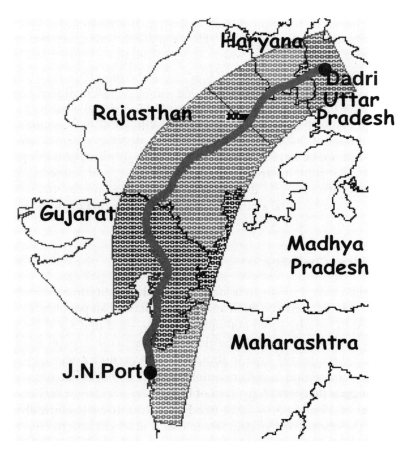

Figure 2.7   Delhi–Mumbai Industrial Corridor: Project Influence Area
Source: Delhi–Mumbai Industrial Corridor Development Corporation Ltd., DMIC
Concept Paper, retrieved from http://www.dmicdc.com/frmDownloads.aspx?pgid=43

The key to DMIC's infrastructure is the multi-modal high axle load dedicated freight corridor (DFC), a high-capacity railway system. Covering 1,483 kilometres and nine new railway stations along which other railroads would connect, the DFC is set to lay a wide network in the transportation of goods and services in the north-western part of the country. Other infrastructure plans include logistics hubs, feeder roads, power generation facilities, upgrades of existing ports and airports, development of greenfield ports, environment protection mechanisms, and social infrastructure.

The basic provision of trunk infrastructure is unlikely to be commercially viable, at least initially.[10] Hence, public financing is required to build this infrastructure, which includes land improvement, roadworks, earthworks, sewerage, storm water drainage, flood management, and solid waste management. There are major implementation challenges including land acquisition, power, water management, and environmental protection. Once such infrastructure is in place, the subsequent addition of cities would become commercially viable and can be implemented through public–private partnerships (PPPs). The trunk infrastructure, industrial zones, and linked cities are all part of an integrated vision of economic development that will require very substantial amounts of financing. How that might occur is discussed in a later section.

The Urban Challenge

The single largest urban transformation of the twenty-first century will be in India. Between 2014 and 2050, India's urban population is expected to grow by about 400 million people—just under a million a month. About one-sixth of the global increase in urban population until 2050 is expected to be in India (China, with under one-eighth, will have the second largest increase).[11] India's demographic projections suggest that over 65 per cent of Indians are going to be between the ages of 15 and 65 by 2032 (see Figure 2.1). If we (realistically) expect the labour participation rate to rise from 60 per cent to 70 per cent and the population of India to be around 1.5 billion in 2032, this points towards an active and young labour force that is 730 million strong. These numbers are unprecedented. A large part of this hugely expanding labour force is expected to move out of agriculture and into urban occupations.

Currently, India has 54 cities with populations of more than one million. As classified by the government census, these include three megacities, or census-defined urban agglomerations with at least 10 million residents (Mumbai, Delhi, and Kolkata); six major metros, or urban agglomerations with between 5 and 10 million residents (Ahmedabad, Bengaluru, Chennai, Hyderabad, Pune, and Surat); and 45 large cities, or urban agglomerations with between 1 and 5 million residents.

In comparison to other countries at similar stages of development, India's urbanization rate is relatively low. Only about a third of India's population is urban compared to 45 per cent in China, 54 per cent in Indonesia, 74 per cent in Mexico, and 87 per cent in Brazil.[12] Typically there are four key drivers of urban growth: natural increase, net rural–urban migration, expansion of boundaries, and net reclassification. Contrary to the standard theory,[13] India's story suggests that rural–urban differentials in productivity have widened in the last few decades and rural to urban migration has not kept pace. The share of agriculture in GDP has consistently been declining, whereas the sectoral composition of the workforce has changed only moderately (Figure 2.8 and Table 2.4).

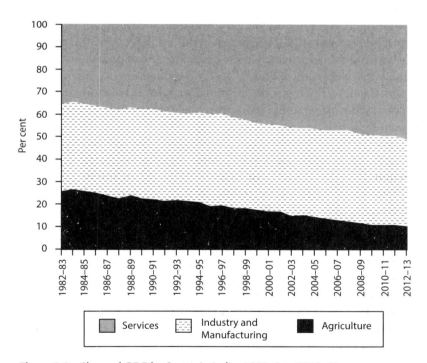

Figure 2.8   Share of GDP by Sector in India, 1982–3 to 2012–13
Source: Planning Commission, Government of India, 'GDP at Factor Cost at 2004–05 Prices, Share to Total GDP and % Rate of Growth in GDP', 2014, retrieved from http://planningcommission.gov.in/data/datatable/data_2312/DatabookDec2014%202.pdf on 4 September 2015.

Table 2.4   Share of Employment by Sector in India (Per Cent), 1999–2000 to 2009–10

Sectors	1999–2000	2004–5	2009–10
Agriculture	59.9	56.6	53.2
Manufacturing	11.1	12.2	11.0
Non-manufacturing	5.3	6.5	10.5
Services	23.7	24.7	25.3
Total	100	100	100

Source: Various rounds conducted by the National Sample Survey Organization under the Ministry of Statistics and Programme Implementation.

Managing this urban transformation will be a Herculean challenge, and addressing it will require India to sharply improve urban governance and rapidly increase urban infrastructure investment. While the former is largely endogenous to India's political economy, the latter will require India to access large amounts of international capital and technologies. As an initial step, India has launched a 100 'smart cities' programme to improve the quality of life in India's burgeoning urban spaces.

India's urban infrastructure investment requirements are vast. A recent report by the McKinsey Global Institute estimated that India required US$1.2 trillion of investment in urban infrastructure by 2030, to be financed by public finance, monetizing land assets, leveraging debt and PPPs, and accessing private investment.[14] The Government of India's High Powered Expert Committee Report of 2011 called for Rs 39.2 lakh crore (about US$670 billion) of investment in urban infrastructure over a similar time period, with increasing private financing and reliance on PPPs.[15] In 2014, India's Ministry of Urban Development estimated that India needs to invest about US$250 billion over the next 20 years for basic urban infrastructure relating to transport, water supply, sanitation, and solid waste management alone.[16]

As a resource-scarce country—especially in land and energy— Japan has had to develop technologies, regulations, systems, and practices that are well adapted to its natural endowments. In particular, its land scarcity has led to dense urban metropolitan areas, where Japan has developed a comparative advantage in public transport systems and solid waste management, both of which are critical gaps in India's urban expansion. The Tokyo–Yokohama metropolitan area is a prime example of high-density urban management in Japan.

India will need to fund public transport investments to: provide high-capacity and quality transport infrastructure in both existing urban areas as well as in emerging greenfield urban areas; integrate intermediate public transport for better connectivity at public transport nodes; and creatively design cities to integrate land use and transport infrastructure to ensure good-quality access to a broad range of transportation modes.

From 2002 to 2011, the transport sector received 25 per cent of JICA's total assistance to India. Within this sector, subway (or local city train) systems account for the largest share (77 per cent), followed by railways (12 per cent), roads (10 per cent), and ports (1 per cent).[17] Japanese aid has been supporting the construction of subway systems in Delhi, Bengaluru, Kolkata, Mumbai, and Chennai. The model has been the Delhi Metro Rail Corporation, which began construction in Delhi in 1998. Yen loans covered about 60 per cent of the costs for the first phase and roughly half the costs for the second phase, and Japanese companies received orders in a broad range of areas including construction, signal systems, and rail cars.[18] With the Indian government having decided to develop subway system projects in all cities with a population of over 2 million—22 currently—subway projects offer a sustained investment and commercial opportunity for Japanese companies.

Urban India is poorly equipped to handle waste—both sewage as well as solid waste. According to data from the Central Pollution Control Board, in 2012–13 around 133,000 tonnes of municipal solid waste was generated in the country daily.[19] A report by the McKinsey Global Institute projected a tripling in per capita waste generation because of higher incomes and consumption resulting in a six-fold increase in waste generation to reach 377 million tonnes per annum inclusive of construction debris, or almost 1 million tonnes a day.[20] Already only about two-thirds of India's urban waste is being collected and barely a fifth is treated, with the remainder littered and often burned, further adding to pollution.[21] Much of the collected waste goes to landfill sites, which are scarce and poorly used. Clearly, developing better landfill technologies (for instance, with systems for compaction); separating the biodegradable waste in municipal waste (constituting nearly half of municipal solid waste) to produce compost for use as fertilizers; and setting up waste-to-energy plants will all be needed. Indian and Japanese researchers can collaborate on developing new technologies to address these urban waste challenges and make them integral to the green city investments being planned on the DMIC.

Given the enthusiasm in the bilateral relationship, especially economic, there is scope for substantially increasing Japanese investments in developing India's urban infrastructure. In a bid to facilitate and fast-track Japanese investment proposals, the Indian government's Department of Industrial Policy and Promotion (DIPP) set up a special management team known as Japan Plus, comprising officials of both governments. In a later section, we examine the challenges facing this group as it attempts to reduce the obstacles facing Japanese investments into India.

Smart City Bonds

Rome was not built in a day, not only because it is physically a challenging task but also because large building projects need large and reliable flows of resources, financed by long-term debt with appropriate maturity structures. For this purpose, a prominent policy option is a renewed emphasis on local government and municipal bonds.

In India, for a host of policy reasons, the dominance of the sovereign bond market and availability of cheap credit to big corporations has so far stymied all other bonds, particularly corporate and local government. It is well known, and Table 2.3 speaks to the fact, that Japanese investors prefer bonds to equity. Along with Hong Kong (if considered a separate market from Mainland China), India is one of the few countries where the opposite is true, that is, Japanese investors have a higher share of equity than bonds. The major reason for Japanese investors' preferred interest in bonds is of course that the former are widely known to favour longer-term and safer capital investment, and these are typically found in sovereigns and big corporate bonds.

So far, Japanese investments in Indian infrastructure have been exclusively in the form of loans. There is a strong case to be made for encouraging Japanese insurance and pension funds to invest in what may be called 'smart city bonds', or financial debt instruments designed to raise capital for the building of new industrial clusters and economic zones. A key constraint on this proposal is the perceived and actual quality of the debt issued through these bonds, especially for Japanese investors, who are known to be quite risk averse. To allay investor fears, a holding entity can be created which has the sovereign guarantees of both the Indian and Japanese governments. A holding entity would be essential to keep the bonds at an arm's length from the governments' balance sheets, which are already stressed.

There are very good economic reasons for Japanese interest in Indian infrastructure. In the current macroeconomic scenario, there are very few countries with growth rates at the level of India's (from the perspective of both base and level effects), and there are certainly very few with the demography to generate sustained demand. Investing through FDI instead of simple loans will also give Japanese firms greater access to Indian markets and create supply chain linkages. Critically, however, given the very low levels of interest rates in Japan, the country's pension funds and insurance companies have to look offshore for profitable investments. As Table 2.3 shows, so far the US, Europe, UK, Hong Kong, and Brazil have been their preferred destinations. But, with financial sector reforms under way in India, the institutional infrastructure to attract long-term capital into the country is being put into place. India's demand for long-term capital with the promise of good returns is perfectly matched with Japan's need to export capital to generate healthy returns.

Railways

Connectivity is the bedrock of growth in a modern economy. While digital connectivity is growing rapidly, India continues to be severely constrained in physical connectivity, that is, the movement of goods and people. While roads and highways have received a much-needed push in policy, investments in railways have been languishing for many decades.

In his 1960 opus, *The Stages of Economic Growth*, W.W. Rostow argued, 'The introduction of the railroad has been historically the most powerful single initiator of take-offs. It was decisive in the United States, France, Germany, Canada, and Russia; it has played an extremely important part in the Swedish, Japanese, and other cases.'[22] One can now surely add China to that list.

The Indian railway system has unfortunately suffered from a lack of investment, both in terms of capacity addition and technology upgrades. Figure 2.9 shows capacity addition in India and China from 1990 to 2010. The progressive difference is quite striking. Comparing this with the investment data available in Figure 2.10 completes the sorry picture.

Other than congested passenger travel, the biggest casualties of underinvestment in railways in India have been the manufacturing

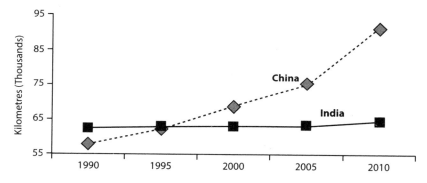

Figure 2.9   Addition to Railway Capacity (Route Km, '000s) in India and China, 1990–2010

Source: World Bank database; *Economic Survey of India, 2014–15*, p. 92.

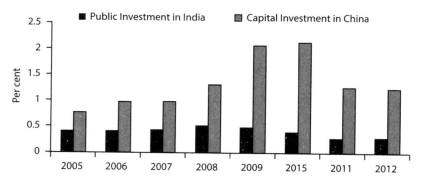

Figure 2.10   Investment in Railways (Per Cent of GDP) in India and China, 2005–12

Source: World Bank database; *Economic Survey of India, 2014–15*, p. 92.

and power sectors. Access to markets and the flow of raw materials, specifically coal and iron ore, are constrained. Low passenger ticket prices are often cross-subsidized with high freight rates. Rail freight rates in India are therefore expensive and have been growing steadily. This has ensured a decline in the share of railways in freight from over 60 per cent in the 1970s to about 33 per cent today, with most of the difference being compensated by roads. Figure 2.11 shows the figures for India with respect to some other countries. This shift has had adverse consequences for the environment and is logistically more cumbersome.

How Can Japan Help and Make a Profit?

Given the large investment needs of railways in India, opportunities abound and there are many options from an investor's perspective. Earlier we had pointed to Japan's involvement in urban transport in India through investments in subway systems. In addition, Japanese excellence in railways can be leveraged through the production of

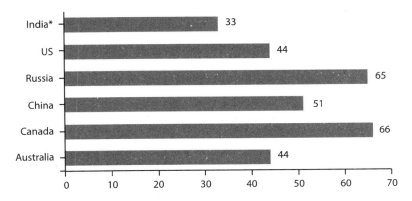

Figure 2.11   Modal Share of Railways (Per Cent) in Domestic Freight for Selected Countries, 2011
Source: P. Amos, *Freight Railways Governance, Organization and Management: An International Round-Up*, World Bank paper submitted to the National Transport Development Policy Committee, Government of India, 2011, cited in *Economic Survey of India, 2014–15*, p. 94.
* Estimate for 2011–12 provided in the report of the National Transport Development Policy Committee, 2014.

state-of-the-art locomotives, rolling stock, and signalling equipment. Collaboration with Indian Railways in producing locomotives in India will allow for the transfer of technology, which is essential for the development of domestic capacity in railways.

In terms of current and prospective Japanese investments in the Indian railways, for the western DFC project currently under implementation, Japanese ODA of ¥646 billion (US$5.4 billion) is envisaged and loan agreements for ¥226 billion (US$1.9 billion) have already been signed.[23] This ODA has a condition of 30 per cent goods being sourced from Japan, which includes electric locomotives, rails, high-capacity electric transformers, and signalling equipment. The total value of these goods sourced from Japan would be approximately ₹ 12,000 crore (US$2 billion), and it would flow over the next three to four years. While this would undoubtedly be beneficial for India, it nonetheless highlights that Japan's economic engagement with India continues to be in the form of loans and not direct long-term investment in physical assets. Another area where there is long-standing Japanese technological leadership is that of high-speed trains. Following feasibility studies on the Mumbai–Ahmedabad corridor, in October 2015 Japan offered to finance India's first bullet train, estimated to cost US$15 billion, at an interest rate of about 1 per cent. However, the high investment required means that the opportunity costs of such investments are substantial. Given other investment priorities, investments in high-speed Shinkansen-type train corridors might need to wait.

Financial Flows and Monetary Stability

In addition to deepening financial markets through much-needed financial sector reforms, India needs a well-developed corporate bond market. Infrastructure development in emerging markets has been driven in large part by non-secured loans and bonds. Unfortunately, both the quality of credit and the nature of the corporate bond market have left much to be desired in India. Japanese pension funds should be encouraged to invest more in debt flows and the corporate bond market in India, where interest rates are considerably higher than the very low rates in Japan and other developed countries.

Central bank liquidity swaps have become a key tool for hedging exchange rate risk and providing liquidity amongst developed countries. Developing countries have now begun this process as well, and India has taken modest steps in this direction. The US$50 billion swap arrangement that India signed with Japan in 2013 could be widened to include other bilateral and multilateral partners.[24]

Education and Labour Mobility

There is going to be a massive need for workers in agriculture, nursing and old age care, and other low- and medium-skill services in Japan in the years to come. India and Japan can develop temporary worker programmes (such as the one between Canada and Mexico) where Indian workers can either go seasonally (for agriculture) or for short-to-medium-term stays of three to five years. In addition, in higher-skill service jobs, such as IT, Japan can draw lessons from programmes such as the H1-B visa programme in the United States to take advantage of India's acknowledged expertise in this area.

But if Indian labour is to be able to serve the Japanese market, it needs to be trained to meet the exacting standards of Japanese employers. India's National Skill Development Corporation (NSDC) needs to partner with Japanese educational institutions and vocational training schools to develop training programmes that will impart both hard skills and the soft cultural skills necessary for the Japanese labour market as well as Japanese firms operating in India. On the other side, Japan needs to have less stringent visa norms at least for academic and research-related travel so as to better leverage India's burgeoning human capital.

Japan Plus

Following Prime Minister Modi's visit to Japan in September 2014, the Indian government established a special cell called Japan Plus in the MoCI to attract and fast-track Japanese investments in India.[25] According to government documents, the mandate of Japan Plus

> runs through the entire spectrum of investment promotion—research, outreach, promotion, facilitation and aftercare. The team will support the Government of India in initiating, attracting, facilitating, fast tracking and handholding Japanese investments across sectors. The team will

also be responsible for providing updated information on investment opportunities across sectors, in specific projects and in industrial corridors in particular. In addition, the 'Japan Plus' team will identify prospective Japanese companies, including Small and Medium Enterprises (SMEs) and facilitate their investments in India.[26]

The cell has been organizationally placed in the DIPP in the MoCI. Currently the team is composed of six members—four from the Government of India and two from Japan's METI. The decision to place two members of a foreign government directly within a unit of the Indian government is exceptional and conveys the priority that both governments attach to facilitating and implementing the agreements reached between them.

The four major objectives of Japan Plus are as follows. First, handholding existing Japanese companies and their investments in India. Second, investment in industrial parks, particularly in identifying locations and working with Indian states. Third, an e-forum to find potential partners on both sides for joint ventures. Finally, facilitating technology transfers from Japanese firms. A key fact that emerged out of our discussions with members of the team is that the main roadblocks that have arisen are located in contractual agreements with state governments. The role of the central government is to help Japanese companies identify potential locations, to provide central tax incentives, and to build basic external infrastructure. The state government addresses the nuts and bolts of location-specific issues such as land acquisition, power supply, and infrastructural connectivity including roads, power, water, and sewage. Coordination between the centre and states is therefore critical to the smooth implementation of projects.

The sequencing is typically as follows. An investor approaches the central government for a project, typically with a region in mind. The central government is tasked with obtaining clearances (mostly tax- and licence-based) from the relevant central ministries. After identifying a particular region, the central government may facilitate land acquisition and external infrastructure. The rest requires the involvement of the relevant state government, which gets reflected in a memorandum of understanding (MoU) between the state government and the investor. It is thus not surprising that a substantial chunk of investments, especially in manufacturing and IT, are clustered in very few states. For example, states in the Hindi heartland

and the north-east have not found favour with big investors because of a general weakness in institutional capacity and infrastructure. A key facilitating tool in reducing bottlenecks is investment through joint ventures. Suzuki did not just succeed as a standalone company in India; its association with Maruti played an important role. If public sector companies were the joint venture of choice in the 1980s, market-driven private firms fit the bill today. Thus, finding suitable partners can significantly reduce the setup costs in terms of navigating the bureaucracy. Table 2.5 lists some prominent joint ventures between Indian and Japanese firms in the last 10 years.

The emergence of a more cooperative (centre–state) and competitive (inter-state) federalism in India means that Japanese investments are likely to cluster where states make special efforts to facilitate these investments. Greater fiscal autonomy for the states that has been recently proposed by the central government will ensure that the next stage of federalism will bode well for international investors.[27] For example, the state of Andhra Pradesh is currently in the process of

Table 2.5   Selected Joint Ventures between Indian and Japanese Firms, 2005–15

	Product	Indian Side	Japanese Firm
1.	High Voltage Cables	Sterlite Technologies (Vedanta Group)	VISCAS Corporation
2.	Alloy Wheels	Minda Industries	Kosei Group
3.	Drugs	Lupin Pharma	Yoshindo Inc.
4.	Mutual Funds	LIC	Nomura
5.	Auto Parts	Lumax Auto Technologies	Mannoh
6.	Food and Food Processing	Ruchi Soya Industries	KMDI International
7.	Construction Machinery	Tata	Hitachi
8.	Steel Wire Ropes	Usha Siam Steel	TESAC Wire Ropes
9.	Telecommunications	Tata	NTT DoCoMo
10.	Telecom and E-commerce	Bharti Airtel	Softbank

Source: Constructed by authors using information available on www.moneycontrol.com.

building a new capital after the creation of the new state of Telangana from the erstwhile united Andhra Pradesh. The chief minister of Andhra Pradesh has already travelled to Japan and been assured monetary and technical expertise by the Government of Japan.

As a final thought on Indian and Japanese collaboration in the private sector, the lack of cultural diplomacy cannot be overemphasized. The reason why Japanese involvement in Indian industry has been limited somewhat to providing technical assistance rather than full-scale FDI is not just regulatory but also cultural. In reply to our questions, a former head of the India–Japan Chamber of Commerce wrote:

> [O]pportunities are significant but Japanese risk aversion, unwillingness to get deeply involved with unique India issues, and lack of successful role models is acting as a constraint on closer economic participation. India is definitely not Thailand/Indonesia and here schools, karaoke bars, and entertainment parlours are as important as opaque regulations and shifting stands. Moreover, new age Indian companies are more culturally in tune with the Western ones.

Geopolitical Considerations

There are two strong underlying reasons for closer economic links between Japan and India. The first is the complementarity between the strengths (and weaknesses) of their respective economies. The second rationale is strategic, a response to the changing geopolitical environment in the region. To that extent, the two countries should also explore closer ties in defence production in areas where Japan has state-of-the-art technologies such as naval vessels, maritime reconnaissance aircraft, and defence electronics (see Chapter 6 in this volume for more on India–Japan strategic economic cooperation). This type of cooperation would also lower the unit costs of production for Japan.

One issue we have not addressed in this chapter is a strategic partnership between the two countries in global economic governance. This issue is especially important in the case of global trade where two mega trade blocs—the Trans-Pacific Partnership (TPP) and the Transatlantic Trade and Investment Partnership (TTIP)—are likely to account for about half of world trade. For Japan, this is important for economic as well as strategic reasons, including being able to get energy imports from the United States. Therefore, over the medium term, the developments that take place in the TPP would begin to underpin the consideration of investments made by Japanese businesses. The most important policy aspects would include standards, intellectual property rights, and digital trade (especially data transfer issues). India has for long focused on the Regional Comprehensive Economic Partnership (RCEP), another mega regional agreement which will likely have less stringent standards and discipline than the TPP. Indian policies and standards at present are below the levels likely to prevail as a result of mega regional trade agreements such as the TPP and TTIP. This is one area where cooperation with Japan could focus on improving Indian standards in line with those emerging in the largest free-trade agreements and developing value chains for foreign markets.

Notes

1. P.A. George (ed.), *East Asian Literatures: An Interface with India*, New Delhi: Jawaharlal Nehru University, 2006.
2. MoFA, 'Overview of Japan's ODA to India', June 2011, retrieved from http://www.in.emb-japan.go.jp/Japan-India-Relations/ODA_Eng_Jun2011.pdf on 2 September 2015; MOFA, 'India', n.d., retrieved from http://www.mofa.go.jp/policy/oda/data/pdfs/india.pdf on 2 September 2015.
3. Authors' estimates from Japanese government data.
4. JBIC, 'Survey Report on Overseas Business Operations by Japanese Manufacturing Companies', 2014, retrieved from https://www.jbic.go.jp/wp-content/uploads/press_en/2014/11/32994/20141128English1.pdf on 2 September 2015.
5. Planning Commission, Government of India, 'Faster, Sustainable and More Inclusive Growth: An Approach to the Twelfth Five Year Plan', 2011, retrieved from http://planningcommission.gov.in/plans/planrel/12appdrft/approach_12plan.pdf on 2 September 2015.
6. N. Smith, 'Japan's Debt Trap', Bloomberg View, 24 September 2014, retrieved from http://www.bloombergview.com/articles/2014-09-24/japan-s-debt-trap on 1 November 2015.
7. OECD, 'FDI in Figures', 2014, retrieved from http://www.oecd.org/daf/inv/FDI-in-Figures-April-2014.pdf on 2 September 2015.

8. For an overview of the evidence, see M. Nathan and H. Overman, 'Agglomeration, Clusters, and Industrial Policy', *Oxford Review of Economic Policy*, 29(2), 2013, pp. 383–404.

9. This section draws on Government of India, *Economic Survey of India 2012–13*, 2013, chapter 2, Box 2.2.

10. Trunk infrastructure refers to the support to large-scale infrastructure projects to allow them to be functional on the ground. It includes water supply, sewage, connecting roads, flood management, community spaces, etc.

11. High Powered Expert Committee, Ministry of Urban Development, Government of India, *Report on Indian Urban Infrastructure and Services*, 2011, retrieved from http://icrier.org/pdf/FinalReport-hpec.pdf on 4 September 2015.

12. High Powered Expert Committee, *Report on Indian Urban Infrastructure and Services*.

13. W.A. Lewis, 'Economic Development with Unlimited Supplies of Labour', *Manchester School*, 22(2), 1954, pp. 139–91; J.R. Harris and M.P. Todaro, 'Migration, Unemployment and Development: A Two-Sector Analysis', *American Economic Review*, 60(1), 1970, pp. 126–42.

14. McKinsey Global Institute, *India's Urban Awakening*, 2010, retrieved from http://www.mckinsey.com/insights/urbanization/urban_awakening_in_india on 4 September 2015.

15. High Powered Expert Committee, *Report on Indian Urban Infrastructure and Services*.

16. The numbers are based on a speech delivered by India's urban development minister, cited in: 'India Needs $250 Billion in the Next 20 Years for Infrastructure', *Economic Times*, 7 October 2014.

17. See JICA, 'India', n.d., retrieved from http://www.jica.go.jp/india/english/ on 4 September 2015.

18. S. Ray, 'Japan to Fund Metro's Phase III from December', *Hindustan Times*, 24 July 2011.

19. Ministry of Environment, Forests and Climate Change, Government of India, *Annual Report 2014–15*, 2015, p. 120, retrieved from http://envfor.nic.in/sites/default/files/Environment%20Annual%20Report%20%20Eng..pdf.

20. McKinsey Global Institute, *India's Urban Awakening*.

21. Ministry of Environment, Forests and Climate Change, *Annual Report 2014–15*, p. 120.

22. W.W. Rostow, *The Stages of Economic Growth: A Non-communist Manifesto*, Cambridge, UK: Cambridge University Press, 1960, pp. 55–6.

23. The data in this paragraph were acquired by the authors from the Indian Ministry of Railways.
24. Ministry of Finance, Government of India, 'Bilateral Currency Swap Arrangement between the Reserve Bank of India and Bank of Japan Enhanced from US $15 billion to US $50 billion', 18 December 2013, retrieved from http://pib.nic.in/newsite/PrintRelease.aspx?relid=102007 on 4 September 2015.
25. This section is based on interviews with members of the Japan Plus unit by one of the authors on 26 February 2014.
26. DIPP, Government of India, '"Japan Plus" constituted to fast track Japanese investments', 9 October 2014, retrieved from http://dipp.nic.in/English/acts_rules/Press_Release/japanPlus_09October2014.pdf on 4 September 2015.
27. See Finance Commission of India, *Report of the Fourteenth Finance Commission*, 24 February 2015, retrieved from http://finmin.nic.in/14fincomm/14fcreng.pdf on 4 September 2015.

Part II

ENERGY AND CLIMATE CHANGE

3

Towards a Co-beneficial Energy Partnership

Nobuo Tanaka and Anthony Yazaki

With up to 400 million Indians currently living without access to electricity, the expansion of energy access is one of the major challenges facing the Indian government. At the same time, Japan also faces significant questions about its energy future following the Fukushima disaster in March 2011. In this context, there are substantial opportunities for mutually beneficial cooperation between the two countries on policies relating to energy security, efficiency, and sustainability. The possibilities for cooperation range from an overarching policy like the Joint Crediting Mechanism to short-term initiatives such as the re-indexation of Asian natural gas prices and long-term goals such as the creation of a regional energy security forum. Such initiatives would not only strengthen the bilateral relationship between Japan and India, but would also necessarily involve Chinese cooperation, which would likely help to strengthen the often strained relationships between some of Asia's most powerful nations.

Japan

For the residents of north-east Japan, 11 March 2011 was a day that began like any other. It was cold and cloudy, but nothing out of the ordinary for a population hardened by centuries in this harsh climate. That all changed in an instant when a magnitude 9.0 earthquake rocked the coast, sending a massive tsunami up to 40 metres tall hurtling across the Japanese mainland, taking with it cars, homes, entire villages, and over 15,000 lives. However, the effects of the disaster went far beyond the immediate death toll and instantaneous destruction. It soon became apparent that the tsunami had overcome the seawall at the Fukushima Daiichi Nuclear Power Plant, causing crippling damage to the plant's cooling system, eventually leading to a core meltdown and the worst nuclear disaster since Chernobyl.

This triple disaster—earthquake, tsunami, and nuclear meltdown—shook Japan to its core, causing the government and the country's citizens to fundamentally re-evaluate the nation's energy systems. As the government temporarily shut down all of the country's nuclear power plants heading into the summer months, the country's dependence on nuclear energy became readily apparent. Still, public opinion created massive uncertainty about the future of an energy source that had previously seemed to be a perfect fit for Japan—in an energy-poor country, nuclear power had reduced reliance on costly energy imports while keeping greenhouse gas emissions to a minimum. The anti-nuclear sentiment following Fukushima eventually manifested in street protests that called for making the temporary moratorium on nuclear energy permanent, an act that would dramatically alter Japan's energy supply.

Four years later, the country's energy future continues to be a major question facing both the Japanese government and the public. How will the country meet its energy needs following the marginalization of nuclear power? Will it be possible to meet these needs while keeping costs within an acceptable range and also protecting the environment at a time when climate change mitigation is becoming an issue increasingly discussed at the highest levels?

India

While the Japanese have now spent several years debating their energy future, India has faced questions of its own regarding how it will handle the growing need for energy in the future. Before taking the reigns as the prime minister of India in May 2014, Narendra Modi spent nearly 13 years serving as the chief minister of Gujarat state in India's far west. In that position, one of Modi's principal accomplishments was the electrification of virtually the entire state with over 60 million residents, roughly the population of Italy. By one account, he claimed in a 2012 interview that '[e]very village in Gujarat has 24/7/365 three-phase power'.[1] Though this is indeed an impressive track record in a country with millions still living in dire poverty, the challenge Modi faced in Gujarat pales in comparison to what he currently faces as the Indian prime minister.

According to various estimates, anywhere from 300 to 400 million Indians currently live without access to electricity, which constitutes roughly 25–33 per cent of the nation's population of 1.2 billion.[2] Energy access is clearly a major development issue in terms of both proportional and absolute figures. India's demand for energy is poised to increase significantly in the coming decades as the country endeavours to continue its rapid economic growth. According to one forecast, India will likely overtake China as the number one driver of global growth in energy demand by 2035.[3] Furthermore, as climate change and environmental sustainability continue to become focal points of international policy making, the Indian government will be faced with a number of challenging questions. Will India be able to expand electricity access to its most impoverished citizens and provide the energy necessary to support economic growth, all while playing a positive role in the global drive to reduce greenhouse gas emissions and mitigate climate change? Can these seemingly conflicting imperatives be balanced? Or even better, is there a way to achieve all of these goals in synergistic and co-beneficial ways?

In a sense, Japan and India are facing situations that are dramatically different yet uniquely similar. While Japan is fundamentally rethinking its existing energy system that had been operating with relative success, India is still trying to determine how it will provide energy to millions of people for the first time while meeting demand that is likely to increase dramatically in the near future. Despite the clear differences between these contexts, the fact is that both countries are currently facing a crossroads, a transformative moment where decisions made in the present will likely have far-reaching consequences in the future. It is prudent therefore to ask how Japan and India may be able to cooperate in such a way that they would both be able to meet their varied challenges. How can they work together so that the outcomes would create co-benefits for the two countries, while also creating co-benefits between energy security and environmental sustainability? This kind of cooperation may not be easy, but there is a basis for saying that it can be done. The options range from highly feasible short-term policies that should be prioritized to long-term policies that may be difficult to execute but would generate considerable benefits for both countries.

Japan's Energy Interests

One of the most significant problems facing Japan's strategic planners has long been the country's virtually complete dependence on energy imports in order to fulfil its energy requirements. Japan has historically been known as an energy-poor country with few indigenous sources of raw energy inputs, meaning that its post-industrialization reliance on fossil fuels has been virtually synonymous with a reliance on imports. One way in which the government had tried to reverse this external dependence was through the use of nuclear power. This was thought of as a doubly beneficial policy for Japan, because a shift from fossil fuels to nuclear energy would not only reduce the need for energy imports, but would also help the country to cut its carbon emissions. Indeed, the 2010 version of Japan's Strategic Energy Plan envisioned that by 2030, nuclear energy would jump from roughly 26 per cent to 50 per cent of the country's electricity generation.[4]

However, the 2011 Fukushima disaster suddenly and dramatically altered Japan's energy outlook. With the abrupt shutdown of Japan's nuclear power plants, the country had to fill the gap by increasing its imports of fossil fuels such as coal, oil, and natural gas, which pushed

Japan's overall dependency on imported fossil fuels to 88 per cent of its total electrical power consumption in 2013, as opposed to 62 per cent in 2010.[5] In terms of electricity generation, the country's dependence on coal increased from 25 per cent in 2010 to 30 per cent in 2013, oil from 7.5 per cent to 15 per cent, and natural gas from 29 per cent to 43 per cent in the same time period.[6] In 2012, Japan's energy source distribution across all sectors (not only electrical power generation) was 47 per cent oil, 24 per cent natural gas, 23 per cent coal, 5 per cent renewables, and 1 per cent nuclear.[7]

With the future of the nuclear industry remaining highly uncertain, it is unsurprising that Japan's 2014 Strategic Energy Plan did not enumerate specific numerical targets for the future of the country's energy portfolio. Rather, it outlined broader goals 'aimed at reducing reliance on nuclear power as much as possible and building a flexible, diversified, multilevel supply-and-demand structure'.[8] The plan also 'encourages Japanese companies to increase energy exploration and development projects around the world to secure a stable supply of oil and natural gas',[9] which suggests that the Japanese government is taking a realist view that even the rapid deployment of renewable energy on a large scale will not be enough to fill the void left by the absence of nuclear power. This in turn means that fossil fuels will continue to play a major role in Japan's energy landscape, at least for the near future.

Although Japan's total energy demand is trending downwards at a rate approaching 1 per cent per annum and is projected to continue on this path,[10] the reality remains that one of the country's core interests is still the need to maintain stable and cost-effective access to fossil fuels. At the same time, Japan will have to make efforts to reduce its dependence on these imported fuels in order to reduce the country's vulnerability to external influences and shocks, while also reducing its carbon emissions. In order to achieve this balance, the government will have to work strategically in global fossil fuel markets while also continuing to encourage the deployment of renewable energy and attempting to overcome public opposition to nuclear power.

The Current State of Japan–India Cooperation on Energy

To date, Japan and India's energy cooperation has been symptomatic of their larger relationship. That is to say that great potential exists in a strong Japan–India partnership and both sides have made verbal commitments to this effect, but meaningful execution has been lacking.

The most recent iteration of relations between Japan and India can be traced back to 2000, when Japanese Prime Minister Yoshiro Mori visited India to thaw the countries' strained relations following India's nuclear tests of 1998. At the time, he and Indian Prime Minister Atal Bihari Vajpayee agreed to declare a 'Global Partnership between Japan and India in the 21st Century', but the scope of issues on the table was limited to subjects such as nuclear non-proliferation, United Nations Security Council (UNSC) reform, the Kashmir issue, and information technology (IT) cooperation, with no specific mention of cooperation on energy security.[11]

The Japan–India relationship was subsequently upgraded in 2006 when Prime Ministers Shinzo Abe and Manmohan Singh declared that their countries would now enter into a 'Strategic and Global Partnership'. This time, the scope of discussions and cooperation was expanded considerably. Abe and Singh's joint statement said that '[the] two sides are determined to tackle global energy security issues jointly' and that they endorsed the creation of the Japan–India Energy Dialogue to be held between the Japanese Ministry of Economy, Trade and Industry (METI) and the Planning Commission of India.[12] Although the Modi government disbanded the latter in mid-2014 soon after coming to power and replaced it with the NITI Aayog (National Institution for Transforming India), the dialogue is one of the main vehicles for energy cooperation between the two countries. There are also a number of working groups that meet within this framework to discuss specific issues including energy efficiency and conservation, renewable energy, electricity, coal, petroleum and natural gas, and nuclear energy.

Although the existence of the energy dialogue and its host of working groups suggests that robust energy cooperation already exists, a deeper look tells a slightly different story. Despite having these structures in place, Japan and India's cooperation appears to be more episodic and ad hoc rather than systematic. For example, the statement released following the most recent energy dialogue describes the progress being made on a number of joint projects, but these projects appear to be taking place within their own silos, with few linkages between them.[13] In other words, cooperation seems to be project-based rather than being based on an overarching strategy for how the two countries can jointly work towards achieving their energy interests. With this in mind, it is necessary to consider how better to support the existing framework for cooperation in order to create a stronger and more institutionalized pattern of cooperation, not just at the level of prime ministers and cabinet ministers, but at the working level as well.

One policy that could play a crucial role in facilitating Japan–India relations in the energy field is the Joint Crediting Mechanism (JCM). Negotiations are already under way between the two countries and should be urgently concluded with the signing of a memorandum of understanding (MoU). The JCM would be beneficial on a number of levels because it would help to advance India technologically while improving its energy security, and would also help both countries to move towards a more environmentally sustainable future.

In practice, the JCM would operate like a bilateral version of the clean development mechanism (CDM), which was outlined in the Kyoto Protocol. Japanese companies would be able to transfer new, clean, and potentially expensive technologies to Indian firms, and in exchange would receive carbon credits corresponding to the reduction or slowing of growth in India's carbon emissions. This policy would be mutually beneficial in that India would be able to receive technologies that may otherwise be difficult or too expensive to obtain, while Japan would be able to better meet its own emissions reduction targets. The downside for either side to enter into such an agreement would be minimal. Furthermore, this arrangement could be applied across a number of different energy sectors, as will be discussed in greater detail later in this chapter. The JCM would also help to address India's hesitancy in making multilateral commitments on energy and climate change issues by keeping the programme within a bilateral context. One potential pitfall of the JCM for Japanese firms is the possibility that their technology would be reproduced by their Indian counterparts at a lower cost, so it will be necessary to create mechanisms for protecting intellectual property rights (IPR). Although the implementation of India's IPR laws does not yet meet global benchmarks, the country's policies in this field are gradually being strengthened and, when interviewed, METI officials did not mention any concerns about potential IPR infringement.[14]

Discussions on the JCM are already ongoing between the two countries. Feasibility studies for the introduction of Japanese technologies have been conducted at a number of locations around India, which range from projects such as the improvement of energy efficiency at a data centre to the construction of a new hydropower plant.[15] With abundant reasons to conclude the MoU negotiations and few potentially negative consequences if any, it appears both highly realistic and prudent that the two sides move expeditiously towards turning the Japan–India JCM into reality. Japan has already concluded 12 such agreements with other countries around the world and has completed dozens of model projects.[16] With the JCM appearing to be a framework that will play an increasingly important role in Japan's overseas development and climate change mitigation strategies, there are plenty of reasons for India to become involved as well.

Near-Term Policies

Clean Coal

One area where the JCM could be effectively implemented is in India's coal sector. According to the US Energy Information Administration, coal accounted for 44 per cent of India's total energy use in 2012, and the country had 'the world's fifth-largest coal reserves, and ranked third largest in terms of both production and consumption'.[17] It is thus unrealistic to expect that India will be able to entirely wean itself from coal consumption and its accompanying carbon emissions at any time in the near future. Accordingly, India should look to harness new technologies like the integrated gasification combined cycle (IGCC) and carbon capture and storage (CCS) that allow for the continued use of coal energy while minimizing negative impacts on the global climate.

Under the JCM, Japan could commit to transferring relatively expensive IGCC and CCS technologies to India at a reduced cost, which would allow India to continue the use of coal energy while also slowing the growth of carbon emissions. In return for financing such projects, Japan would earn carbon credits to help meet its own emission reduction targets. At least three feasibility studies have already been conducted on coal projects under the JCM; hence, this seems to be an especially realistic possibility.

Not only would this type of cooperation ensure that India could continue to make use of its coal resources moving forward, it is also likely that it would encourage India to more proactively join a binding international climate change agreement. India has been generally reticent to make major multilateral commitments on the climate change front largely due to its position that developed countries are responsible for the vast majority of historical carbon emissions, and that the mitigation of emissions should not come at the expense of India's development. However, if the country were to be able to guarantee its ability to continue using coal energy, thus helping to maintain its development trajectory while also reducing or slowing the growth of its emissions, it would be more likely to agree to a legally binding framework. Clean coal initiatives would not guarantee India's willingness to sign a multilateral agreement, but at minimum these measures would address one of the country's major concerns. Considering the array of mutually beneficial and reinforcing benefits mentioned earlier, both Japan and India should see this bilateral initiative as a high priority for the near future.

Renewable Energy

As climate change and sustainability continue to become more significant issues on the international agenda, renewable energy should begin to form an incrementally larger proportion of countries' energy portfolios. This means that renewable energy is another field in which the Japan–India JCM should be applied. Although Japan needs to tend to its immediate energy security while nuclear power remains at a virtual standstill, it should be looking to the future with an understanding that investments in renewables are likely to pay off greatly over time. Meanwhile, India should be looking to make renewables an important pillar of its drive to provide energy for the first time to millions of its citizens.

Indeed, both countries have already made commitments in this vein. For example, India's Five Year Plan—a periodic exercise in

priority setting and financial allocation for socio-economic development prepared by the now-defunct Planning Commission—spanning 2012–17 targets a roughly 30 GW increase in the deployment
of renewables.[18] More recently, the secretary of India's Ministry of
New and Renewable Energy has been quoted saying that the country
would aim to raise US$100 billion in investments that would increase
the country's solar capacity 33-fold.[19] Meanwhile, Japan's most recent
Strategic Energy Plan did not outline a concrete renewable energy
target, but it did commit more broadly to '[a]ccelerating the introduction of renewable energy'.[20] Japan's interest in renewables has also
been demonstrated by the introduction of a feed-in tariff programme
in 2012, which has created incentives for the implementation of
renewable energy projects by paying renewable energy producers for
their power generation at a predetermined above-market rate over a
fixed period of time.[21] Further, the two prime ministers' September
2014 joint statement said that they had 'decided to spur cooperation'
on renewable energy.[22] Both countries have clearly identified renewable energy as a goal, and cooperation is both realistic and mutually
beneficial, especially if carried out through the JCM.

Beyond the verbal commitments made by Japan and India's
respective prime ministers to cooperate on renewable energy, there is
an added degree of possibility considering that a number of renewable energy projects including solar power and hydropower have
already undergone feasibility studies in the context of JCM negotiations.[23] Considering India's explicit commitment to the expansion of
solar power, this would be a reasonable field to begin with. Japanese
firms could use their technical expertise to collaborate with Indian
counterparts both on research and development of new technologies
and in terms of the deployment of solar power projects. This type
of collaboration could be especially helpful for rural electrification
projects in India through the use of decentralized micro power grids.
Although the Indian government has pledged to expand the country's national power grid, smaller-scale projects would help improve
India's energy access in the interim. India already has abundant experience with decentralized power grids, especially small hydropower
projects. Therefore, combining this expertise with Japan's technical
capabilities in the solar power field could be an effective means to
expand energy access in a way that can more easily reach remote areas

and also reduce the substantial electricity losses that occur during transmission and distribution. (The World Bank estimates that over 20 per cent of power generated in India between 2010 and 2014 was lost during the transmission and distribution process).[24]

Aside from solar power, there is also room for cooperation on other forms of renewable energy such as hydro, geothermal, and wind power. Like solar power, small hydropower projects could be effective in electrifying remote areas because of their constant power output (unlike solar or wind energy which have inherently intermittent power output) and relatively small environmental impact.[25] Given that both countries are already among the world's largest hydroelectricity producers, their joint expertise in this field could prove effective.

Next, India stands to benefit from the development of its geothermal resources, a source of energy that the country has only recently begun to explore. According to one Indian government publication, the Geological Survey of India has identified roughly 340 locations that could be conducive to geothermal power production.[26] Considering that Japan has one of the highest levels of installed geothermal capacities in the world, it should be able to assist India on the latter's own projects through the JCM. Lastly, although India is already one of the world's largest producers of wind power, it continues to have immense untapped potential, making it an area where cooperation with Japan could have a meaningful impact.[27]

With India's immense territory and varied landscapes, it has the potential to house a diverse renewable portfolio, which would contribute greatly to improving the country's energy security. Japan could play an integral role in making this a reality at a relatively modest cost. Considering the rapid rate at which India's energy demand is likely to continue growing, this would be a worthwhile investment.

Energy Efficiency

While the stability of energy supplies is clearly a vital issue for any government, increasing energy efficiency and thus reducing or slowing the growth of energy demand is another viable way to reduce energy costs while also helping to minimize adverse impacts on the global climate and environment. With this in mind, it would be realistic and useful for Japan to assist India in adopting energy efficiency technology, know-how, regulations, and standards. In particular, Japan's 'Top Runner' programme could serve as a model for India to improve the efficiency of its consumer products.

Initiated in Japan in 1998, the Top Runner programme created a set of efficiency standards for certain appliances, equipment, and automobiles, based on the most efficient products in their particular categories. In other words, efficiency standards for air conditioners are set by the most efficient air conditioners on the market, while the most efficient gasoline-powered cars on the market set the standards for gasoline-powered cars. Products that meet the efficiency standard are given a Top Runner label in stores, while companies that fail to meet standards are faced with increasingly severe penalties for non-compliance. With companies having to constantly improve the efficiency of their products, the Top Runner approach has led to a voluntary increase in corporate outlays for research and development.[28]

The programme has proven to be extremely effective in improving the efficiency of a wide range of consumer products. Between 1998 and 2010, the efficiency of Japanese computers improved by an astonishing 99.1 per cent, air conditioners by 67.8 per cent, refrigerators by 55.2 per cent, fluorescent lights by 35.6 per cent, televisions by 25.7 per cent, and gasoline-powered cars by 22.8 per cent.[29] Although efficiency gains should naturally be expected over time, research indicates that the rate of improvement for some appliances increased significantly following the enactment of the Top Runner programme, suggesting that the law played an important role in driving these improvements.[30]

In terms of transplanting the Top Runner approach to India, there are a number of considerations to keep in mind. First, Indian firms that would like to take advantage of Japanese technology could potentially do so under the framework of the previously mentioned JCM, meaning that Japanese companies would receive the benefit of carbon credits towards meeting emissions reduction goals, while Indian companies would benefit from receiving leading technologies at a reduced rate. Second, efficiency measures would likely be easier to implement than other forms of energy infrastructure investment, meaning that the adoption of a Top Runner scheme should be a cost-effective way to slow the growth of India's energy consumption and carbon emissions.

Third, although compliance with Top Runner standards is mandatory in Japan, with persistent non-compliance carrying a number of increasingly severe penalties, in the Indian context it may be better to start by making compliance voluntary. While some companies may at first be hesitant to bind themselves to new standards which could increase their costs and the prices of their products, the availability of Japanese technology through the JCM would mean that less money would be required for research and development activities, and that more efficient products may not be significantly more expensive. Even if the Top Runner certified products do end up being more expensive to produce and sell than their uncertified counterparts, at least some consumers from India's growing middle class are likely to opt for appliances that are more efficient and likely to save money over the long term.

Finally, it is important to note that the Indian government already has some of the necessary institutions in place to be able to effectively implement the Top Runner approach. There already exists a Bureau of Energy Efficiency (BEE), which was set up in 2002 under the Energy Conservation Act of 2001. The bureau is tasked with developing 'minimum energy performance standards and labelling design for equipment and appliances'.[31] One particular programme under the bureau's purview is India's 'Standards and Labelling' programme, which is similar to the Top Runner programme in that it mandates certain efficiency standards and labels electric appliances based on their performance. However, one of the main differences between the two programmes is in how the standards are determined. Whereas Top Runner standards are essentially determined by the appliance producers themselves and therefore are inherently achievable, the Indian standards are determined by the BEE based on its own assumptions and analyses. There is evidence to suggest that the latter system has shortcomings. For example, according to a 2014 study, virtually all refrigerators in India received efficiency ratings between three and five stars (out of five), even though India's standards were less stringent than those set in places like China and the US, which indicates that the BEE's standards are too loose and are not keeping up with the efficiency gains of products in the Indian market.[32]

Taking all of this into consideration, adoption of the Top Runner approach in India would not require a fundamental shift in India's existing efficiency plan. Rather, it would be an adjustment that could improve the ability of government institutions to carry out pre-existing mandates. These factors, combined with the possibility of using advanced Japanese technology through the JCM, should make this an attractive option for policy makers in both countries.

The larger point to take away from these discussions is the significant role that the JCM can play in spurring energy cooperation between Japan and India. Although some options for effective collaboration are described here, they will remain much more difficult to execute without the JCM. As such, the conclusion of an MoU should continue to be a top priority for the relevant policy makers in both countries. In this regard, an interview with Japanese officials from METI revealed a degree of perplexity about the fact that numerous Indian agencies are involved with the negotiations, thus creating delays and confusion as to who would be making a final decision for Delhi on this count. Still, the Japanese officials expressed optimism that the MoU could be concluded sooner rather than later. Once that is done, Japan and India will have greater incentive to work together due to the benefits that will be derived by each side.

Natural Gas Prices

Another issue that merits Japan–India cooperation in the short term is the re-indexation of natural gas prices in Asia. Japan is currently the world's largest importer of natural gas, accounting for roughly 37 per cent of global liquefied natural gas (LNG) consumption in 2012, while natural gas made up 24 per cent of the country's total energy consumption that year. Meanwhile, although only 7 per cent of India's energy was derived from natural gas in 2012, the country has been a net importer since 2004 and was the world's fourth largest importer of LNG in 2013.[33] These current conditions, combined with the projected growth in India's energy demand, suggest that more favourable gas pricing practices would be of great benefit to both countries.

Currently, the dominant practice in Asia is for natural gas prices to be indexed to oil prices, rather than indexing them to other gases or using a free market system based on supply and demand. Although this kind of gas price regulation is practised throughout much of the world, Asia does so at a particularly high rate largely due to the monopolies held by government-controlled natural gas suppliers in the region, as opposed to many Western countries where gas market liberalization has led to a market-based pricing mechanism.[34] In 2010, 88 per cent of natural gas traded in the Asia Pacific was priced using oil indexation, while this was the case for 67 per cent of gas traded in Europe and 0 per cent of gas traded in North America.[35] According to a study conducted by the International Energy Agency (IEA), '[T]his [indexation] has helped keep Asian gas prices much higher than those in other parts of the world, leading to competitiveness concerns and serious questions about whether such a system can last.'[36]

In order to change this status quo, it would be beneficial for Asian countries to begin a system of joint procurement of natural gas. This is because individual countries would face difficulty in overturning the existing system due to government-run Asian gas companies having a vested interest in maintaining the current system that generally features prices above the market rate. Russia, for example, is the largest natural gas exporter in the world and continues to support oil indexation.[37] However, it is likely that if a number of large gas-importing Asian countries were to cooperate, they would have the economic and diplomatic clout necessary to alter the current pricing mechanisms. While this task may seem difficult at the moment, it is important to note that '[v]ery few experts believed back in 2008 that oil indexation could lose its supremacy in European gas markets, yet in a few years' time it did'.[38] Furthermore, the shale gas revolution in the US may help to bring down costs and increase pressure on sellers to abandon distortionary pricing practices.

This measure would also help to bring together a broader coalition of Asian natural gas importers including South Korea, Taiwan, Thailand, and most notably China. Although one important dimension of the growing relationship between Japan and India will be to counteract China's growing power and assertiveness, it will also be important to create an atmosphere where cooperation and coexistence between the three major Asian powers will be possible. Joint efforts on natural gas pricing could present an opportunity to turn historical mistrust and antagonism into mutually beneficial cooperation, while also creating stronger ties with the rapidly growing economies of Southeast Asia. Such an effort among Asian nations would likely face opposition from gas-exporting countries who stand to gain from high natural gas prices, such as Russia, Indonesia, and Malaysia, but if major economies and natural gas purchasers such as Japan, India, and China were to present a united front, these exporters would face a much more difficult battle. Considering the intra-regional competition and rivalries that tend to hamper cooperation within Asia, it may be necessary for India and Japan—possibly alongside other like-minded countries—to cooperate in reducing natural gas prices before expanding cooperation with China. Regardless of such sequencing issues, natural gas may be an avenue through which to create greater pan-Asian cooperation, which has been elusive through the twentieth and twenty-first centuries.

There is reason to be optimistic that Japan and India can move towards joint procurement. During their 2014 summit meeting in Tokyo, Prime Ministers Shinzo Abe and Narendra Modi issued the so-called Tokyo Declaration, which stated that '[t]hey shared the intention that Japan and India would explore a higher level of strategic collaboration in the global oil and natural gas market, including the joint procurement of LNG.'[39] Furthermore, one such arrangement between Japan and India has actually been signed between Japan's Chubu Electric Power Company and India's natural gas distributor, the Gas Authority of India Limited (GAIL), in March 2014, in which the two companies pledged to 'discuss the possibility of collaboration in joint LNG procurement'.[40] If this arrangement proves to be successful, the partnership between the two companies could provide a model for how cooperation in the natural gas field could be widened and deepened in the future. Overall, the two companies' agreement combined with the stated commitment of the two heads of government should bode well for the future of Japan and India's relationship in this arena.

Finally, in the realm of natural gas but separate from joint procurement, it would also be beneficial to create greater interconnectivity between gas pipeline networks throughout Asia, with Russia acting as a core supplier. Notwithstanding the current sanctions and diplomatic standoff between Russia and a number of Western countries, Russia could act in the future as a relatively stable and nearby gas supplier for rapidly growing Asian economies. Due to the sanctions associated with the Ukrainian conflict, Russia has few options available in terms of selling its natural gas, which is a major source of the state's revenues. This has unsurprisingly pushed it into sealing a number of deals with China, which is not participating in sanctions and stands to be one of the greatest beneficiaries of the standoff between Russia and the West. However, sanctions against Russia cannot last forever and will eventually have to be lifted. It therefore behoves Japan, India, and the rest of Asia to be prepared for that moment. Considering the extended amount of time that would be necessary to regionally integrate gas pipelines, it would be worthwhile to begin making such plans now. With China already planning to connect its pipelines to Central Asia and Russia, it is incumbent upon Japan and India to think in such strategic terms as well.[41]

If joint procurement and pipeline integration were to succeed, Japan, India, and Asia as a whole would benefit greatly from stable supplies along with more reasonable pricing. Given the region-wide benefits that would be derived from such arrangements, these policies should be prioritized by both Tokyo and Delhi.

One additional measure worth considering would be to create a greater level of reciprocity between Japan and India by tying together the suggested policies on natural gas and clean coal. On the one hand, Japan has more to gain from natural gas cooperation due to its higher dependence, while on the other hand India stands to benefit more from enhanced coal cooperation. By committing to both of these policies in tandem, the two governments would be taking reciprocal measures so that they are each working towards securing their own primary interests, while also assisting the other country. Such mutually beneficial cooperation should be the basis for building the confidence and trust necessary to continue expanding and deepening the bilateral relationship.

Mid- and Long-Term Policies

Nuclear Energy

As mentioned previously, the 2011 Fukushima disaster brought Japan's nuclear energy industry to a standstill. Prior to that, nuclear energy accounted for roughly 26 per cent of the country's power generation, meaning that it was an especially important energy source for a country that now 'meets less than 10% of its own total primary energy use from domestic sources'.[42] Although the government has recently restarted power generation at one nuclear plant, a majority of the country opposed the move.[43] As such, it is clear that rebuilding the public's confidence in nuclear power is imperative for the Japanese government, since the resumption of nuclear power generation on a large scale would allow the country to reduce its carbon emissions and its dependence on expensive imported energy resources.

Looking beyond Japanese public opinion, the global outcry against the environmental damage being caused by radioactive leaks from the Fukushima power plant shows that harmonizing nuclear safety standards around the world and rebuilding public confidence in nuclear power is a global imperative. In order to do so, the world will have to move beyond its current generation of nuclear reactors towards a more sustainable reactor and fuel cycle design with enhanced passive safety (safety features inherent to the system requiring minimal additional engineering), improved non-proliferation mechanisms, and easier management of nuclear waste. As negotiations on a civil nuclear agreement between Japan and India continue to progress, it appears realistic that the two countries will be able to jointly contribute to this effort.[44]

As of 2013, there were 31 countries around the world (including Taiwan) generating nuclear power.[45] Of the 439 nuclear reactors operating in these countries, roughly 85 per cent were variations of the light water reactor (LWR).[46] However, the LWR is also the design that is responsible for most of the concerns associated with nuclear power. The lack of passive safety features was acutely highlighted by the Fukushima disaster, when the failure of the plant's cooling system due to the tsunami led to a core meltdown. Moreover, LWRs create the dilemma of how to deal with spent fuel. Although the waste can be reprocessed back into usable fuel, this process cannot be carried out at all LWR-operating plants, meaning that fuel must oftentimes be reprocessed off-site, which in turn can lead to nuclear proliferation concerns. On the other hand, if fuel cannot be reprocessed, it must be safely stored, which raises a plethora of related issues. Therefore, moving towards a so-called Generation IV reactor that is more advanced and sustainable than the current generation of LWRs appears to be a sensible goal in which both Japan and India have an interest. There are a number of available options within the Generation IV family of reactors, but the reality is that Japan–India collaboration does not hinge on any particular reactor type. The larger imperative is that the two countries should work to see which one is the most sustainable and operationally efficient.

At the moment, India is working on a thorium-based reactor (due to the abundance of thorium in India), which is an area where Japan could potentially act as a partner. Notwithstanding the fact that this project has been in development for decades, Japan may be able to assist in bringing India's latest attempt to fruition.[47] Another possibility would be to revive the integral fast reactor (IFR), which was originally developed at the Argonne National Laboratory in the United States. Considering that the project was killed by the Clinton administration during the 1990s due mostly to political rather than scientific concerns, there are still reasons to be optimistic about the potential of the technology. At the time, some American officials opposed the continuation of research citing the cost, the difficulty of creating commercial success for the reactor, and the fact that continued research would have undermined the Clinton administration's non-proliferation policy.[48] However, IFR technology would actually reduce proliferation risks due to its closed fuel cycle, meaning that radioactive waste would be reprocessed on-site using pyroprocessing and would help to remedy the long-standing issue of nuclear waste management.[49] Furthermore, passive safety would be enhanced through the use of metal fuel rods rather than the oxide fuel used in LWRs. This would reduce the risk of overheating, thus reducing the risk of a disaster similar to what happened at Fukushima due to the loss of on-site power and cooling.[50]

Again, there are a number of possible nuclear reactor and fuel cycle designs that could be the focal point for Japan–India nuclear collaboration, and it will be up to the countries' policy makers to decide which would be the most appropriate and effective. However, the larger and more important imperative is that the two countries should make the most of their emerging agreement to collaborate in developing a more sustainable nuclear system that can help to rebuild international public confidence in nuclear energy. Doing so would improve both countries' abilities to provide greater energy security for their populations in a more sustainable manner.

The IEA and the Energy Charter

At present, there is limited regional cooperation within Asia to promote energy security. Whereas North America, Europe, and a limited number of other developed countries benefit from the services of the IEA—which provides emergency preparedness for petroleum supply disruptions through strategic stockpiles and peer reviews of member states' energy policies—Asia is lacking a similar institution.

As a first step towards remedying this, it would be important to have China and India, two massive players in the international energy market, join the IEA before moving on to the far more ambitious goal of establishing a similar energy security body for the Asian region. Though India and China may be hesitant to join the Western-led IEA, it does not make sense that the two biggest drivers of energy demand growth in the foreseeable future are not part of the dialogue that takes place among the world's top energy consumers. In fact, with India and China poised to become the two most important countries in the global energy market, it would be in both of their interests to make sure that they have a seat at the table.

As major energy importers, it may also be possible for Japan and India to push for the Energy Charter to play a larger role in the international energy architecture. The charter was originally signed in 1991; a more binding Energy Charter Treaty was signed in 1994, with the purpose of protecting foreign energy investments, ensuring an open energy market with uninhibited transit for energy resources, providing dispute resolution mechanisms, and promoting energy efficiency and sustainability, all of which were intended to boost investments (especially from the Organisation for Economic Co-operation and Development [OECD]) in fossil fuels originating from the former Soviet Union.[51] Russia has since withdrawn from the treaty, which has diminished the agreement's role in the international energy market. However, China—currently an observer—has become increasingly involved in the organization, which could help to bring the latter back into greater prominence.[52]

At present, the treaty has 54 signatories spanning from Western Europe to Japan, while other major countries such as the United States, China, and Pakistan have either charter membership or observer status.[53] India is currently neither a member nor an observer. However, as India's energy consumption and imports grow, it will have a greater interest in protecting its investments by first becoming an observer before moving on to charter membership and eventually becoming a treaty signatory. If Japan and India could push to make the treaty a more significant part of the international energy architecture, they would be better able to ensure the stability and affordability of their energy supplies.

Regional Energy Security Forum

One final recommendation for Japan and India's energy cooperation is the creation of a regional energy security forum for Asia that would act as a parallel organization to the IEA. This may be an uphill battle due to the persistent and substantial discord in the region, but taking into account the combined economic and diplomatic power of Japan and India, the two countries could play a major role in making this important but difficult goal a reality. Asian member states would potentially benefit greatly from such an organization and, if successful, it could prove to be a good confidence-building measure among countries that may otherwise view each other with suspicion.

In operational terms, this forum would have a number of goals. First, it would attempt to integrate energy grids and pipelines throughout the region, which would enhance the stability of both energy supplies and distribution, while also creating a fairer pricing scheme for gas and electricity around Asia. This would clearly be a highly ambitious endeavour with hefty costs, but it would offer benefits that would make the initial investment of financial and diplomatic capital worthwhile (this policy would also overlap with the regional integration of gas pipelines that was recommended earlier in this chapter). Second, the creation of regional oil stockpiles like those held by the IEA would act as a hedge against the potential geopolitical risks of oil imports from the Middle East. Third, member states could consider expanding energy preparedness by stockpiling hydrogen as methylcyclohexane in order to facilitate a region-wide transition to the increased use of clean hydrogen energy in thermal power and fuel cell vehicle technology. This measure would help both advanced and developing economies across the region to shift towards a cleaner energy model. Fourth, much like the IEA, member states would undergo periodic peer reviews to assess their energy policies and to generate policy recommendations that would enhance energy security. Finally, the forum could provide a venue for discussing regional efforts to secure sea lanes as a matter of energy security.

Given the immense logistical and political difficulties, along with the long time horizon that would be necessary to implement all of these actions, it would be beneficial to take intermediate steps to create momentum and confidence among the parties. With this in mind, the countries involved may find it useful to begin by establishing a joint working group for energy security, which would be a modest step towards the ultimate goal but would still generate positive returns.

* * *

With up to 400 million citizens currently living without electricity, the expansion of energy access—especially in rural areas—is one of the major challenges facing the Indian government. At the same time, Japan is also facing significant questions about its energy future following the nuclear disaster at the Fukushima Daiichi nuclear plant in March 2011. In this context, there should be substantial opportunities for mutually beneficial cooperation between the two countries on policies relating to energy security and efficiency, as well as the increasingly significant issues of climate change and environmental sustainability.

As discussed, the possibilities for cooperation range from short-term initiatives such as the re-indexing of natural gas prices in Asia to long-term goals such as the creation of a regional energy security forum. Such initiatives would not only act as a means to strengthen the bilateral relationship between Japan and India, but would also necessarily involve cooperation with Russia, China, South Korea, and Southeast Asia, which would likely help in strengthening the often strained relationships between some of Asia's most powerful nations. Considering the numerous mutual benefits that are likely to arise from energy cooperation, these issues should form one of the main pillars of increasing collaboration between Japan and India.

Notes

1. W.J. Antholis, 'Narendra Modi's Power Obsession: Indian Energy Reform', PlanetPolicy blog, The Brookings Institution, 28 July 2014, retrieved from http://www.brookings.edu/blogs/planetpolicy/posts/2014/07/28-india-modi-power-energy-reform-antholis on 7 September 2015.
2. S.J. Ahn and D. Graczyk, *Understanding Energy Challenges in India*, Paris: International Energy Agency (IEA), 2012, p. 29; IEA, Energy Access Database, n.d., retrieved from http://www.worldenergyoutlook.org/resources/energydevelopment/energyaccessdatabase on 7 September 2015; World Bank, *Energy— Access to electricity (% of population)*, n.d., retrieved from http://data.worldbank.org/indicator/EG.ELC.ACCS.ZS on 7 September 2015.
3. British Petroleum, *BP Energy Outlook 2035*, London: British Petroleum, 2014, p. 5.
4. METI, 'The Strategic Energy Plan of Japan: Meeting Global Challenges and Securing Energy Futures', Tokyo: METI, 2010 (revised in June 2010), p. 10.
5. METI, 'FY2013 Annual Report on Energy (Energy White Paper 2014) Outline', Tokyo: METI, 2014, p. 8.
6. METI, 'FY2013 Annual Report'.
7. EIA, 'Japan', n.d., retrieved from http://www.eia.gov/countries/cab.cfm?fips=JA on 7 September 2015.
8. H. Hiranuma, 'Japan's Energy Policy in a Post-3/11 World: Juggling Safety, Sustainability and Economics', Tokyo Foundation, 2014, retrieved from http://www.tokyofoundation.org/en/articles/2014/energy-policy-in-post-3-11-world on 7 September 2015.
9. EIA, 'Japan'.
10. Asia-Pacific Economic Cooperation (APEC), *Energy Demand and Supply Outlook*, 2013, 5th edn, p. 31.
11. MoFA, 'Japan-India Summit Meeting (Summary)', 23 August 2000, retrieved from http://www.mofa.go.jp/region/asia-paci/pmv0008/india_s.html on 7 September 2015.
12. Kantei, 'Towards Japan-India Strategic and Global Partnership', 2006, pp. 8–9.

13. See METI, 'Joint Statement on the occasion of the 7th India-Japan Energy Dialogue between the Planning Commission of India and the Ministry of Economy, Trade and Industry of Japan', retrieved from http://www.meti.go.jp/press/2013/09/20130913002/20130913002-12.pdf on 1 November 2015.

14. Global Intellectual Property Center, *Unlimited Potential: GIPC International IP Index*, Washington, D.C.: US Chamber of Commerce, 3rd edn, 2015, p. 25; and information based on author's interview with METI officials.

15. Information based on author's interview with METI officials.

16. Global Environment Centre, *Projects/Studies*, n.d., retrieved from http://gec.jp/jcm/projects/index.html on 7 September 2015.

17. EIA, 'India', n.d., retrieved from http://www.eia.gov/countries/cab.cfm?fips=IN on 7 September 2015.

18. Planning Commission of India, *Twelfth Five Year Plan (2012–2017): Economic Sectors*, New Delhi: Government of India, 2013, p. 194.

19. K.N. Das and S. Gopinath, 'India's Modi Raises Solar Investment Target to $100 Bln by 2022', Reuters, 2 January 2015, retrieved from http://www.reuters.com/article/2015/01/02/india-solar-idUSL-3N0UG13H20150102 on 7 September 2015.

20. Government of Japan, *Strategic Energy Plan*, 2014, p. 42.

21. METI, 'Feed-In Tariff Scheme for Renewable Energy', n.d., retrieved from http://www.meti.go.jp/english/policy/energy_environment/renewable/pdf/summary201109.pdf on 7 September 2015.

22. MoFA, 'Tokyo Declaration for Japan-India Special Strategic and Global Partnership', 2014, p. 8.

23. Information based on author's interview with METI officials.

24. World Bank, 'Electric Power Transmission and Distribution Losses (% of Output)', n.d., retrieved from http://data.worldbank.org/indicator/EG.ELC.LOSS.ZS on 7 September 2015.

25. Japan and India may also find it beneficial to cooperate on research to bring down the cost of batteries that could be used to store energy generated by intermittent renewable sources.

26. O.P. Sharma and P. Trikha, 'Geothermal Energy and Its Potential in India', *Akshay Urja*, 7(1), 2013, pp. 14–18.

27. Ernst and Young, *Mapping India's Renewable Energy Growth Potential: Status and Outlook 2013*, 2013, p. 9.

28. M. Hamamoto, 'Energy Efficiency Regulation and R&D Activity: A Study of the Top Runner Program in Japan', *Low Carbon Economy*, 2(2), 2011, pp. 91–8.

29. O. Kimura, 'Japanese Top Runner Approach for Energy Efficiency Standards', Tokyo: Central Research Institute of Electric Power Industry, 2010, p. 5; A. Kodaka, 'Japan's Top Runner Program: The Race for the Top', Tokyo: METI, n.d., p. 7.

30. Kimura, 'Japanese Top Runner Approach', p. 6.

31. BEE, 'About Us', n.d., retrieved from http://beeindia.in/content. php?page=about_bee/about_bee.php?id=1 on 7 September 2015.

32. A. Chunekar, 'Standards and Labeling Program for Refrigerators: Comparing India with Others', *Energy Policy*, 65, 2014, pp. 626–30.

33. EIA, 'India'; International Gas Union, *World LNG Report—2014 Edition*, 2014, p. 9.

34. Leidos, Inc., 'Global Natural Gas Markets Overview: A Report Prepared by Leidos, Inc., under Contract to EIA', Washington, D.C.: EIA, 2014, pp. 38, 47–8.

35. W. Ten Kate, L. Varro, and A. Corbeau, *Developing a Natural Gas Trading Hub in Asia*, Paris: IEA, 2013, p. 13.

36. Ten Kate *et al.*, *Developing a Natural Gas Trading Hub*, back cover.

37. S. Komlev, 'Oil-Indexed Gas Best Bet for Asia Pacific', Presented at the LNG Global Congress Asia Pacific, Singapore, 2014.

38. A. Corbeau, A. Braaksma, F. Hussin, Y. Yagoto, and T. Yamamoto, *The Asian Quest for LNG in a Globalising Market*, Paris: IEA, 2014, p. 15.

39. MoFA, *Tokyo Declaration*, p. 7.

40. Chubu Electric Power Company, 'Chubu Electric and GAIL Agree Memorandum of Understanding in Collaboration Study of Joint LNG Procurement', 24 March 2014, retrieved from http://www.chuden.co.jp/english/corporate/ecor_releases/erel_pressreleases/3237991_18939.html on 7 September 2015.

41. J. Jiang and J. Sinton, 'Overseas Investments by Chinese National Oil Companies: Assessing the Drivers and Impacts', Paris: IEA, 2011, p. 8.

42. EIA, 'Japan'.

43. 'Japan PM Abe's Support Slips, Majority Oppose Nuclear Restart', Reuters, 10 August 2015, retrieved from http://www.reuters.com/article/2015/08/10/us-japan-abe-support-idUSKCN0QF0A820150810 on 7 September 2015.

44. One major hurdle in civil nuclear negotiations—India's desire to reprocess spent fuel—was overcome in June 2015 when Japan agreed to allow reprocessing, which signalled a potential breakthrough in what had been long-drawn-out negotiations. For more information, see D. R. Chaudhury, 'For the First Time, Japan May Allow India to Reprocess Spent Nuclear Fuel from Japanese-Made Reactors', *Economic Times*, 19

June 2015, retrieved from http://articles.economictimes.indiatimes. com/2015-06-19/news/63617216_1_fukushima-nuclear-fuel-spent-fuel on 7 September 2015.

45. International Atomic Energy Agency (IAEA), 'Nuclear Share of Electricity Generation in 2013', Power Reactor Information System, n.d., retrieved from http://www.iaea.org/PRIS/WorldStatistics/ NuclearShareofElectricityGeneration.aspx on 7 September 2015.

46. IAEA, 'Operational & Long-Term Shutdown Reactors', Power Reactor Information System, n.d., retrieved from http://www.iaea.org/PRIS/ WorldStatistics/OperationalReactorsByType.aspx on 7 September 2015.

47. V. Ghunawat, 'Design of World's First Thorium Based Nuclear Reactor Is Ready', *India Today*, 14 February 2014, retrieved from http://india-today.intoday.in/story/worlds-first-thorium-based-nuclear-reactor-barc/1/343569.html on 7 September 2015.

48. G.M. Gaul and S.Q. Stranahan, 'Military Scientists Cast About for Work—On Catfish Farms Workers from a Former Weapons Plant Are Trying to Keep Fish from Suffocating', *Philadelphia Inquirer*, 8 June 1995; A. Hazard, 'Senate Defeats Bid to Cut Argonne Funds', *Chicago Tribune*, 1 October 1993, p. 1; M. Locin, 'Congress Pulls Plug on 10-Year Argonne Project', *Chicago Tribune*, 5 August 1994, p. 1.

49. G.S. Stanford, 'What Is the IFR?', Argonne, IL: Argonne National Laboratory, 2013, p. 7.

50. Stanford, 'What Is the IFR?', p. 4.

51. Energy Charter, 'The Energy Charter Treaty', n.d., retrieved from http://www.energycharter.org/process/energy-charter-treaty-1994/ energy-charter-treaty/ on 7 September 2015; R. Kemper, 'New Charter to Govern International Energy Transit', *Oil & Gas Journal*, 100(9), 2002.

52. Z. Wang, 'Securing Energy Flows from Central Asia to China and the Relevance of the Energy Charter Treaty to China', Brussels: Energy Charter Secretariat, 2015, p. 36.

53. Energy Charter, 'Members and Observers', n.d., retrieved from http:// www.encharter.org/index.php?id=61 on 7 September 2015.

4

Energizing India–Japan Cooperation on Clean Energy and Climate Change

Shyam Saran and Radhika Khosla

India and Japan enjoy a geopolitical and economic relationship that is gathering momentum.[1] We argue that cooperation on clean energy provides a natural conduit to enhance existing cooperation and to meet the shared energy challenges of growth and security, and in the process address climate change. India's energy demands and imports are increasing and Japan, post-Fukushima, is heavily reliant on imported energy. Both countries are also acutely vulnerable to climate change impacts and recognize that their long-term energy strategies necessitate a shift towards actions that limit their greenhouse gas emissions. While the bilateral relationship reflects this perspective, it has not acquired scale. A considered shift is needed to look beyond and address constraints in the current engagement. This chapter analyses India and Japan's bilateral cooperation and suggests a focus on energy efficiency, solar energy, and clean coal technologies, including their respective implementation frameworks, to enhance mutual benefits.

India and Japan are central to the emerging economic and security architecture in the Indo-Pacific region. Their bilateral relations too, in recent years, have witnessed remarkable progress. Japan is the largest bilateral donor and fourth largest investor in India.[2] The two countries share multiple interests such as economic opportunities in each other's markets, concern over China's emergence as a rising Asian power, and a recognition that both countries have a stake in each other's geopolitical success. A part of the growing relationship and shared interests between India and Japan is also the recognition that cooperation on clean energy can bring significant opportunities to both.

Historically, India and Japan developed strong diplomatic ties after the Treaty of Peace in 1952.[3] The relationship has waxed and waned since, but India has remained a major recipient of Japanese official development assistance (ODA). The countries renewed their engagement after India's 'Look East' policy began in 1992, and Japan was one of the first countries to invest in a post-economic-reform India. More recently, the India–Japan relationship has been marked by successive declarations related to security and defence, including ongoing, albeit slow, negotiations on civil nuclear cooperation.[4] Some examples include the Joint Declaration on Security Cooperation (2008) and the India–Japan Strategic and Global Partnership in the Next Decade (2010). During the 2014 visit of Indian Prime Minister Narendra Modi to Japan, the word 'Special' was added to the countries' relationship, making it a Special Strategic and Global Partnership.

Clean energy, with its linkages to economic growth, energy security, and climate change, is increasingly seen as an area of synergy between the two countries. This agenda was initially pursued through the high-level bilateral dialogue on Energy Security and Climate Change in 2006, which was led by the deputy chairman of the Planning Commission on the Indian side and the minister for economy, trade, and industry on the Japanese side. The basis for engagement is clear: both India and Japan are characterized by heavy import dependence and vulnerability to external energy prices. India currently imports over 70 per cent of its oil, 30 per cent of its coal, and a similar percentage of its gas requirements.[5] These figures are likely to increase significantly over the next two decades, with the high end of 2030 projections being roughly 90 per cent of oil, 50 per cent of coal, and 70 per cent of gas.[6] For Japan, the Fukushima nuclear accident in 2011 and the subsequent halt of nuclear power generation has reduced its energy self-sufficiency to amongst the lowest in industrialized countries. Consequently, fossil fuels will be central to its energy landscape in the near term. The country is virtually 100 per cent dependent on energy imports (except for local hydropower), threatening its economic competitiveness and consequentially its national security.[7] Finally, both India and Japan face severe threats from the impacts of climate change, which bolsters their basis for engagement.

In this context, there is a persuasive case for a long-term partnership between India and Japan to lead an energy transformation away from fossil fuels towards clean energy, supporting each other's efforts. The timing of the collaboration is of the essence, since both countries are in the midst of fundamental shifts. India is undergoing an unprecedented urban, demographic, and infrastructure transition, and Japan must rethink its energy future in light of diminishing nuclear power. Policy choices made in the present will thereby have long-term implications for both energy economies. The countries already have a series of working groups under their bilateral energy dialogue. However, these initiatives remain relatively ad hoc and do not add up to significantly assisting either country in overcoming their respective challenges.

This chapter examines the shared energy and climate priorities of both countries and their incentives for bilateral cooperation. It discusses India's primary interests in these two areas and assesses the strategies adopted so far to achieve them. The chapter outlines India's current scope of cooperation with Japan on energy and climate change, and sheds light on why such cooperation has not achieved its full potential. We then suggest an approach focused on clean energy for future engagement. The three suggested elements of the engagement on clean energy are solar energy, energy efficiency, and clean coal, with specific institutional hubs to oversee progress on the Indian side. This three-fold package will serve India and Japan beyond their immediate energy and energy security needs. It will also, in the process, enable them to address climate change impacts and contribute to their respective national and international climate responses.

Such an approach, which avails of the linked opportunities from addressing development and climate change is consistent with the co-benefits framing of the Intergovernmental Panel on Climate Change (IPCC), defined as '[t]he positive effects that a policy or measure aimed at one objective might have on other objectives, irrespective of the net effect on overall social welfare'.[8] Further, the engagement would be consistent with India's own framework for meeting its development, energy, and climate objectives. Finally, it will help foster collaboration between the two countries and position them as serious actors at the multilateral level when engaging on climate change, where they often take divergent stands.

We argue that the suggested focus on clean energy pathways can bring momentum to the existing bilateral relationship and multiple benefits to both India and Japan. For instance, the Japanese and Indian prime ministers issued a joint statement in 2010 to reaffirm the importance of strengthening bilateral discussions on climate change, but the promise has not translated into much action. Renewing this focus would also be tactical in light of recent geopolitics with China's shifting position on climate change, an occurrence which turns global attention towards India and Japan as the other important players and major economies in the region. The move towards a collaborative India–Japan framework will serve both countries' domestic economic, energy, and climate interests if dealt with strategically, and can be the basis of a larger geopolitical strategy between the two countries.

Energy and Climate Change in India

India's Energy: State of Play

How India's energy sector plays out in the next couple of decades will be a defining factor in the country's development. At present, the country is in the midst of large-scale transitions that place extraordinary pressures on energy demand. Most salient of these is urbanization, with one of the largest shifts to urban centres in world history projected to occur in India in the next few decades.[9] It is estimated that the middle class in Indian cities will grow from 31 million in 2013 to 114 million in 2025.[10] An analogous transformation is taking place in infrastructure, with a projected investment of US$1 trillion between 2012–13 and 2017–18.[11] In addition, the quantity of real estate is expected to quadruple by 2050, and it is estimated that two-thirds of the commercial and high-rise buildings that will exist in the country between 2010 and 2030 are yet to be built.[12]

Such rapid transformations raise pertinent questions about India's energy future. How will India simultaneously meet its rising energy demand, ensure access to quality supply, safeguard its energy security, and prevent damaging socio-environmental effects? In the course of meeting these multiple objectives, how will India also reduce its vulnerability to climate change?

So far, excessive fossil fuel reliance and high import dependence have dominated the country's energy landscape. India's installed electric power capacity is about 255 GW (as of early 2015), which consists of thermal (177 GW), hydro (40 GW), renewable (31 GW), and nuclear power (5 GW).[13] At present, India's import dependence is over 40 per cent for coal, oil, and gas. Without changes in policy, the imports are projected to increase up to 50 per cent by 2030, raising serious concerns about energy security.[14]

Coal is the largest contributor (65 per cent) to current energy supply, and India is the second largest consumer of coal in the world.[15] However, over a fifth of India's total coal consumption is imported.[16] In spite of this, existing energy studies uniformly predict that coal will continue to play a prominent role in the fuel supply mix over the next couple of decades, singling India out as one of the few large economies with high future coal dependence.[17] Any transition towards a fossil-free energy ecosystem for the country should thus be contextualized within this reality, and should not ignore the need for cleaner coal during the transition period.

On the non-fossil fuel side, renewable energy production has increased in the last few years driven by economic and regulatory incentives. The installed power capacity of renewables grew to 31,702 MW in March 2014, a growth of over 20 per cent over the preceding five years.[18] Solar energy in particular has received policy emphasis as a future fuel source, with the government targeting 100 GW of installed solar capacity by 2022. Wind energy too has received a boost, more than doubling its original target capacity to 60 GW by 2022.[19] For nuclear power, the planned target is to achieve 63 GW installed capacity by 2032.[20] However, these ambitious targets should be considered with caution if they are not accompanied by a clear set of actions and institutional arrangements required to achieve them.

Renewables, in particular, are gaining importance with policy makers and businesses, and can play a key role in the country's fuel mix if addressed in conjunction with broader issues in the power sector. Further, they would enable additional benefits by addressing energy security, providing viable solutions for energy access, and reducing harmful environmental and climate impacts.

Any discussion of India's energy also requires acknowledging the range of existing structural inefficiencies and financial losses, in spite of increasing electricity production and policy targets. Lack of efficiency in power production, transmission, and utilization remain major concerns, and it is estimated that one-third of power generated is 'lost'.[21] In terms of power outages, an overall economy shortage of 8.5 to 10 per cent is experienced in off-peak and peak hours, with immense financial implications.[22] To circumvent the system, diesel generators now add up to a cumulative capacity of 90 GW or 36 per cent of India's installed generation capacity.[23] Further, lack of energy access remains the overarching characteristic of the sector, with a disproportionate cost on the poor: more than 400 million people have no access to electricity.[24] As per the 2011 census, of the 55 per cent of rural households that have access to electricity, 86 per cent still depend on non-commercial sources such as firewood, crop residues, and dung cakes, pointing to the challenges of fuel quality even when there is supply.[25]

India's rising energy demand in light of large-scale urban and infrastructure transitions, its increase in production capacity, and the structural realities that characterize the power sector point to an uncertainty about how the energy system will evolve over the next couple of decades.[26] What are evident, though, are opportunities for a timely and strategic transition to a clean energy future. Actions in renewables, energy efficiency, and clean coal have the potential to be the linchpin of such a transition. Further, there are economic, energy, and climate rationales for investing in these sectors, and this is where India–Japan cooperation acquires considerable significance. The opportunities will be discussed in detail in later sections of this chapter.

India's Approach to Climate Change

India's approach to climate change takes multiple considerations into account. The first is the country's high vulnerability to the impacts of climate change. India faces imminent effects of global warming such as irregular monsoons, flooding, rising sea levels, and higher heat stress. The poorest population groups of the country, which have the least energy access, are the most vulnerable to these effects.[27] Climate change, therefore, is an urgent and compelling concern.

The second factor influencing India's climate approach is the development imperative. India has roughly 400 million people with no access to electricity.[28] In terms of development indicators, the country ranks at 135 of 187 on the UN's human development index and multidimensional poverty index.[29] This is marginally above countries in the least developed category. As an economically growing country with a young population, India's energy-related needs are significant and essential to its development. They include the ability to provide sufficient and quality energy for all, be energy secure, and limit local environmental concerns. Further, the energy sector is inextricably linked to, and the largest determinant of, the country's contribution to climate change: the energy sector is responsible for 77 per cent of India's greenhouse gas emissions.[30] Any climate policy for India thus needs to be informed by its energy strategy. Further, its mitigation and adaptation actions must be embedded within the overriding sustainable development objectives.

A third factor shaping India's approach to climate change is its engagement with the ongoing multilateral negotiations under the UN Framework Convention on Climate Change (UNFCCC). India is currently amongst the top five CO_2 emitters in the world, and some projections suggest that it could be the second largest global emitter within the next decade. At the same time, the per capita emissions picture looks very different, with India's projected per capita emissions in 2030 falling well below the 2011 world average.[31] This duality in the emissions scenario does not allow for an easy answer to the climate problem. Traditionally, India, together with a majority of developing countries, insisted upon the principle of 'common but differentiated responsibilities and respective capabilities' (CBDR-RC), which is enshrined in the UNFCCC. The principle implies that any burden sharing for meeting the challenge of global climate change must take into account the historical responsibilities of industrialized countries for accumulated greenhouse gas emissions, which are the cause of anthropogenic climate change. While this principle was endorsed in the Conference of Parties (COP) to the UNFCCC at Bali in 2007, a shift in narrative took place in subsequent negotiations away from a top-down approach premised on CBDR-RC with multilaterally negotiated targets and actions. Japan and India took opposing stands on burden sharing in these negotiations. Japan, along with other developed countries, stressed the 'common' rather than the 'differentiated' aspect of the CBDR principle, arguing that emerging economies like India were now significant emission sources and should therefore assume mitigation commitments of the same legal form, even if not stringency, as developed economies. It is for this reason that India and Japan find themselves on opposite sides of the fence at the multilateral level. India was also disappointed by Japan joining other developed countries in rendering the Kyoto Protocol inactive, especially since the protocol was associated with Japan and its commitment to the UNFCCC. More recently, the distinctions between developed and developing countries have become blurred at the international negotiations. The multilateral negotiating process under the UNFCCC has now evolved towards a pledge-and-review approach, whereby each country puts forward its domestically defined contribution towards global climate change action in the form of an 'intended nationally determined contribution' (INDC). The outcome of the 21st COP to the UNFCCC at Paris, in December 2015, is sought on the basis of this approach. It is expected that the Paris COP should result in a new agreement that will govern, regulate, and incentivize the next generation of climate actions.[32]

Accounting for these different evolving factors, India's INDC, in the lead-up to the Paris COP, is to reduce its emissions intensity by 33–5 per cent from a 2005 baseline; to increase the share of non-fossil-fuel-based electricity to 40 per cent of total capacity, with the help of transfer of technology and low cost finance; and to create an additional carbon sink of 2.5 to 3 billion tonnes of CO_2 equivalent through forest cover.[33]

The above pledge builds on India's National Action Plan for Climate Change (NAPCC), which was launched in 2008, ahead of the COP in Copenhagen. India's NAPCC contains eight missions, of which the national solar mission is the most developed.[34] The solar mission aims to increase the share of solar power in the energy mix by investing in and creating a favourable investment climate. The current government has increased the solar energy target from 20 GW in 2022 to 100 GW in 2022 within the last year; however, the implementation roadmap to achieve the target is less clear.[35] On the demand side, the government's relatively successful mission on enhanced energy efficiency focuses on increased efficiency for industrial, commercial, and domestic sectors. The mission targets savings potentials of 23 million tonnes of oil equivalent, which corresponds to 98 million tonnes of CO_2 equivalent emissions.[36] An important component of the NAPCC is its focus on a co-benefits-based framework to inform domestic policy making.[37] The framing keeps the focus on development as the basis for climate action, yet allows a linkage between India's domestic priorities and its international engagement.

In spite of the detailed climate plan, however, many of the NAPCC missions are yet to see progress. The reasons for the slow progress can be traced to institutional failures and the lack of a consistent approach to guide efforts. Sound implementation of the NAPCC requires a complex institutional response that enables climate policy to be interwoven into existing policy-making constructs and institutions. However, India does not have a formal role for an agency or individual to coordinate such a process. Further, the limits of government capacity and governance styles also do not enable the driving of climate policy beyond fragmented efforts.[38]

This growing domestic interest in clean energy and climate change efforts in India allows for significant opportunities for collaboration when approached strategically. If India and Japan focus on advancing a clean energy agenda, it is possible to advance interests that simultaneously link energy and climate concerns, and enhance the bilateral relationship, which has thus far achieved mediocre outcomes. In addition, such cooperation would create a constructive dialogue on climate change that can help bridge the countries' differing positions at the UNFCCC. The untapped potential of the energy transition would be significant if properly harnessed: it would provide access to new markets and the resulting economic growth, increase energy security which is a pressing need for both countries, and enable climate and socio-environmental benefits. The next section discusses opportunities for partnership for India and Japan within this context.

Ongoing and Future Partnership Opportunities

Status of Ongoing Bilateral Initiatives

Energy cooperation between India and Japan was emphasized by the joint statement on the Enhancement of Cooperation on Environmental Protection and Energy Security in 2007.[39] The recurring priorities under the dialogue are: energy security, environment and conservation, renewables, industrial and research cooperation, and the transfer of Japanese technologies to India. From the Japanese side, technical assistance is provided primarily by Japan's New Energy and Industrial Technology Development Organization (NEDO), with support from the Ministry of Economy, Trade and Industry (METI) and the Japan External Trade Organization (JETRO). Funding is provided by the Japan Bank for International Cooperation (JBIC) and the Japan International Cooperation Agency (JICA).

Focus areas under the dialogue are currently categorized by several working groups. To name a few, under 'energy efficiency', the major activities are capacity building and research and development (R&D) programmes. Under 'renewable energy', projects include the Delhi–Mumbai Industrial Corridor (DMIC), which utilizes Japanese technologies for solar power, smart urban transportation, and so on. Under 'electricity and coal', the Japan Coal Energy Centre (JCOAL) works towards improving the efficiency of equipment and facilities at Indian sites and to introduce clean coal through supercritical and ultra-supercritical coal power generation.[40]

While the architecture for cooperation is in place and some early initiatives are under way, the actual impact of the bilateral relationship under the energy dialogue has not been significant. The cooperation so far does not reflect a larger strategy of working towards the interests of both countries. It is worth taking a deeper look at the nature of the engagement to understand why this is so, especially if we are to assist transformational changes in the energy economies of both countries. Experience from the energy dialogue shows that while at the level of heads of state there is a positive commitment to cooperation, the enthusiasm and leadership does not filter down to implementing ministries and agencies.[41] There are both public and private sector reasons for this. At an institutional level, there is no coordinating agency that oversees or can take forward the working group relationships. The objectives of the working groups require engagement from different ministries, yet the ministries operate in silos with respect to working group goals and seldom participate in the same discussions. The members of working groups themselves often have minimal engagement with ministry officials responsible for taking forth the groups' agendas. Lastly, there is no accountability with regard to fulfilling targets, and progress is therefore fitful and slow.

In the absence of follow-up implementation and careful monitoring by an empowered governmental mechanism, there could still be private sector opportunities to pursue. However, this has not been the experience so far. While Indian businesses see immense opportunities in the Japanese market, their efforts to avail of these are largely unsuccessful. Prevailing explanations for this failure highlight the deep differences between the business cultures of the two countries.[42] While Indian businesses prefer contractual agreements with short-term gains, Japanese industry prefers to own business stakes in projects and rely on long-term relationships, an approach which is often perceived as too insular for Indian industry to penetrate. On the other hand, such a longer-term approach has allowed Japanese industry to be somewhat more successful in India than vice versa. Importantly, the high cost of Japanese technology prevents its penetration into the Indian market at scale.

It is unfortunate that in spite of the common energy priorities of the two countries, the scope of significant cooperation to mainstream clean energy remains untapped. Any serious bilateral collaboration must thus address the institutional shortcomings and cultural differences just mentioned if it is to leapfrog from the status quo. Given the current India–Japan relationship where the two countries are increasingly looking to each other as partners, the political context is conducive to imparting a new thrust to clean energy cooperation. The effort would require a clear identification of opportunities and agencies responsible for implementation, with a rethinking of the bilateral approach as one that prioritizes the simultaneous objectives of sustainable economic growth, energy security, and addressing climate change. Clean energy cooperation itself should be seen as part of a larger strategic partnership that can evolve to other areas over time. The next section lays forth recommendations for such collaboration.

Opportunities for Partnership

We recommend three major partnership opportunities for India and Japan: energy efficiency, solar energy, and clean coal. The following sub-sections discuss these opportunities, including institutional recommendations for coordination and accountability. If the bilateral focus starts with prioritizing these win–win areas, it will lay the foundation for working together on more politically challenging areas in the longer term, such as strategic collaboration in global oil and natural gas markets which has been discussed in some forums, or partnering in Japan's Joint Crediting Mechanism. The recommendations below are based on research and consultations with public and private sector stakeholders.

Energy Efficiency

India and Japan have a successful history of collaborating on energy efficiency. Starting in 2006 under the energy dialogue, the countries collaborated on the development of India's Energy Conservation Act. The act is the cornerstone of India's domestic strategy on energy efficiency in appliances, buildings, industry, and transportation.

Cooperation currently entails workshops in partnership with India's Bureau of Energy Efficiency (BEE), India's Petroleum Conservation Research Association (PCRA), and the Energy Conservation Center, Japan; capacity-building programmes for Indian state-designated agencies, small and medium enterprises, and energy managers and auditors; training of Indian trainers and technical assistance from METI; and cooperation on energy conservation in the textile industry. Demonstration projects on energy efficiency and smart community projects in the DMIC that utilize Japanese technologies are also under way. In the last two years, the countries have placed special emphasis on energy-intensive sectors and discussed technology transfers, financial support, and training programmes for Indian experts to exchange information with their Japanese counterparts.[43] We recommend further collaboration on energy-intensive industries—such as iron and steel, cement, pulp and paper, petrochemicals, and power generation and distribution—for formulating benchmarks, undertaking energy audits, and recommending energy efficiency measures.

For appliances, India could adopt a local version of Japan's extremely successful 'Top Runner' programme to improve appliance energy efficiency by setting efficiency standards to match the most efficient products in the market (see Chapter 3 in this volume for more on this programme). Indian appliances account for a large share of energy consumption and, with a rising middle class, the consumer appliances market will experience immense growth.[44] While the BEE has led a relatively successful programme of standards and labels, the untapped potential for energy efficiency from an efficient consumer appliance stock remains high particularly as the market grows. Japan's Top Runner programme, adapted to the Indian scenario, could help achieve this potential.

Further, there should be a focus on energy efficiency in buildings. India has an energy conservation building code which, if widely implemented, can result in significant energy and cost savings, especially since the bulk of real estate growth will occur in the next 15 years, as mentioned earlier. Since Japan is a leader in energy conservation and enhancing energy efficiency, cooperation in this sector would benefit India and also create opportunities for Japanese energy service companies. The initial effort may need to be supported by the two governments, but it should eventually be driven by their respective private sectors.

Transport, one of the fastest-growing energy-intensive sectors in the Indian context, is another area for collaboration. Japanese foreign direct investment (FDI) in India forms a 15 per cent share in automobiles, making opportunities for fuel-efficient automobile technology easier given existing Japanese market penetration.[45]

In India, there are few energy service companies that can provide full-spectrum services. Banking services to support the energy service business are also lacking since banks are conditioned to seek collateral, which energy service businesses cannot provide as they lend against future energy cost savings. The limited availability of financial instruments is a barrier to scaling up energy efficiency in India. Japan's experience in this regard, combined with the creation of India–Japan joint ventures in the energy service business, could create a promising line of commercial cooperation.

On the Indian side, the BEE in the Ministry of Power can coordinate the bilateral activities discussed above. The BEE is the nodal agency for the implementation of the Energy Conservation Act; the Perform, Achieve and Trade scheme for energy-intensive sectors; appliance ratings; and the energy conservation building code. Identification of activities and coordination by the BEE can bring immense benefits to energy efficiency collaboration.

Solar Energy

Solar energy projections dominate India's renewable energy future. The Government of India launched the Jawaharlal Nehru National Solar Mission in January 2010 with the aim of making solar energy a progressively more significant component of the country's energy mix. The original target was to install 20 GW of grid-connected capacity and 200 MW of off-grid decentralized applications by 2022. In late 2014, the already ambitious target was raised to 100 GW of solar power by 2020.[46] So far, the mission has achieved an installed capacity of approximately 4,000 MW, and has a long way to go to achieve its objective.[47] The target is challenging considering that the Indian solar industry faces constraints on account of its limited domestic technological capacity and its substantial reliance on imported technology. Further, the enhanced target will require adequate financing. In both respects, Japan could be a partner to India. Such collaboration is also in line with Japan's recalibrated post-Fukushima energy strategy to increase the share of renewables in its overall energy mix, as per its 2014 Strategic Energy Plan.[48] However, technological and space constraints can hinder growth in the Japanese solar market.[49]

India, like Japan, needs to reduce the space required per megawatt of solar power through technology applications (for example, nanotechnology). In order to reduce intermittency to achieve parity with the current grid, it is also necessary to advance battery storage technologies. This could be a key joint R&D project between India and Japan. Japanese companies at the forefront of solar technologies could be a source for India's expanding solar market and assist in creating an Indian manufacturing base. The Indian government is promoting solar manufacturing parks, and Japanese companies can be invited to set up wholly owned subsidiaries or joint ventures.

The two governments have already initiated technological cooperation on solar power as part of the bilateral relationship. A large-scale micro-grid solar photovoltaic demonstration project and smart community projects in the DMIC utilize Japanese technologies to develop next-generation energy infrastructure.[50] NEDO has also initiated a feasibility study for the greening of India's telecommunication towers using a photovoltaic system. Both countries intend to initiate a joint research programme towards energy access improvement in non-electrified areas and to establish appropriate investment environments for renewables.

Solar energy collaboration thus has the potential to become an important joint initiative. By expanding the scope of the current relationship, in line with the two prime ministers' 2014 statement on spurring renewables cooperation, India and Japan can develop their respective industries, increase competition in the global renewable energy market, and reduce the cost of generation. Knowledge sharing, in the form of exchanges between technical experts and joint projects, can facilitate productive engagement. Institutionally, from the Indian side, the nodal agency for bilateral cooperation could be the Solar Energy Corporation of India, a Government of India enterprise that was set up in 2011 as a non-profit company. The Solar Energy Corporation of India is mandated to promote solar power, facilitate the implementation of projects, and promote and guide R&D in this sector.

Clean Coal

Coal-based thermal power continues to be an important part of the overall energy mix in India and Japan. Both countries also face pressures to reduce coal use with the need to address climate change. It is likely that coal will thus be a bridging fuel towards a substantially renewable future. Since the energy mix can only be altered in a gradual manner, it is in their interest to enhance the efficiency of coal-based power, reduce harmful emissions post-combustion, and find economic uses for carbon effluents from power plants.

For India, coal is the largest contributor (65.3 per cent) to the energy supply and the country is the second largest global consumer of coal. India also has the world's fifth largest coal reserves.[51] However, the sector is mired in inefficiencies of production and supply, and security of supply is weak as over a fifth of India's coal is imported. In spite of these drawbacks, projections of future coal use are relatively consistent: coal generation is expected to grow at approximately 7–9 per cent annually over the next two decades. The high rate of projected growth is greater than the historical growth rate of 6 per cent in the last decade.[52] It is thus clear that any transition to a clean energy economy will involve a significant coal share in the near future, during which India can prioritize the use of efficient coal technologies. India is already developing a programme for indigenous ultra-supercritical technology, which could raise the efficiency of coal combustion from the current 33–6 per cent to 47–9 per cent. Japanese technologies could aid in meeting these objectives.

The foundation for collaboration on clean coal technologies already exists. Technology for coal washeries has been exchanged by JCOAL through the invitation of Indian experts to Japan since 2001. Currently, NEDO is engaged in a commercial-scale demonstration project to reduce the ash content of Indian coal using highly efficient coal washery technology, and is also implementing a feasibility study to combine upgraded brown coal technology using Indian lignite with ultra-supercritical technology. The National Thermal Power Corporation of India (NTPC) and JBIC have entered into a loan agreement for the Kudgi supercritical coal-fired power project in the state of Karnataka under the India–Japan Energy Dialogue.[53] To enhance this collaboration, Japanese entities could be identified and invited to join the ultra-supercritical technology R&D project, which commenced under a memorandum of understanding between NTPC, the Indira Gandhi Centre for Atomic Research (IGCAR), and Bharat Heavy Electricals Limited (BHEL).

The success of these initiatives will require an institutional anchor, and the collaboration would benefit from a nodal agency that is accountable for progress. While the Ministry of Coal is already the nodal agency for India–Japan cooperation on clean coal, the scope of cooperation may be widened to include other relevant and informed entities such as NTPC, which is India's main thermal power producer.

* * *

India and Japan have enjoyed a long and relatively harmonious bilateral relationship. Their engagement rests on shared geopolitical concerns, and of late a common clean energy agenda is coming into focus. The basis for the latter is a growing recognition of the multiple and mutual benefits that clean energy engagement can bring in the form of economic returns, energy security, and sustainable development. Focusing collaboration in these areas will also address climate change, a major concern in both countries.

While there are several ongoing clean energy collaborations between India and Japan, the scope of mainstream activities remains untapped in spite of their common priorities. This is in part due to the absence of an institutional agency that can oversee, coordinate, and be accountable for the different bilateral working groups in India. Further, while Japan provides a role model for technology in India, government and private sector collaborations so far have not translated into widespread dissemination, primarily for reasons of cost. Japanese technology continues to be too expensive for India and there are instances of Japanese ideas being implemented by the Indian private sector using lower cost Chinese technologies (for example, for waste heat recovery). Innovative business models led by industrial associations and individual corporations are thus necessary to bring down costs and overcome differences in business cultures. An additional recommendation is for Japanese technologies to be designed for production in Indian plants. This would require companies to have a Japanese design bureau in India, which would also serve the role of finding creative ways to increase cost effectiveness.

The current political context is conducive to imparting impetus to cooperation in the clean energy sector, and can establish an institutional foundation for longer-term engagement. This cooperation should serve as the basis for a larger geopolitical relationship between India and Japan, with an eye towards growing to other areas. As mentioned previously, this effort would require a clear identification of mutual opportunities and agencies responsible for implementation, with a rethinking of the ways in which the relationship has thus far been approached.

This chapter has recommended three areas for collaboration: energy efficiency, solar energy, and clean coal. All will require systemic institutional coordination. The BEE in the Ministry of Power; the Solar Energy Corporation of India; the Ministry of Coal; and the

NTPC are ideally placed to act as the nodal implementing agencies for energy efficiency, solar power, and clean coal, respectively. Further, an overarching coordinating body should be appointed to oversee the work of the nodal agencies. During the Indian prime minister's visit to Japan in 2014, it was decided that a senior Japanese official would be deployed in the Indian prime minister's office to monitor and facilitate the implementation of key bilateral projects such as the East–West Freight Corridor. The official is in fact deployed in the Department of Industrial Policy and Promotion (DIPP). The recommended clean energy cooperation would be well placed within his or her mandate.

On the private sector side, major industrial associations in India (the Federation of Indian Chambers of Commerce and Industry [FICCI] and the Confederation of Indian Industry [CII]) should prioritize the work of their subgroups that focus on India–Japan corporate-sector ties and enable private–public collaboration that interfaces with the government for successful cooperation.

In all cases, increasing interaction between government officials and independent experts will be fruitful for both countries. Government-to-government exchanges are better influences on policy making, compared to a direct transplantation of policies which may not account for differing politics, levels of development, and federal structures. A longer-term goal should be to increase student exchanges in promising areas for clean energy business and capacity building.

Cooperation on clean energy provides a natural conduit to enhance existing cooperation between India and Japan. Not only will such collaboration increase economic relations between the countries, it will also simultaneously achieve the countries' shared and multi-objective energy goals. The untapped potential of supporting a clean and efficient energy transition will be significant, and a bilateral move in this direction would be tactical in light of recent international climate politics, which have turned global attention towards India and Japan as important players and major sources of emissions in the Asian region. A move towards the suggested collaborative framework will serve the countries' mutual economic, energy, and climate interests if dealt with strategically, and will result in domestic and international accomplishments for both.

Notes

1. The authors are thankful to Ajay Mathur and Ameet Nivsarkar for their inputs, and to Ashwini Hingne for research assistance.
2. Ministry of External Affairs (MEA), Government of India, 'India-Japan Relations', 2014, retrieved from http://www.mea.gov.in/Portal/ForeignRelation/Japan_January_2014.pdf on 9 September 2015.
3. MEA, 'India-Japan Relations'.
4. Nuclear power is on the agenda for both India and Japan. However, we do not believe that it should be prioritized as an issue for immediate cooperation, for three reasons. First, India–Japan negotiations on civil nuclear cooperation are unlikely to culminate in an agreement in the near term. Nuclear power could thus be an important component of future cooperation, but it is not imminently feasible. Second, for India, nuclear energy makes for a modest part of the overall energy mix and is likely to remain so. There are thus limited reasons to be optimistic about the use of nuclear energy increasing dramatically in India. Lastly, in Japan, the public outcry against nuclear power is significant. The country is changing course to reduce its dependence on nuclear energy. The immediate opportunities for growth are thus in other fuels, such as the ones we suggest in this chapter.
5. US Energy Information Administration (EIA), 'India Is Increasingly Dependent on Imported Fossil Fuels as Demand Continues to Rise', *Today in Energy*, 14 August 2014, retrieved from http://www.eia.gov/todayinenergy/detail.cfm?id=17551 on 9 September 2015.
6. N.K. Dubash, R. Khosla, N.D. Rao, and K.R. Sharma, 'Informing India's Energy and Climate Debate: Policy Lessons from Modelling Studies', Research Report of the Climate Initiative, Centre for Policy Research, New Delhi, 2015.
7. Center for Strategic and International Studies, 'Japan Chair Platform: Japan's Energy Security Post-Fukushima', 2014, retrieved from http://csis.org/publication/japan-chair-platform-japans-energy-security-post-fukushima on 9 September 2015.
8. Intergovernmental Panel on Climate Change, 'WGII AR5 Glossary', 2013, retrieved from http://ipcc-wg2.gov/AR5/images/uploads/WGIIAR5-Glossary_FGD.pdf on 9 September 2015.
9. United Nations, Department of Economic and Social Affairs, Population Division, *World Urbanization Prospects*, 2011, retrieved from http://esa.un.org/wpp/ppt/CSIS/WUP_2011_CSIS_4.pdf on 9 September 2015.

10. 'India's Middle Class Population to Touch 267 Million in 5 Yrs', *Economic Times*, 2011, retrieved from http://articles.economictimes.indiatimes.com/2011-02-06/news/28424975_1_middle-class-households-applied-economic-research on 9 September 2015.

11. M.S. Ahluwalia, 'Prospects and Policy Challenges in the Twelfth Plan', *Economic and Political Weekly*, 46(21), 2011, pp. 88–105.

12. Global Buildings Performance Network, 'Mitigation Potential from India's Buildings—Status Report', 2013; S. Kumar, R. Kapoor, R. Rawal, S. Seth, and A. Walia, 'Developing an Energy Conservation Building Code Implementation Strategy in India', Report for the USAID Energy Conservation and Commercialization (ECO-III) Project, May 2010, retrieved from http://eco3.org/wp-content/plugins/downloads-manager/upload/Developing%20an%20ECBC%20Implementation%20Strategy%20in%20India-%20Report%20No.1028.pdf on 9 September 2015.

13. Centre for Study of Science Technology and Policy, 'A Sustainable Development Framework for India's Climate Policy', 2015, retrieved from http://www.cstep.in/uploads/default/files/publications/stuff/306 83f0adbd6f81820ab9a37eb55c7b0.pdf on 9 September 2015.

14. Dubash *et al.*, 'Informing India's Energy and Climate Debate'.

15. British Petroleum, *Statistical Review of World Energy 2014*, 2014, retrieved from http://www.bp.com/en/global/corporate/about-bp/energy-economics/statistical-review-of-world-energy.html on 9 September 2015.

16. EIA, 'India Is Increasingly Dependent on Imported Fossil Fuels'.

17. Dubash *et al.*, 'Informing India's Energy and Climate Debate'.

18. Ministry of New and Renewable Energy, Government of India, *Annual Report 2013–14*, 2014, retrieved from http://mnre.gov.in/file-manager/annual-report/2013-2014/EN/index.html on 9 September 2015.

19. United Nations Framework Convention on Climate Change, 'Submission by India: India's Intended Nationally Determined Contribution', 2015, retrieved from http://www4.unfccc.int/submissions/INDC/Published%20Documents/India/1/INDIA%20INDC%20TO%20UNFCCC.pdf on 30 October 2015.

20. Ibid.

21. Planning Commission of India, *High Level Panel on Financial Position of Distribution Utilities*, 2011.

22. Federation of Indian Chambers of Commerce and Industry, 'Lack of Affordable & Quality Power: Shackling India's Growth Story', 2012, retrieved from http://www.ficci.com/sedocument/20218/power-report 2013.pdf on 9 September 2015.

23. 'Gensets Add up to under Half of Installed Power Capacity', *Indian Express*, 2014, retrieved from http://indianexpress.com/article/india/india-others/gensets-add-up-to-under-half-of-installed-power-capacity/99/ on 9 September 2015.
24. Census of India, Government of India, 'Houses, Household Amenities and Assets Data 2001–2011: Visualizing through Maps', 2011, retrieved from http://censusindia.gov.in/2011-Common/NSDI/Houses_Household.pdf on 9 September 2015.
25. Ministry of New and Renewable Energy, *Annual Report 2013–14*.
26. Dubash *et al.*, 'Informing India's Energy and Climate Debate'.
27. Intergovernmental Panel on Climate Change, *Climate Change 2014: Impacts, Adaptation, and Vulnerability*, Part B: *Regional Aspects*, Contribution of Working Group II on the Fifth Assessment Report of the Intergovernmental Panel on Climate Change, Cambridge, UK, and New York: Cambridge University Press, 2014, pp. 1327–70.
28. Census of India, 'Houses, Household Amenities and Assets Data'.
29. United Nations Development Programme, Multidimensional Poverty Index, 2013, retrieved from http://hdr.undp.org/en/content/multidimensional-poverty-index on 9 September 2015; United Nations Development Programme, 'Table 1: Human Development Index and Its Components', 2013, retrieved from http://hdr.undp.org/en/content/table-1-human-development-index-and-its-components on 9 September 2015.
30. Indian Network for Climate Change Assessment, *Greenhouse Gas Emissions 2007*, Ministry of Environment and Forests, Government of India, 2010, retrieved from http://www.moef.nic.in/downloads/public-information/Report_INCCA.pdf on 9 September 2015.
31. Dubash *et al.*, 'Informing India's Energy and Climate Debate'.
32. Rajamani, L., *The Devilish Details: Key Legal Issues in the 2015 Climate Negotiations*, 2015. *The Modern Law Review*, 78(5), 826–53.
33. United Nations Framework Convention on Climate Change, 'Submission by India: India's Intended Nationally Determined Contribution', 2015, retrieved from http://www4.unfccc.int/submissions/INDC/Published%20Documents/India/1/INDIA%20INDC%20TO%20UNFCCC.pdf on 30 October 2015.
34. Prime Minister's Council on Climate Change, Government of India, *National Action Plan on Climate Change*, 2008, retrieved from http://www.moef.nic.in/modules/about-the-ministry/CCD/NAP_E.pdf on 9 September 2015.
35. Sustainable Business, 'India Quintuples Solar Target'.
36. BEE, *Perform, Achieve and Trade*, 2012, retrieved from https://beenet.gov.in/ on 9 September 2015.

37. Prime Minister's Council on Climate Change, *National Action Plan on Climate Change*.

38. N. Dubash and N. Joseph, 'The Institutionalization of Climate Policy in India: Designing for Co-benefits and Mainstreaming', Working paper, Centre for Policy Research, New Delhi, 2014.

39. MoFA, 'Joint Statement on the Enhancement of Cooperation on Environmental Protection and Energy Security', 2007, retrieved from http://www.mofa.go.jp/region/asia-paci/pmv0708/joint-3.html on 9 September 2015.

40. MEA, 'Joint Statement on the Occasion of the 6th India-Japan Energy Dialogue between the Planning Commission of India and the Ministry of Economy, Trade and Industry of Japan', 2012, retrieved from http://www.mea.gov.in/bilateral-documents.htm?dtl/20657/Joint+Statement+on+the+occasion+of+the+6th+IndiaJapan+Energy+Dialogue+betwee n+the+Planning+Commission+of+India+and+the+Ministry+of+Econ omy+Trade+and+Industry+of+Japan on 9 September 2015; JCOAL, *Japan Coal Energy Center*, 2015, retrieved from http://www.jcoal.or.jp/eng/work/05/ on 9 September 2015.

41. Discussion with MEA officials in March 2015.

42. Discussion with CII members in March 2015.

43. MEA, 'Joint Statement on the Occasion of the 7th India-Japan Energy Dialogue between the Planning Commission of India and the Ministry of Economy, Trade and Industry of Japan', 2013, retrieved from http://www.mea.gov.in/bilateral-documents.htm?dtl/22192/Joint+Statement+on+the+occasion+of+the+7th+IndiaJapan+Energy+Dialogue+betwee n+the+Planning+Commission+of+India+and+the+Ministry+of+Econo my+Trade+and+Industry+of+Japan on 9 September 2015.

44. BEE, 'Overview of Energy Efficiency Standards and Labeling Program', APP Workshop, New Delhi, 2011.

45. DIPP, 'FDI Synopsis on Country: Japan', 2012, retrieved from http://dipp.nic.in/English/Publications/SIA_NewsLetter/AnnualReport2012/Chapter6.1.A.iv.pdf on 9 September 2015.

46. Ministry of New and Renewable Energy, *Annual Report 2013–14*.

47. Central Electricity Authority, Ministry of Power, 'All India Installed Generation Capacity Report', 2015.

48. International Renewable Energy Agency, 'IRENA's Renewable Energy Roadmap (REmap 2030): REmap Countries Renewable Energy Targets Table', 2012, retrieved from http://irena.org/remap/IRENA_REmap_RE_targets_table_2014.pdf on 9 September 2015; Government of Japan, *Strategic Energy Plan*, 2014.

49. 'Data Analysis: Can Japan Exceed 10 Gigawatts of Solar Capacity Installation in 2014?', *Renewable Energy World*, 2014, retrieved from http://www.renewableenergyworld.com/rea/news/article/2014/12/data-analysis-can-japan-exceed-10-gigawatts-of-solar-capacity-installation-in-2014 on 9 September 2015.

50. Central Electricity Authority, 'All India Installed Generation Capacity Report'.

51. British Petroleum, *Statistical Review of World Energy 2014*.

52. Coal Controller, Government of India, *Coal Directory of India and Provisional Coal Statistics*, 2014.

53. MEA, 'Joint Statement on the Occasion of Official Visit of the Prime Minister of Japan to India (January 25–27, 2014)', 2014, retrieved from http://www.mea.gov.in/in-focus-article.htm?22772/Joint+Statement+on+the+occasion+of+Official+Visit+of+the+Prime+Minister+of+Japan+to+India+January+2527+2014 on 9 September 2015.

Part III

SECURITY AND DEFENCE

5

Japan–India Security Cooperation

In Pursuit of a Sound and Pragmatic Partnership

Noboru Yamaguchi and Shutaro Sano

The rise of India and Japan's new policy of 'proactive contribution to peace' have created opportunities for bilateral cooperation on the promotion of democratic values, nation building, anti-terrorism, anti-piracy, UN peacekeeping operations (PKO), humanitarian assistance and disaster relief (HADR), cyber security, and the sharing of new technologies. Furthermore, the security environment requires Japan and India to respond in a positive manner to China's rise. However, the two countries do not necessarily have common perceptions, priorities, and strategies on various issues: first, India's possession of nuclear weapons has been a concern for Japan; second, Japan and India's engagement in the reconstruction effort in Afghanistan may fuel tensions with Pakistan; and finally, Beijing may perceive Japan–India security cooperation as an antagonistic action against China, and thus react adversely. It is important, therefore, for both Japan and India to embrace available opportunities for security cooperation and pragmatically develop common perceptions, policy priorities, and strategies.

Cooperation between Japan and India has become an increasingly important issue for the security and safety of the Asia Pacific region in recent years. The rise of India and Japan's policy of 'proactive contribution to peace' have expanded the need and opportunity for the two countries to work collectively.[1] Meanwhile, a number of regional security situations have begun to pose challenges for both countries. In this light, Prime Minister Narendra Modi's visit to Japan in August–September 2014 took place at a crucial moment. The visit was strategically important as Tokyo and Delhi upgraded their relationship to a 'Special Strategic and Global Partnership'. This chapter explores the critical issues surrounding Japan–India bilateral security cooperation from Japan's perspective. First, it will focus on Japan's primary security interests and strategies. Second, it will clarify the growing opportunities and challenges for bilateral security cooperation. Finally, it will provide short- and long-term recommendations for the strengthening of ties between the two countries.

Japan's Primary Security Interests and Strategies

Maintaining the peace and security of Japan and ensuring its survival are the primary responsibilities of the Government of Japan (GoJ). This has been stipulated up front in Japan's first ever National Security Strategy (NSS) issued in December 2013. The NSS declared Japan's determination 'to maintain its sovereignty and independence; to defend its territorial integrity; to ensure the safety of life, person, and properties of its nationals; and to ensure its survival while maintaining its own peace and security grounded on freedom and democracy and preserving its rich culture and tradition'.[2] Furthermore, the strengthening of the global free trade regime and the maintenance of an international order based on rules and universal values including freedom, democracy, respect for fundamental human rights, and the rule of law are also set forth as Japan's national interests. In light of these interests, Japan opposes any attempt to change the status quo by force. The NSS, together with the newly established 2013 National Defense Program Guidelines (NDPG) and the National Security Council, is based on the belief that Japan needs to become a 'proactive contributor to peace' with its active involvement in the security realm both in the Asia Pacific region and in the international milieu. Japan has set forth six strategic approaches, including the need to strengthen diplomacy and security cooperation with Japan's partners for peace and stability in the international community.[3]

For over 60 years, Japan has made full-scale efforts on its own initiative to secure its safety and prosperity, and to this end has continuously strengthened its alliance with the United States and abided by the rules and norms set forth by the United Nations, including the establishment of cooperative mechanisms. In short, the GoJ regards the Japan–US alliance to be the pillar of its security strategy and has other bilateral or trilateral partnerships and cooperative mechanisms to supplement its alliance with the United States.[4] This fundamental policy has not changed since the end of the Second World War and will probably not change in the near future. The GoJ acknowledges that Japan's security arrangements with the US 'constitute the cornerstone for Japan's national security' and function as 'public goods that contribute to the stability and prosperity of Japan, the Asia Pacific region and the world at large'.[5] Furthermore, the GoJ has been clear that 'it has become more important than ever for Japan to strengthen the Japan-US Alliance and make it more balanced and effective'.[6]

Today, the international community is experiencing a significant geopolitical realignment, and the global centre of gravity is shifting from the Euro-Atlantic to the greater Asia Pacific region.[7] Notably, a newly emerging China and the American rebalancing strategy have changed the balance of power between the two countries. Furthermore, recent security challenges have compelled the international community, including Japan and other Asia Pacific countries, to take proactive measures on various security issues. Meanwhile, Japan at present acknowledges that there have been a number of so-called 'grey zone' situations that are neither considered to be pure peacetime situations nor contingencies over territory, sovereignty, and maritime economic interests.[8]

In the Asia Pacific, North Korea's nuclear and missile challenges have become a particularly serious concern for Japan. This is evident from the fact that North Korea is cited first in the 2013 NDPG as a country that poses a challenge to Japan. Meanwhile, it is important to note that the 2013 NDPG is the first official Japanese security document to characterize North Korea as an actual 'threat' to Japan, going as far as to say that North Korea poses 'a serious and imminent threat to Japan's security'.[9] Specifically, North Korea's 'Military First' policy, its development and proliferation of weapons of mass destruction and ballistic missiles, and its provocative rhetoric and behaviour suggesting a missile attack on Japan have been direct concerns. Furthermore, the abduction of Japanese citizens remains one of the major concerns of the Japanese public. The GoJ officially recognizes that North Korean agents abducted 17 Japanese citizens in 12 cases in the late 1970s and early 1980s.[10]

China's growing assertiveness in the East and South China Seas and the wider western Pacific has also become an increasing concern in Japan, and has become a major focus of attention within security policy circles over recent years. Since the mid-to-late 2000s, Chinese maritime enforcement ships have been increasing their activities and have often intruded into Japan's territorial waters. What is most concerning is that Chinese aircraft and naval vessels have also been expanding their areas of operation around the Senkaku Islands, which China claims. In February 2013, a Chinese vessel, in a couple of cases, directed its fire control radar on a Japanese Maritime Self-Defense Force (JMSDF) helicopter and ship, risking escalation into a possible military confrontation. In November 2014, China infringed upon the freedom of overflight above the high seas by unilaterally announcing the establishment of an Air Defense Identification Zone (ADIZ) over Japanese airspace. In light of these challenges, the GoJ acknowledges that these actions 'can be regarded as attempts to change the status quo by coercion based on [Beijing's] own assertions, which are incompatible with the existing order of international law in the maritime and aerial domains'.[11] Even if these actions do not accurately reflect China's true intentions, the GoJ perceives these challenges as reflecting China's aspiration to pursue a so-called 'salami-slicing tactic', which aims to establish a new territorial fait accompli by coercive means short of an armed attack.

China has also showed a greater interest in the Indian Ocean over recent years, especially through its 'string of pearls' policy. Furthermore, China has increased its presence in the region through low-intensity operations driven by overseas commercial and human security needs.[12] These include the deployment of a frigate and military transport aircraft to safeguard the evacuation of Chinese citizens from Libya in February 2011; the dispatch of anti-piracy forces to the

Gulf of Aden since December 2008; and the deployment of hospital ships to the Indian Ocean in the summer of 2010, the Caribbean in autumn 2011, and the Philippines in November 2013 after Typhoon Haiyan.

Despite China's increasingly worrying attempts to change the status quo by coercion, Japan still sees 'stable relations with China as an essential factor for peace and stability of the Asia-Pacific region', and encourages China to 'play a responsible and constructive role for the sake of regional peace, stability and prosperity'.[13]

Meanwhile, with globalization and growing interdependence among nations, security risks can no longer be confined to a specific country or region. The issues at hand include the proliferation of weapons of mass destruction and ballistic missiles, the presence of weak and failed states, the spread of international terrorism and piracy, climate change, natural disasters, pandemics, and issues related to the global commons such as cyberspace, the Arctic, and outer space. Notably, the threat of international terrorism has become a major concern for the GoJ and the Japanese public with the killings of two Japanese hostages in Syria by Islamic State extremists in early 2015, as well as the killings of Japanese businessmen and technicians in Algeria in early 2013. In light of these security challenges, it has become crucially important for the country to promote a variety of cooperative initiatives with the United States and other partners.

With regard to India, the GoJ clearly acknowledges that the country has become increasingly influential and geopolitically important for Japan. At present, Japan considers India to be the fifth most important country behind the US, the Republic of Korea, Australia, and Association of Southeast Asian Nations (ASEAN) members. The GoJ understands that India is projected to have the world's largest population and become a prominent economic power, and that India shares interests with Japan in a broad range of areas.[14] This view is in line with the statement made by Prime Minister Modi in early September 2014 in Tokyo, where he emphasized the need to pursue a new economic development initiative based on India's young labour force, the vast markets within and west of India, and a stable industrial environment. At present, however, bilateral cooperation has been relatively symbolic. As stated, there is a need to enhance deeper strategic cooperation that promises to give each side a broader security role.[15]

Expanding Opportunities for Cooperation

Today, Japan–India cooperation can no longer be limited to the economic realm. Both countries have come to view each other as key partners that share various foreign policy and security interests. Essentially, the promotion of democratic values has been the core political and security foundation for both countries domestically. Furthermore, Japan's 2013 NSS has pledged to pursue diplomacy through partnerships with countries who share with Japan universal values such as freedom, democracy, respect for fundamental human rights, and the rule of law.[16] India has functioned as a responsible democratic country since its independence in 1947, and shares these universal values with Japan. Needless to say, like any two countries, both Japan and India face various difficult domestic problems, but the common values shared by both countries can form the basis for closer cooperation.

Based on this foundation, opportunities for cooperation can further expand in the following four areas. First, Japan and India share an interest in engaging in international cooperation activities including United Nations Peacekeeping Operations (UNPKOs) and humanitarian assistance and disaster relief (HADR). India has historically been the leading contributor to UNPKO missions. It has participated in more than 44 missions and dispatched nearly 180,000 troops, the highest number in the world.[17] As of June 2015, India has lost 159 of its soldiers in 24 missions.[18] Currently, India is ranked second only to Bangladesh among UN members with a total of 8,008 dispatched personnel.[19] In contrast, Japan's first overseas deployment of peacekeepers was in 1992, when it dispatched over 1,200 personnel to Cambodia. Despite this short history, Japan has now sent its forces to Mozambique (1993–5), Rwanda (1994), the Golan Heights (1996–), East Timor (2002–4, 2010–), Afghanistan (2001), Nepal (2007–11), Sudan (2008–11), Haiti (2010–), and South Sudan (2011–). The role of Japan's international contributions has been limited by the country's pacifist constitution, but the Japan Self-Defense Forces (JSDF) have thus far been greatly appreciated by local governments and populations for their high level of performance and discipline. In light of the increasing commitment to UN peacekeeping activities by Japan and India, this area can be a field for further cooperation between the two countries, as will be described in greater detail later in this chapter.

In July 2014, Prime Minister Shinzo Abe's cabinet expanded the JSDF's mandate to use weapons to include the protection of non-Japanese peacekeepers (the so-called *kaketsuke-keigo*) and the conditional use of weapons for the purpose of executing UNPKO missions. This decision will also increase the functions and areas in which the JSDF will be allowed to operate, thereby expanding the opportunities for increased cooperation between India and Japan.

Another area where Japan and India have played significant roles is HADR. This can also be an area for further cooperation between the two countries. For example, India has provided aid in post-conflict situations in countries such as Sri Lanka and Afghanistan and has also allocated resources to improve its own disaster management capabilities since the 2004 Indian Ocean tsunami.[20] In 2007, India acquired a landing platform dock from the United States to bolster its HADR capabilities. The dock is capable of carrying six helicopters and, along with its landing craft, would be able to deploy relief supplies and manpower faster to debris-littered shores.[21] In November 2013, India used its C-130 aircraft to send relief goods to the Philippines. Similarly, Japan has also been actively engaged in HADR missions. Since November–December 1998, when the JSDF were sent to Honduras for the first time in an overseas HADR mission, the GoJ has deployed the JSDF to places such as Turkey (1999), India (2001), Iran (2003–4), Thailand (2004–5), Indonesia-Sumatra (2005), Russia (2005), Pakistan (2005, 2010), Indonesia-Java (2006), Indonesia-West Sumatra (2009), Haiti (2010), and New Zealand (2011).

It is worth noting that in retrospect, the 2004 tsunami served as a watershed moment for Japan's HADR missions overseas. The International Disaster Relief Law that enables the overseas deployment of the JSDF was enacted in 1992, but it took six additional years for the GoJ to actually deploy its troops overseas for such a mission, and it was only after the 2004 tsunami that Japan began to be actively involved in overseas HADR.

Second, the protection of sea lines of communication (SLOC) against piracy in the Asia Pacific region has become increasingly important for both Japan and India, as well as for other Asian countries including China, because the Indian Ocean and the South and

East China Seas serve as a source of human capital, underground resources (including oil reserves, gas, gold, uranium, diamonds, iron, titanium, chromate, and manganese), and raw materials (including rubber). Moreover, the entire area also serves as a vital conduit for global trade. Altogether, this has made 'the Asia-Pacific more inter-reliant and symbolic as a region'.[22] Furthermore, India is geopolitically well positioned as it sits at a key juncture in South Asia along the waterway from Africa and the Middle East to the Far East.

For Japan, the protection of the SLOC in the western Pacific, the East and South China Seas, and the Indian Ocean has been a vital national security interest, most notably because the country imports most of its crude oil from the Middle East. In this sense, India's effort to strengthen its capabilities to secure the safety of the SLOC in the Indian Ocean is of great importance to Japan. India's growing interest in the South and East China Seas has also been encouraging for Japan and many other Asian countries, as they share an interest in securing the safety of these waters. In 2005, former Indian chief of naval staff Arun Prakash said that it was essential for India to take adequate security measures to safeguard its assets and interests, including those in the Persian Gulf, Central Asia, Southeast Asia, and Africa.[23] In June 2012, at the 11th International Institute for Strategic Studies (IISS) Asia Security Summit in Singapore, Indian Minister of Defence A.K. Antony underlined the importance of maritime security and suggested two ways in which India seeks to ensure its maritime security: through safeguarding its territories against seaborne threats, and by ensuring maritime access for all.[24] Meanwhile, the Indian Ocean has increasingly become strategically important for India since the late 1990s, as Delhi decided to explicitly link India's maritime power with the protection of its economic interests.[25]

In recognition of the need to secure the SLOC in the Asia Pacific, Japan and India have strengthened their military relations in recent years. For example, the two countries conducted their first ever bilateral naval exercise in Japan's Sagami Bay in 2012. An additional exercise was held off the coast of Chennai in India in 2013. Furthermore, India is currently planning to purchase JMSDF US-2 search and rescue amphibious aircraft for its navy.[26] This purchase should strengthen India's HADR capabilities, given that US-2s are known for their ability to cruise at extremely low speeds (approximately

90 kilometres per hour) and take off and land on water within a very short distance, with a range of over 4,500 kilometres. More importantly, this sale may become a precedent for boosting Japan's arms exports, despite the fact that in the past Japan had essentially banned all overseas military sales including transfers of technology. Easing this restriction on arms exports has been one of Prime Minister Abe's key security initiatives. The administration's intention to relax Japan's policy on arms exports will allow the country to develop arms with its allies and give the Japanese defence industry access to overseas markets. Furthermore, Japan's Ministry of Defense (MoD) has recently decided to expand the number of defence attachés in India. Traditionally, Japan has sent one officer of the Japan Ground Self-Defense Force (JGSDF) to India, but now dispatches officers from JMSDF and the Japan Air Self-Defense Force (JASDF) as well, making a total of three defence attachés.

Third, anti-terrorism can also be an area of cooperation. The war on terror has become a serious global issue since the 9/11 incident. The Indian Ocean region is located at 'the intersection of two main reservoirs of Islamic extremism, the Middle East and Southeast Asia',[27] and encompasses a large portion of the 'arc of instability',[28] enabling violent extremists including al-Qaeda and associated groups to attack 'civilians and military entities in Yemen, Jordan, Bahrain, the United Arab Emirates, the Strait of Hormuz, and the Strait of Malacca'.[29] Furthermore, Southeast Asia has become an important secondary front against radical extremist terrorism, making countries such as Singapore a critical hub for US military operations.[30] The safety of the Indian Ocean littoral region, which contains one-third of the world's population, is therefore essential to both Japan and India as the two countries seek to strengthen their political and economic relationships in the area. In light of this reality, the two countries, together with the international community, need to clear what one analyst has called the 'lake of Jihadi terrorism'.[31] Specifically, Japan and India can contribute to the capacity building of countries in the region, for example, by strengthening the latter's coastguards through defence equipment cooperation and solidifying information-sharing networks.

Finally, issues related to the global commons such as cyber security and the Arctic Sea are also areas in which Japan and India can cooperate. Cyber security has become a major concern for many countries including Japan and India. Cyber espionage has been widely reported, and it is reasonable to expect that Japan and India will be targeted more in the future. Furthermore, as Caroline Baylon notes, the international community is confronted with major cyber security challenges that are similar to the concerns raised in terms of space security, such as the blurring of the line between 'non-military' and 'military' roles including a rise in dual-use technologies, as well as between 'offensive' and 'defensive' actions in the cyber field; and asymmetric threats in the cyber domain (that is, offence is easier and cheaper than defence).[32] Together with these challenges, Japan and India both face unique drawbacks. Japan's major strength lies in its public–private partnership (PPP), and it acknowledges 'cyber security not only as important for defense but also as an opportunity for its industry to improve its international competiveness'.[33] However, Japan's weakness is that it views cyber security as 'an issue that concerns primarily the security of IT systems but not the underlying critical infrastructure such as power plants and electricity grid, telecommunications, and railway systems'.[34] In the case of India, its major strengths are its large pool of available talent and capabilities as well as its pursuit of a blend of national security and social harmony. In Rajeswari Pillai Rajagopalan's view, India perceives cyber security as a tool to protect its critical infrastructure and to strengthen India's social harmony and cohesion.[35] However, India has its weaknesses in areas such as insufficient private sector input, including PPPs that involve only large corporations.[36] In light of this reality, the two countries seem to be able to cooperate by supplementing each other's weaknesses: unlike India, Japan has a strong PPP but does not necessarily have sufficient talent and capabilities in cyber security or a strong sense of protecting its infrastructure. It must be noted, however, that cyber security needs to be solely defensive if the two countries should seek cooperation in this field, as an offensive action runs counter to the basic spirit of Japan's pacifist constitution.

Meanwhile, the Arctic has also become a focus of the international community due to receding ice, which is enabling increased human access and creating economic opportunities while also raising security concerns. As US President Barack Obama noted in the White House's National Strategy for the Arctic Region released in May 2013, the region needs to be 'peaceful, stable, and free of conflict'.[37] In this regard, Japan and India together with the United States can contribute to the peaceful and stable use of the region by supporting and preserving the international legal principles of freedom of navigation and overflight and other uses of the sea and airspace, protecting the free flow of resources and commerce, as well as protecting the environment.

Growing Challenges

Despite these common national interests, however, Japan and India face challenges in areas such as nuclear issues, the reconstruction effort in Afghanistan, and their responses to China's assertive actions. To begin with, the nuclear issue remains a very sensitive one for Japan, as it is the only country to have been victimized by the actual use of these weapons. Furthermore, the North Korean nuclear programme and its continuous launching of missiles have raised concerns in Japan. Meanwhile, India's geopolitical position seems, at least from the Japanese point of view, to be leading the country to take a unique stance on nuclear issues. By 1974, India had tested its own peaceful nuclear device in response to both the 1964 Chinese nuclear test and the US's entry into the Bay of Bengal in 1971.[38] In May 1998, India and Pakistan each conducted five and six nuclear tests, respectively, igniting a great deal of condemnation from the international community, which feared a possible nuclear confrontation. Japan joined the condemnation and sanctioned India from 1998 until 2000, when Prime Minister Yoshiro Mori visited Delhi and announced a number of aid and investment projects such as the Delhi Metro and the beginning of an Indo-Japanese Global Partnership for the Twenty-First Century.[39] Some have argued that India's and Pakistan's nuclear tests made the South Asian region far more volatile, such that a relatively small incident like a terrorist attack or a large conventional attack could easily turn into a nuclear war.[40] On the other hand, others have argued that nuclear weapons have made large-scale war less likely due to the doctrine of mutually assured destruction, but that this has actually created incentives for low-intensity warfare so long as a certain threshold is not crossed.[41] Furthermore, according to Neil Padukone, the overt nuclearization of South Asia also revealed India's potential military might and its great power ambitions, particularly vis-à-vis China.[42]

Pakistan's nuclear capabilities remain a constant threat to India. According to *The Economist*, Pakistan's arsenal of warheads—developed with Chinese assistance—is at least as large as India's and probably larger. Its Chinese-designed missiles are within reach of most Indian cities and, unlike India, Pakistan does not have a no-first-use policy.[43] In light of these security situations, the possibility remains that Pakistan may, at least from an observer's perspective, resort to using its nuclear weapons if a small-scale conventional war with India were to escalate into an all-out war. Although India's decision to possess nuclear weapons is not targeted solely at Pakistan, a grave situation may arise in which Pakistan will be forced to use these weapons, as Islamabad is in an inferior position to India with regard to the capabilities of its conventional forces. During the border conflict of 1999 in Kargil, Pakistan was believed to have been on the verge of using its nuclear weapons when Pakistan's foreign secretary had warned, 'We will not hesitate to use any weapons in our arsenal to defend our territorial integrity.'[44] Needless to say, such a situation would jeopardize the overall security situation in the Asia Pacific and is totally unacceptable for Japan. Undoubtedly the Indo-Pakistani relationship needs to improve, and both Japan and India must exert their utmost effort to control the Indo-Pakistani nuclear rivalry. Specifically, India needs to exert stronger control over its superior conventional forces so that Pakistan can implement a no-first-use policy for its nuclear arsenal. In particular, India needs to scale back its conventional defence spending so that Pakistan will not be encouraged to use its nuclear arsenal in order to compensate for its inferior conventional forces. As for Japan, it needs to continuously emphasize the importance of a nuclear-free world and firmly maintain its current non-nuclear principles of not producing, possessing, or allowing the entry of nuclear weapons into its territory.

In relation to North Korea, it is imperative for the international community including Japan and India to prevent the proliferation of North Korea's weapons of mass destruction, including its missiles. It is believed that, in the past, North Korea exported its missile technologies to Pakistan for the development of the latter's Ghauri I missiles.[45] The Proliferation Security Initiative (PSI) can serve as a framework to prevent these actions from occurring again in the future. Japan was one of the initial members of the PSI along with

10 other countries, and at present the PSI has expanded into a global effort with over 100 countries. However, several countries including India and Pakistan are yet to subscribe to the PSI framework. India should change its passive position on the issue.

Second, both Japan and India have engaged themselves extensively in the reconstruction effort in Afghanistan to facilitate the development of the country, which remains a common challenge. In the case of India, Afghanistan has been at the centre of Delhi's Central Asia strategy and the geographic hub of the 'New Silk Road'—China's recent economic integration initiatives seeking to link East and Central Asia. According to Padukone, since the fall of the Taliban regime in 2001, India's strategic interests in Afghanistan have been: (*a*) balancing against China's growing footprint in the region; (*b*) preventing the spread of Islamic militants into India, especially Indian-administered Kashmir, and restricting the Pakistani influence in Afghanistan that may assist those militants; and (*c*) developing an economic infrastructure that will stabilize the country and enable it to reconnect to the rest of the region.[46] India, along with Afghanistan, was the lead organizer of the Delhi Investment Summit on Afghanistan in June 2012, and has helped to attract foreign investment in Afghanistan, particularly in sectors such as mining, hydrocarbons, infrastructure, telecommunications, agriculture, education, and health care.[47] Furthermore, India and Afghanistan signed a security and trade pact in October 2011, agreeing to step up cooperation in counterterrorism operations, training of security forces, and trade, as well as to boost political and cultural engagement.[48] Similarly, Japan has also been an active contributor to Afghanistan. In July 2012, Japan hosted the Tokyo Conference on Afghanistan, and as of April 2014 it had delivered nearly US$5.4 billion in aid since September 2001.[49]

Despite these efforts by both countries, the activities may cut both ways—that is, facilitating the development of Afghanistan on one hand and fuelling tensions with Pakistan on the other. The withdrawal of foreign military forces from Afghanistan may have created conditions that will intensify competition between India and Pakistan. India has strategic interests in Afghanistan as an access route for energy from Central Asia, and is one of the largest contributors to Afghanistan's reconstruction, having given over US$2 billion in aid.[50] However, some believe that Pakistan sees the growing Indian presence in Afghanistan as a form of strategic encirclement.[51] Islamabad has long accused Delhi of fuelling a separatist movement in Pakistan's Balochistan region in partnership with Afghan officials.[52] To complicate the situation, China and Russia also have a stake in Afghanistan. That said, regardless of these countries' intentions, it is important for Afghanistan to be a stable country in the region. Japan and India will therefore need to give considerable attention to engagement and cooperation on Afghanistan in a way that will not jeopardize the India–Pakistan relationship.

Finally, China has also posed a challenge in the Asia Pacific region in recent years. Notably, the South and East China Seas, including the Paracel Islands, Spratly Islands, Scarborough Shoal, and Senkaku Islands have been hotspots between China and its neighbours over territorial claims. In some cases, there have been direct confrontations between the countries concerned. Regardless of the legitimacy of the claims to these waters, the countries need to manage the issue to keep it from escalating into a military confrontation. To this end, the formulation of a code of conduct (CoC) for the South and East China Seas will be essential. Unfortunately, no real movement was made on the CoC during the ASEAN Regional Forum (ARF) in Myanmar in August 2014. The CoC is a major focal point for most ASEAN members, and something China has been hesitant to make progress on in light of its claim to a vast majority of the South China Sea.[53] Both Japan and India need to support the formulation of the CoC, as this will contribute greatly to the security of the Asia Pacific region as a whole. Furthermore, Japan needs to set up a maritime communication mechanism with China as quickly as possible in order to avoid any miscommunication that may lead to the escalation of a confrontation. In January 2015, Japan's and China's defence authorities resumed talks over the issue after two years of suspension. The resumption may lead to the implementation of a consultative mechanism to govern contacts in the East China Sea.

Policy Recommendations

Japan–India bilateral cooperation is still in its primary stages. The question at hand is how consistently and continuously policies can be pursued to strengthen security ties between the two countries. There are short- and long-term recommendations for Japan and India. In the short term, first and foremost, it is crucially important for both countries not to be perceived by Beijing as trying to contain China through their bilateral cooperation efforts. Undoubtedly, China's recent assertive actions have not positively contributed to the security and safety of the Asia Pacific region as a whole, including both Japan and India. Countervailing China, however, may only provoke additional hard-line responses from Beijing. Sourabh Gupta recently stated that the US–India strategic relationship was 'too important to be constructed solely or even primarily through a China-management lens', and that their defence cooperation 'should be constructed rather on more modest but firmer foundations that are geared to nudging the Indo-Pacific region's multilateral security relations toward a more consociational model of international relations where power is shared and balanced within'.[54] By the same token, Japan and India will need to both hedge against and engage with China through a multilateral security framework, as will be discussed shortly, so that China can become a responsible stakeholder that will not try to change the status quo of the region by force. This is in line with Abhijit Singh's proposal that India needs to become a gentle 'stabilizer' in the Indo-Pacific.[55]

It is also important to note that the India–China relationship is very sensitive, and that Japan needs to give due consideration to the ambivalent relationship between the two. Retired Indian brigadier general Arun Sahgal stresses the need for India to take a dual approach to China, by achieving 'the right balance of pragmatism and nationalism in pushing Sino-Indian relations forward'.[56] Furthermore, an Indian senior government official stated that the country was absolutely committed to a pragmatic approach in dealing with sensitive bilateral issues, and that it did not want war with China as it wanted to develop their relationship further and faster, but in a way that would not hurt India's pride in the process.[57] These comments illustrate that a simple containment effort aimed at China will not serve the interests of either India or Japan.

Meanwhile, both Japan and India need to implement the idea of 'putting more eggs into the basket' in order to create greater regional stability. That is, it is imperative to involve more participants in building a multilateral regional security cooperation framework (the basket), including China, and encouraging each participant not to infringe upon the interests of the other participants (the eggs) or of the mechanism as a whole. Current mechanisms such as the ARF, ASEAN Defence Ministers Meeting Plus (ADMM Plus), and ASEAN Maritime Forum may provide the foundation for a more comprehensive security mechanism. For India, as Jagannanth Panda clarifies, comprehensive engagement with ASEAN and reviving its Look East policy by advocating in favour of the ARF and ADMM Plus are important and immediate priorities.[58] Furthermore, India is 'fully committed to ASEAN processes and will participate in and contribute to the ARF as well as the ADMM Plus, Expanded Maritime Forum and others'.[59] Indeed, ASEAN members have urged India to take a more decisive stance towards the region, including the South China Sea. For example, President Nguyen Tan Dung of Vietnam has asked for direct intervention by India in maritime issues.[60] In the case of Japan, the government has actively engaged in various multilateral gatherings including the ARF, East Asia Summit, ADMM Plus, and the IISS Asia Security Summit to promote and establish relationships based on multi-layered security cooperation.[61]

In relation to the deepening and widening of multilateral cooperation mechanisms, the formulation of a Japan–US–India trilateral security mechanism may also benefit all three countries. To begin with, the US acknowledges the Japan–US alliance as a 'cornerstone of regional security' in the Asia Pacific,[62] and 'the indispensible linchpin of [its] forward military and diplomatic presence in Asia and the foundation of a stable equilibrium in the region'.[63] Furthermore, India has become an important partner for the US. In November 2011, President Obama, in the context of US strategic interests in the Asia Pacific, praised India's Look East policy and welcomed India to play a larger role as an 'Asian power'.[64] Later, in June 2012, Secretary of Defense Leon Panetta stated that '[d]efense cooperation with India is a linchpin' in the US defence strategy of rebalancing towards the Asia Pacific region, and that 'India shares with the United States a strong commitment to a set of principles that help maintain international security and prosperity.'[65] Furthermore, President Obama visited India in November 2010 and January 2015, becoming the first American president in history to visit the country twice during his presidency. During the January 2015 visit, President Obama and Prime Minister Modi announced that they had agreed on a new 10-year military cooperation agreement to replace the Indo-US agreement that was set to expire later in 2015, including more intensive joint military exercises and increased collaboration in maritime security. In addition, the 'U.S.–India Joint Strategic Vision for the Asia-Pacific and Indian Ocean Region' statement affirmed 'the importance of safeguarding maritime security and ensuring freedom of navigation and over flight throughout the region, especially in the South China Sea'.[66] Meanwhile, India has stressed the importance of maintaining maritime freedom. During his speech in September 2012, India's external affairs minister S.M. Krishna stated that India 'will work to build a regional architecture that promotes cooperation and reinforces convergence, reduces the risks of confrontation and conflicts, and draws all countries of the region into a common framework of norms and principles of engagement'.[67] India has conducted more joint naval exercises with the US than any other country.[68] As explained previously, Japan regards its alliance with the US to be a vital pillar of its security strategy, and uses other cooperative mechanisms and partnerships, including with India, to support the alliance. Japan, together with the US and India, fully respects the rule of law, as reflected in Prime Minister Abe's keynote address during the 13th IISS summit: 'What the world eagerly awaits is for our seas and our skies to be places governed by rules, laws, and established dispute-resolution procedures. The least desirable state of affairs is having to fear that coercion and threats will take the place of rules and laws and that unexpected situations will arise at arbitrary times and places.'[69] In sum, the United States, India, and Japan all have a common interest in working more closely together.

With regard to the Indian Ocean, the strategic importance of the island of Diego Garcia can play a significant role in strengthening the Japan–US–India trilateral security mechanism. At present, it appears that the Indian government has accepted Diego Garcia as an important and permanent hub for American power projection in the Indian Ocean region; unlike in the past, the American military presence is now seen as a stabilizing factor in an otherwise fragile region.[70] India's strategic ties with the United States can be a vital means of reinforcing India's position in the Indian Ocean. According to Walter C. Ladwig

III *et al.*, it has been acknowledged that the 'American presence in the littoral can complement India's quest for a peaceful and stable regional order' because the US is able to use Diego Garcia as a base for significant air assets and to deploy its naval forces from the Gulf and the Pacific to the Indian Ocean.[71] As an important ally of the US, Japan may also benefit from utilizing the US base in Diego Garcia as a future stronghold in order to reinforce its operations in the Indian Ocean.

The emerging Japan–Australia–India trilateral cooperation may serve as an important element to strengthen ties between Japan and India. In June 2015, the three countries held their first ever high-level dialogue in Delhi. The dialogue seems to be very promising, as the representatives exchanged views on maritime security issues, including freedom of navigation in the South China Sea and trilateral maritime cooperation in the Indian Ocean and Pacific Ocean.[72] As Tokyo and Canberra share common interests as US allies, the two countries may become a catalyst to enhance this trilateral cooperation mechanism. However, there are some potential bilateral hurdles, such as the submarine deal between Japan and Australia and the nuclear agreement between India and Australia, that may hamper closer cooperation among the three countries. Furthermore, it must be noted that the GoJ will not be willing to pursue such cooperation without the due consideration of the US.

The second short-term recommendation is to widen and deepen cooperation in areas such as PKO and HADR. As mentioned earlier, India has played a leading role in UN peacekeeping and has many lessons that it can share with Japan. Currently, both Japan and India have engaged themselves in the same UN peacekeeping operations in places such as South Sudan. The 2014 Japan Defense White Paper emphasized cooperation between the JSDF contingent and Australian forces in South Sudan, where two Australian military personnel were dispatched to assist Japan's coordination team; since August 2012, they have been engaged in the coordination activities of the UN Mission in South Sudan.[73] Likewise, if Japan and India can mutually dispatch military personnel to the headquarters of PKO missions as liaisons, it will promote mutual understanding, thereby strengthening the grounds for mutual confidence.

Meanwhile, Japan is known for its strengths in HADR, both domestically and internationally. In particular, Japan is highly appreciated by local populations for operating with a local perspective (*genba mesen*).[74] By sharing their experiences with each other, Japan and India can benefit greatly from further interactions. Furthermore, in relation to the first recommendation, Japan and India can cooperate through the multilateral route in areas such as UNPKO and HADR. This will also lead the two countries to deepen their relations with China, as Chinese troops have operated in areas close to those in which Japanese and Indian troops have operated in the past during PKO and HADR missions. During the annual Khaan Quest peacekeeping exercise held in Mongolia in June–July 2015, JSDF units trained together with Chinese troops for the first time in such a military exercise.

In addition to short-term recommendations, two long-term recommendations can be proposed. One is to strengthen the connectivity between India's Look East policy and Japan's effort to make more proactive efforts in line with the principle of international cooperation, so that the two countries can share greater common perceptions, policy priorities, and strategies. Recently, during the 12th India–ASEAN meeting in Myanmar, India's external affairs minister Sushma Swaraj referred to the foundation of the ASEAN–India strategic partnership and said, 'The ASEAN-India strategic partnership owes its strength to the fact that Delhi's Look East policy meets ASEAN's Look West policy. There is synergy and a sense of fraternity in our relationship, as we look towards a shared future of peace and stability, economic growth and prosperity in our region.'[75] She went on to emphasize the value of the 'C' of connectivity in foreign policy, which needs to translate into tangible and urgent action on the ground, bringing India's and ASEAN's capabilities together for mutual benefit. In a similar vein, Tokyo and Delhi will need to implement this 'C' strategy in order to strengthen the foundation of their Special Strategic and Global Partnership. Japan and India share universal values such as freedom, democracy, respect for fundamental human rights, and the rule of law. In recent years, Japan and India have been strengthening their security ties through bilateral naval training, defence exchanges, and security dialogues. The two countries have also been strengthening their economic ties. Based on this Special Strategic and Global Partnership, it is imperative that both Japan and India continue these efforts and steadily expand and deepen the scope of cooperation so that it can be of real substance and contribute to the enduring peace and prosperity of the Asia Pacific region and the international community.

The other long-term recommendation is to cooperate continuously to pursue the reform of the UN, most notably the UN Security Council (UNSC) (an issue that is also discussed in detail in Chapters 7 and 8 of this volume). The issue of UN reform has been endlessly discussed, but member states have failed to come to an agreement on what kind of reform is needed and for what purpose. Resistance to change by some permanent UNSC members and the existence of rivalries within each geographic region have also affected the process of reform. Both Japan and India believe that they have the necessary credentials to become permanent members of the UNSC. Japan has for the past 20 years dispatched approximately 9,300 JSDF and police personnel to UNPKO missions. As of March 2015, approximately 350 members of JSDF engineering units and three staff officers are being deployed to South Sudan.[76] Moreover, Japan has served as a non-permanent member of the UNSC for 10 terms, the largest contribution among non-permanent members (alongside Brazil).[77] Japan is also the second largest financial contributor behind only the United States, contributing 10.8 per cent of the UN's regular and peacekeeping budgets.[78] In addition, Japan is committed to promoting non-proliferation while firmly maintaining its three non-nuclear principles of not possessing, producing, or permitting the introduction of nuclear weapons into its territory. Furthermore, Japan has been playing a leading role in the disarmament of conventional arms, including small arms and landmines.[79] Meanwhile, India, together with Germany and Brazil, has sufficient credentials to become a permanent member in the UNSC. India has been elected as a non-permanent member of the UNSC seven times,[80] and is—as noted previously—ranked second only behind Bangladesh in the number of peacekeepers deployed overseas. In light of the difficulty of realizing UN reform in the near future, Japan and India, in cooperation with Germany and Brazil, will need to make persistent efforts—both physically (through troop contributions) and financially—to contribute to international security. To this end, Japan and India need to show through their peaceful intent and actions that they are competent for permanent membership in the UNSC.

Notes

1. MoFA, 'Japan's Security/Peace & Stability of the International Community', 2015, retrieved from http://www.mofa.go.jp/policy/security/ on 9 September 2015. 'Proactive contribution to peace' is one of Japan's basic security policies, which enables Japan 'to contribute more actively to the peace and stability of the region and the international community, while coordinating with other countries including its ally, the United States'.
2. GoJ, 'National Security Strategy', 17 December 2013, p. 14.
3. GoJ, 'National Security Strategy', pp. 28–31.
4. T. Shoji, 'Japan's Perspective on the Security Environment in the Asia Pacific and Its Approach toward Multilateral Cooperation: Contradictory or Consistent?', in NIDS International Symposium on Security Affairs, *Prospects of Multilateral Cooperation in the Asia Pacific: To Overcome the Gap of Security Outlooks*, Tokyo: NIDS, 2014, p. 92.
5. GoJ, 'National Defense Program Guidelines for FY 2014 and Beyond', 17 December 2013, p. 8.
6. GoJ, 'National Defense Program Guidelines for FY 2014 and Beyond'.
7. H. Kissinger, 'Center of Gravity Shifts in International Affairs', *San Diego Union-Tribune*, 4 July 2004.
8. GoJ, 'National Defense Program Guidelines for FY 2014 and Beyond', p. 2.
9. Ibid., p. 3.
10. MoFA, 'Abductions of Japanese Citizens by North Korea', 2012, retrieved from http://www.mofa.go.jp/region/asia-paci/n_korea/abduction/pdfs/abductions_en.pdf on 9 September 2015.
11. GoJ, 'National Defense Program Guidelines for FY 2014 and Beyond', p. 12.
12. W.C. Ladwig III, A.S. Erickson, and J.D. Mikolay, 'Diego Garcia and American Security in the Indian Ocean', in C. Lord and A.S. Erickson (eds), *Rebalancing U.S. Forces: Basing and Forward Presence in the Asia-Pacific*, Annapolis: Naval Institute Press, 2014, p. 162.
13. GoJ, 'National Security Strategy', p. 23.
14. Ibid.
15. A. Singh, 'Rebalancing India's Maritime Posture in the Indo-Pacific', *Diplomat*, 5 September 2014.
16. GoJ, 'National Security Strategy', p. 23.
17. Permanent Mission of India to the United Nations, 'India and United Nations: Peacekeeping and Peacebuilding', 2015, retrieved from https://www.pminewyork.org/pages.php?id=1985 on 9 September 2015.

18. United Nations Peacekeeping, 'Fatalities by Nationality and Mission', 30 June 2015, retrieved from http://www.un.org/en/peacekeeping/fatalities/documents/stats_2.pdf on 9 September 2015.

19. United Nations Peacekeeping, 'Troop and Police Contributors', 2015, retrieved from http://www.un.org/en/peacekeeping/resources/statistics/contributors.shtml on 9 September 2015.

20. N. Samaranayake, C. Lea, and D. Gorenburg, 'Improving U.S.-India HA/DR Coordination in the Indian Ocean', Report for CNA Analysis & Solutions, July 2014, p. 2.

21. S.S. Parmer, 'Humanitarian Assistance and Disaster Relief (HADR) in India's National Strategy', *Journal of Defence Studies*, 6(1), 2012, pp. 91–101.

22. J.P. Panda, 'India's Security Outlook and Views on Multilateral Cooperation: The Emerging Asia-Pacific Theater', in NIDS International Symposium on Security Affairs, *Prospects of Multilateral Cooperation in the Asia Pacific: To Overcome the Gap of Security Outlooks*, Tokyo: NIDS, 2014, p. 71.

23. N. Padukone, *Beyond South Asia: India's Strategic Evolution and the Reintegration of the Subcontinent*, New York: Bloomsbury, 2013, p. 120.

24. A.K. Antony, 'Protecting Maritime Freedoms', Second plenary session of the 11th IISS Asia Security Summit: The Shangri-La dialogue, 2 June 2012.

25. Ladwig *et al.*, 'Diego Garcia and American Security', p. 152.

26. 'Japan, India in Talks to Set Up US-2 Joint Venture', *Japan Times*, 28 March 2015.

27. Ladwig *et al.*, 'Diego Garcia and American Security', p. 135.

28. Ibid., p. 163.

29. Ibid., p. 135.

30. C. Rahman, 'Singapore: Forward Operating Site', in C. Lord and A.S. Erickson (eds), *Rebalancing U.S. Forces: Basing and Forward Presence in the Asia-Pacific*, Annapolis: Naval Institute Press, 2014, p. 123.

31. G.S. Khurana, 'Maritime Security in the Indian Ocean', *Strategic Analysis*, 28(3), 2004, p. 414.

32. Caroline Baylon, 'Overview: Common Challenges in Cyber Security and Space Security—Contributing to an Escalatory Cycle of Militarization?', in Caroline Baylon (ed.), *Challenges at the Intersection of Cyber Security and Space Security: Country and International Institution Perspectives*, Research paper, London: Chatham House, 2014, pp. 7–14. In addition to these two challenges, Baylon emphasizes other factors such as: (*a*) an escalatory cycle of militarization in the cyber field

prompted by the increasing militarization of a small number of states; (*b*) lack or inadequacy of national policy documents in the cyber realm; and (*c*) lack or insufficiency of internationally agreed definitions of key terminology in the cyber domain.

33. K. Suzuki, 'Japan's Cyber and Space Security Policies', in Caroline Baylon (ed.), *Challenges at the Intersection of Cyber Security and Space Security: Country and International Institution Perspectives*, Research paper, London: Chatham House, 2014, p. 29.

34. Suzuki, 'Japan's Cyber and Space Security Policies', p. 29.

35. R.P. Rajagopalan, 'India's Cyber and Space Security Policies', in Caroline Baylon (ed.), *Challenges at the Intersection of Cyber Security and Space Security: Country and International Institution Perspectives*, Research paper, London: Chatham House, 2014, p. 22.

36. In addition to insufficient private sector input, India's weaknesses lie in the lack of a comprehensive policy, insufficient public input, and lack of a strong security culture as well as a lack of an institutional and legal framework. See Rajagopalan, 'India's Cyber and Space Security Policies', pp. 22–3.

37. The White House, 'National Strategy for the Arctic Region', 10 May 2013, p. 1.

38. Padukone, *Beyond South Asia*, p. 29.

39. Ibid., p. 111.

40. Ibid., pp. 55–6.

41. Ibid., p. 56.

42. Ibid., p. 125.

43. 'India as a Great Power: Know Your Own Strength', *Economist*, 30 March 2013.

44. P.R. Chari, 'Nuclear Crisis, Escalation Control, and Deterrence in South Asia', Working paper, Henry L. Stimson Center, Washington, D.C., August 2003.

45. 'North's Missiles Tied to Musharraf Blunder', *Japan Times*, 28 January 2013.

46. Padukone, *Beyond South Asia*, p. 117.

47. G. Sachdeva, 'The Delhi Investment Summit on Afghanistan', IDSA Comment, Institute for Defence Studies and Analyses, New Delhi, 26 June 2012.

48. R. Lakshmi, 'India and Afghanistan Sign Security and Trade Pact', *Washington Post*, 4 October 2011.

49. Permanent Mission of Japan to the United Nations, 'Statement by Ambassador Motohide Yoshikawa, Permanent Representative of Japan to the United Nations, at the Debate of the 69th General Assembly

on the Situation in Afghanistan', 20 November 2014, retrieved from http://www.un.emb-japan.go.jp/jp/statements/yoshikawa112014.html on 11 September 2015.

50. A. Pande, 'Afghanistan's Karzai Presses for Indian Support, Investment', *Voice of America*, 16 December 2013.

51. N. Waintraub, 'India-Pakistan Relations and the Impact on Afghanistan', *Ploughshares Monitor*, 31(4), 2010.

52. J. Chowdhury, 'India-Pakistan-Afghanistan: Will the Triangle Give Peace a Chance?', *RT*, 2 September 2014.

53. C. Richards, 'Code of Conduct for South China Sea Unlikely, yet ASEAN Made Progress', *Diplomat*, 11 August 2014.

54. S. Gupta, 'A US-India Strategic Reset: Getting Back to Basics', PacNet Number 67, Pacific Forum CSIS, Honolulu, 14 August 2014.

55. Singh, 'Rebalancing India's Maritime Posture'.

56. A. Sahgal, 'China's Military Modernization: Responses from India', in A.J. Tellis and T. Tanner (eds), *China's Military Challenge: Strategic Asia 2012–13*, Seattle and Washington, D.C.: National Bureau of Asian Research, 2012, pp. 286–7.

57. S. Bhatt, 'Handle China Like a Test Match, Not a Ranji Match', *Rediff News*, 14 December 2011.

58. Panda, 'India's Security Outlook', p. 84.

59. MEA, Government of India, 'External Affairs Minister's Intervention on "Exchange of Views on Regional and International Issues" at 20th ARF Meeting in Brunei Darussalam', 2 July 2013, retrieved from http://www.mea.gov.in/in-focus-article.htm?21891/External+Affairs+Ministers+Intervention+on+Exchange+of+views+on+regional+and+int ernational+issues+at+20th+ASEAN+Regional+Forum+ARF+meeting+in+Brunei+Darussalam on 11 September 2015.

60. Panda, 'India's Security Outlook', p. 82.

61. MoFA, 'Nihon no anzen hosho seisaku: Tasotekina anzenhosho kyoryoku kakei no suishin kochiku' (Japan's Security Policy: Promoting and Establishing Relations of Multi-layered Security Cooperation), 2012, retrieved from http://www.mofa.go.jp/mofaj/gaiko/anpo/tasouteki.html on 11 September 2015.

62. The White House, Office of the Press Secretary, 'Remarks by President Obama to the Australian Parliament', 17 November 2011, retrieved from https://www.whitehouse.gov/the-press-office/2011/11/17/remarks-president-obama-australian-parliament on 11 September 2015.

63. Foreign Affairs Committee, Subcommittee on Asia and the Pacific, 'Prepared Statement by Michael J. Green for Hearing on the Future of

Japan', House of Representatives, 11th Congress 1st Session, 24 May 2011.

64. The White House, 'Remarks by President Obama to the Australian Parliament'.

65. L. Panetta, 'The U.S. and India: Partners in the 21st Century', Lecture at the Institute for Defense Studies and Analysis, New Delhi, 6 June 2012, retrieved from http://www.defense.gov/speeches/speech.aspx?speechid=1682 on 11 September 2015.

66. The White House, 'U.S.-India Joint Strategic Vision for the Asia-Pacific and Indian Ocean Region', 25 January 2015, retrieved from https://www.whitehouse.gov/the-press-office/2015/01/25/us-india-joint-strategic-vision-asia-pacific-and-indian-ocean-region on 11 September 2015.

67. MEA, Government of India, 'External Affairs Minister on "India's Foreign Policy Priorities for the 21st Century" at launch of the "India Initiative" by Brown University', 28 September 2012, retrieved from http://www.mea.gov.in/Speeches-Statements.htm?dtl/20639/Speech+by+External+Affairs+Minister+on+Indias+Foreign+Policy+Priorities+for+the+21st+Century+at+launch+of+the+quotIndia+Initiativequot+by+the+Brown+University on 11 September 2015.

68. 'India as a Great Power', *The Economist*.

69. S. Abe, 'Keynote Address', 13th IISS Asia Security Summit: The Shangri-La Dialogue, 30 May 2014, retrieved from http://www.mofa.go.jp/fp/nsp/page4e_000086.html on 11 September 2015.

70. Ladwig *et al.*, 'Diego Garcia and American Security', p. 156.

71. Ibid., p. 159.

72. P. Parameswaran, 'India, Australia, Japan Hold First Ever Trilateral Dialogue', *Diplomat*, 9 June 2015.

73. Ministry of Defense of Japan, 'Defense of Japan 2014', 2014, retrieved from http://www.mod.go.jp/e/publ/w_paper/2014.html on 11 September 2015.

74. For example, JSDF operations in Pakistan in 2005 were highly appreciated in person by President Pervez Musharraf (see http://www.mod.go.jp/e/jdf/no01/support.html, retrieved on 11 September 2015). In addition, the performance of the JGSDF contingent was highly respected in Iraq. In May 2004, about 100 Iraqis rallied around the Japanese camp in Samawah with the slogan, 'Honest Japanese. All of us are with you to rebuild our safe city', after the camp was nearly hit by rocket grenades. See N. Yamaguchi, 'Heiwakouchiku to Jieiai: Iraku-fukko-shien wo chuushin-ni' (Self-Defense Forces in Peace Building Missions: What Japan Learned from Its Experience in Iraq),

Journal of International Security, 34(1), June 2006, p. 23. (See also http://www.mofa.go.jp/mofaj/area/iraq/g_forum_0501.html, retrieved on 11 September 2015). Similarly, about 140 Iraqis marched near the Japanese camp to support the performance of the JGSDF in November 2004. Subsequently, groups of Iraqis launched a signature-collecting campaign and collected 1,500 signatures in two days requesting the Japanese contingent to extend its deployment. These events have been confirmed by JGSDF members including then commanders Sato Masahisa and Bansho Koichiro (see also http://www2s.biglobe. ne.jp/~nippon/jogbd_h17/jog378.html, retrieved on 11 September 2015).

75. 'New Delhi's Look East Policy Key to Strong ASEAN-India Strategic Partnership, Says Sushma Swaraj', *Business Standard*, 9 August 2014.

76. Ministry of Defense of Japan, 'SDF's Contribution to UNMISS', n.d., retrieved from http://www.mod.go.jp/e/about/answers/sudan/#a4 on 11 September 2015.

77. UNSC, 'Countries Elected Members of the Security Council', n.d., retrieved from http://www.un.org/en/sc/members/elected.asp on 11 September 2015.

78. UN General Assembly, Implementation of General Assembly resolutions 55/235 and 55/236, Report of the Secretary-General, A/67/224/ Add.1, 27 December 2012, retrieved from http://www.un.org/en/ga/ search/view_doc.asp?symbol=A/67/224/Add.1 on 28 October 2015; UN Peacekeeping, 'Financing Peacekeeping', n.d., retrieved from http://www.un.org/en/peacekeeping/operations/financing.shtml on 28 October 2015.

79. MoFA, 'An Argument for Japan's Becoming Permanent Member: What Is the Stance of Japan on Becoming a Permanent Member of the United Nations Security Council?', n.d., retrieved from http://www.mofa.the GOJp/policy/q_a/faq5.html on 11 September 2015.

80. UNSC, 'Countries Elected Members of the Security Council'.

6

India–Japan Strategic Partnership

Steady Advance amidst Enduring Constraints

C. Raja Mohan and Rishika Chauhan

The rise of China and the consequent power shift in Asia are drawing India and Japan closer than ever before. Yet a number of constraints limit the pace and scope of efforts to construct an enduring strategic partnership between the two countries. These include resistance in national security bureaucracies in both capitals to new ways of thinking about the bilateral relationship, the persistent sentiments of military isolationism in India and pacifism in Japan, and the residual legacy of non-alignment in Delhi and the primacy of the US alliance in Tokyo's calculus. The changing global balance of power in China's favour, paradoxically, both encourages and discourages a strong strategic partnership between India and Japan. If China's rise is pushing India and Japan towards greater strategic coordination in Asia, Delhi and Tokyo are acutely conscious of the importance of cooperation with Beijing and the dangers of sparking a confrontation with it.

In the first decade of the twenty-first century, the India–Japan relationship steadily progressed from a 'global' to a 'global-strategic' partnership. In 2014, it was elevated to the level of a 'Special Strategic and Global Partnership'. The change in terminology is not merely a play on words.[1] It underlines the steady expansion of the scope and substance of the relationship. In September 2014, during his visit to Tokyo, India's Prime Minister Narendra Modi pointed to the many 'special' features of the relationship—expanding economic partnership, growing political dialogue, and the deepening of defence ties at a moment when Asia is witnessing tectonic shifts in the regional balance of power.[2] The current optimism about bilateral relations stands in contrast to the mutual indifference of the past. This chapter begins with a brief review of the evolution of political relations between India and Japan since India's independence and examines the incremental advances in their proclaimed strategic partnership that could shape Asian geopolitics in the future. It also analyses the multiple constraints on a rapid advance in bilateral ties and suggests ways in which some of them could be overcome.

Cold War Years: From Warmth to Indifference

After India's independence, Asia was at the heart of Prime Minister Jawaharlal Nehru's foreign policy vision. Unlike many others in Asia and the world, Nehru was against attempts to isolate Japan after its defeat in the Second World War. In 1947 when the Asian Relations Conference was organized in New Delhi, Nehru insisted that the Japanese delegation be allowed to participate in spite of Japan's status as an occupied nation. He, along with others, maintained that it was an Asian conference and Japan should be included as it was an Asian country.[3] In 1951, India refused to attend the San Francisco Peace Conference organized by the Allies, arguing that the proposed treaty to be concluded there would interfere with the future of Japanese sovereignty.[4] Subsequently, Delhi signed a peace treaty with Tokyo in 1952, waiving India's claims for wartime reparations.[5] Later when the issue of seeking compensation for property destroyed during the 1942–5 Japanese occupation of the Andaman and Nicobar Islands came up in the Indian Parliament, Nehru responded definitively that Delhi did not propose 'to take any further steps for recovery of compensation from the Government of Japan'.[6]

Tokyo deeply appreciated Nehru's positive approach at one of Japan's most difficult historical moments. Japan gave Nehru much attention in the 1950s and early 1960s and saw him as the 'undisputed' leader of the post-colonial world.[7] Another Indian, Justice Radhabinod Pal, became popular in Japan for his dissenting judgement at the Tokyo International War Crimes Tribunal.[8] India also became the first recipient of Japan's official development assistance (ODA) in 1958. However, this warm phase did not last long, as the Cold War in Asia cast a shadow on the bilateral relationship. As Japan's military alliance with the US deepened, non-aligned India opposed American policies in Asia and steadily drifted towards the Soviet Union. As India's relations with China deteriorated in the 1960s and 1970s, Japan normalized ties with China following the Sino-American detente in 1972.

Positioned at opposite ends of the Asian geopolitical spectrum, it was not only hard to find a congruence of interests, but the two Asian states were also unable to understand each other's security compulsions. In May 1974, when India conducted a lone 'peaceful nuclear explosion', Japan condemned India's action and suspended its economic assistance to Delhi.[9] By the end of the year, however, Tokyo tempered the reaction by agreeing to resume yen credits and reschedule debt repayment.[10] While non-proliferation emerged as a problem between the two capitals, Delhi and Tokyo had few shared interests to bind them. On the economic front, the divergence was marked by India's inward turn amidst Japan's spectacular growth from the 1960s to the 1980s.

After the Cold War: The Nuclear Disruption

After the Cold War, the Asian security landscape changed dramatically, making some partnerships more plausible than before. The India–Japan partnership was one such relationship that had the potential and structural complementarity to develop significantly. India's new outward economic orientation from the early 1990s onwards helped Delhi broaden its relations with most major powers in the world, including Tokyo. As India's relationship with the US improved, the latter's ally Japan took more interest in India, and common foreign and security interests emerged. However, India's 1998 nuclear tests sparked a severe reaction in Japan and left India bitter. Terming the tests 'extremely regrettable', Japan became the first state to initiate punitive action against India.[11] Japan suspended yen loans for new projects in India and decided to cautiously examine the loans that international financial institutions were extending to Delhi.[12] Tokyo recalled its ambassador to India in protest against the nuclear tests. Japan also took the lead in getting the UN Security Council (UNSC) to pass a resolution that demanded the rollback of India's and Pakistan's nuclear programmes. With Japan making non-proliferation activism a major plank of its foreign policy in the post–Cold War period and India determined to secure its nuclear option, Delhi and Tokyo found it very difficult to reconcile their differences.

While major powers such as the United States, Russia, France, and Britain left themselves some political room to engage India after the nuclear tests, Japan's vehement reaction left Tokyo with little flexibility. In seeking to prevent Pakistan from following in India's footsteps, in May 1998 Japan offered to take up the Kashmir question in international forums and promised to shift economic assistance earmarked for Delhi to Islamabad.[13] While US officials were talking to India within a month of the tests, it took more than a year for Japan to resume formal dialogue with India. Even then the engagement was testy and tentative. The nuclear question remained a difficult one to get around even after the US successfully changed the international rules on civil nuclear cooperation to accommodate India between 2005 and 2008. Although Japan supported the George W. Bush administration's initiative to end India's atomic isolation, its political leaders have found it difficult to persuade domestic constituencies to finalize a civil nuclear cooperation agreement with India after 2008.

Towards a Strategic Partnership

Prime Minister Yoshiro Mori's August 2000 visit to India, four months after US president Bill Clinton travelled to Delhi, provided some fresh momentum to the India–Japan relationship that was derailed by Tokyo's reaction to India's nuclear tests in May 1998. Mori, personally committed to building relations with Delhi, launched a 'Global Partnership' with India.[14] However, with Japanese sanctions still in place, there was much scepticism in Delhi about the prospects for a robust relationship.[15] Japan eased some of the measures by October 2001, and Prime Minister Atal Bihari Vajpayee visited Japan soon after (in December 2001) to celebrate the 50th anniversary of the establishment of diplomatic relations between the two countries. His visit led to a steady expansion of engagement to cover a wide range of bilateral, regional, and international issues including terrorism, UN reforms, institutionalization of defence exchanges, a comprehensive security dialogue, and military-to-military cooperation in combating piracy. The advent of the George W. Bush administration in Washington and its warmth towards India helped Tokyo take a more strategic view of its relations with Delhi.

It was Prime Minister Junichiro Koizumi's April 2005 visit to India that set the stage for the construction of a stronger bilateral partnership. Koizumi and Prime Minister Manmohan Singh affirmed their desire to deepen the India–Japan global partnership and strengthen the security dialogue. In a major commitment to India's economic growth, Koizumi announced Japanese support to the Delhi–Mumbai freight and industrial corridors.[16] In December 2006, when Prime Minister Manmohan Singh visited Tokyo, the India–Japan relationship was elevated to a 'Global and Strategic Partnership'. The addition of the word 'strategic' was another small step in the steady expansion of the partnership. Singh's new partner was Prime Minister Shinzo Abe, who had an ambitious vision for Japan's role in the world and for the partnership with India.

Importantly, Abe proposed and Singh accepted the creation of a new quadrilateral framework involving four democratic nations: India, Japan, Australia, and the United States. Their joint statement explained that the two leaders agreed on 'the usefulness of having dialogue among India, Japan and other like-minded countries in the Asia-Pacific region'.[17] The idea of a 'democratic quad' had distinct geopolitical overtones as it sought to promote new forums in Asia that brought India in but kept China out. During his 2007 visit to India, Abe put India back into the Japanese strategic imagination by countering the perception that the Indian subcontinent was not a part of Asia. By talking about a 'broader Asia', the 'confluence of two seas' (the Indian and Pacific Oceans), and shared democratic values, Abe was making India central to his vision of an Asian 'arc of freedom and prosperity'.[18] By the time Narendra Modi visited Japan in August–September 2014, the relationship had steadily grown, not least because of the annual summitry since 2005 that kept up political pressure on the bureaucracies in Delhi and Tokyo to ensure sustained progress. Abe, who returned to power at the end of 2012, and Modi, who took charge of Delhi in the summer of 2014, signalled special personal warmth towards each other and raised expectations of a rapid consolidation and expansion of the strategic partnership. Calling their meeting the 'dawn of a new era in India–Japan relations' and noting their importance for 'advancing peace, stability and prosperity in Asia and the world', the two leaders elevated their ties to a 'Special Strategic and Global Partnership'.[19] The word 'special' now took its place in the description of the partnership.

Expanding Defence Engagement

In the first decade of the twenty-first century, the India–Japan security relationship developed steadily. India's defence minister Pranab Mukherjee visited Japan in 2006 and signed a joint statement with his counterpart that laid out the context, objectives, and means to develop bilateral defence and security cooperation.[20] In 2008, during the visit of Prime Minister Manmohan Singh to Tokyo, the two sides signed the Joint Declaration on Security Cooperation.[21] This was only the second such declaration issued by Tokyo outside of its US alliance. It called for a variety of measures to enhance security cooperation, including information exchange and policy coordination, bilateral cooperation within multilateral frameworks in Asia, cooperation between coastguards, safety of transport, counterterrorism and transnational crime, and disarmament and non-proliferation. Since 2010, Delhi and Tokyo have held an annual 'two plus two' dialogue among their foreign and defence secretaries. During Prime Minister Modi's visit to Tokyo in September 2014, Japan wanted to elevate the dialogue to the ministerial level, but India chose to maintain it at the level of top sub-cabinet officials.[22] Delhi has not ruled out the elevation of the defence dialogue to the political level in the future.

Since the mid-2000s, maritime security cooperation has emerged as a primary arena of security cooperation between India and Japan. Well before Abe articulated the idea of the confluence of the two seas, there had been a steady expansion of maritime engagement between the two countries, as the naval communities in both countries began to recognize the growing convergence of their interests in the Indian Ocean.[23] The first exchanges were between the coastguards of the two countries, which began joint exercises focused on anti-piracy as well as search and rescue operations in 2000. At the end of 2004, India and Japan joined hands in the international relief operations that followed the tsunami in the eastern Indian Ocean. In 2007, India invited Japan to participate in naval exercises in the Bay of Bengal along with the United States, Australia, and Singapore. The following year, in the Joint Declaration on Security Cooperation, the prime ministers of India and Japan underlined their shared interest in securing sea lines of communication (SLOC), and agreed to conduct navy-to-navy staff talks.[24] In the 2009 action plan to advance security cooperation, the two countries agreed to hold 'annual bilateral naval exercises, alternately in the waters near India and Japan'.[25]

In November 2011, the defence ministers of the two countries decided to carry out bilateral exercises between the Japan Maritime Self-Defense Force (JMSDF) and the Indian Navy. Prime Ministers Yoshihiko Noda and Manmohan Singh affirmed their commitment to enhancing maritime cooperation when the two met in December 2011 and promised to expand cooperation in the area of maritime security, including safety and freedom of navigation. The first bilateral naval exercise called JIMEX12 was held in June 2012. Two destroyers, one maritime patrol aircraft, and a helicopter participated from the JMSDF, while the Indian Navy's *INS Rana* (a Rajput-class destroyer), *INS Shivalik* (a Shivalik-class frigate), *INS Karmukh* (a Kora-class corvette), and *INS Shakti* (a Deepak-class fleet tanker) took part in the exercise.[26]

In 2014, when Prime Mister Modi visited Japan, the leaders spoke extensively on issues related to maritime security. The subject figured prominently in the Tokyo Declaration that was issued following the summit, which underscored the importance of 'regularization of bilateral maritime exercises as well as ... Japan's continued participation in [the] India-US Malabar series of exercises'. The two prime ministers 'welcomed the existing dialogue mechanism and joint exercises between Indian and Japanese Coast Guards', and 'affirmed their shared commitment to maritime security [and] freedom of navigation'.[27] Modi welcomed the liberalization of Japanese arms transfers, and the two prime ministers 'expressed the hope that this would usher in a new era of cooperation' in the development of the defence relationship.[28] The two leaders also urged their officials to accelerate negotiations on the sale and co-production in India of Japan's US-2 amphibious aircraft.

Since the Tokyo Declaration, positive developments have taken place in the field of defence. India's Defence Minister Manohar Parrikar visited Japan in March–April 2015 and discussed the prospect of bilateral defence exchanges, among other issues.[29] India is also promoting its 'Make in India' policy, as reports suggest that ShinMaywa Industries Ltd—a manufacturer of the US-2 based in Hyogo Prefecture—is in talks with Indian companies to set up a joint company if India and Japan agree to produce the plane jointly.[30] In mid-2015, Delhi confirmed that the Japanese Navy would join the Malabar exercises in the Bay of Bengal in October 2015.[31]

Outer Space and Cyber Security

The Tokyo Declaration also expressed the need to cooperate in the field of outer space. The potential of Indo-Japanese cooperation in this area has been recognized before. In 2003, Madhavan Nair, the chairman of the Indian Space Research Organisation (ISRO), pointed to the shared interests of India and Japan in promoting the peaceful uses of outer space and the importance of sharing experience and technology.[32] In a 2005 memorandum of understanding, ISRO and the Japan Aerospace Exploration Agency (JAXA) agreed to launch collaboration in space sciences, 'including lunar missions and X-ray astronomy, satellite remote sensing and satellite communication'.[33] The 2008 Joint Declaration on Security Cooperation identified cooperation in the area of disaster management as a high priority for ISRO and JAXA.[34] During Prime Minster Modi's visit to Japan in 2014, Tokyo addressed a major concern of India by removing six Indian companies working in the space and defence sector from Japan's list of foreign entities under sanctions. Issued by the Ministry of Economy, Trade and Industry (METI), the list provides names and information on foreign establishments suspected of involvement in activities related to the development of weapons of mass destruction. These entities were denied transfers of sensitive dual-use technology, that is, equipment as well as software.

Although there is considerable convergence in the arena of outer space between India and Japan, such cooperation is likely to remain restricted for some time to come. While many Asian nations including India, Japan, South Korea, and China are rapidly expanding their national space capabilities, their international cooperation has been largely with non-Asian powers rather than with each other.[35] This trend largely applies to India and Japan as well. Given its dual nature—civil and military—even peaceful space cooperation between Delhi and Tokyo has long been constrained by Japan's concerns on proliferation and India's ambivalent position in the global nonproliferation regime. As in the case of nuclear cooperation, Delhi and Tokyo are some distance away from fully realizing their joint potential in the space domain. Deepening the space partnership between Delhi and Washington is likely to provide a better political context for more productive space cooperation between India and Japan. India is also seeking, with US support, membership in the Missile Technology Control Regime (MTCR) that has long restricted space cooperation between the advanced industrial nations and India. Following the US lead on integrating India into global non-proliferation regimes, Japan has expressed its support for India's full membership in four international export control regimes: the Nuclear Suppliers Group (NSG), the MTCR, the Wassenaar Arrangement, and the Australia Group.

Given the dramatic growth in China's military space capabilities, it would seem logical for Delhi and Tokyo to explore the prospects for such cooperation. In the near term, such engagement seems limited by a number of factors. Despite their awareness of the growing national security challenges from China's emerging space weapon capabilities, the establishments are hesitant to openly engage in a public discussion of the need for robust military space programmes. Yet both Delhi and Tokyo have carefully begun to expand their military space activities, and it is not impossible to imagine bilateral military space cooperation in the future.[36] A larger constraint of course is the nature of the bilateral agreements on exclusive missile defence cooperation between Japan and the United States. However, as the United States expands its military space engagement with India, this situation could change as well.

As in space, so in the cyber domain, China's growing capabilities and impact on the evolution of international norms should encourage Delhi and Tokyo to work together increasingly. Some tentative engagement has already begun. At the 6th Japan–India Foreign Ministers' Strategic Dialogue in India during April 2012, the Indian external affairs minister S.M. Krishna and Japanese foreign minister Koichiro Gemba agreed that 'cyber attacks raised serious concerns that could have an impact on national security. They shared the view that they would cooperate on this issue including through discussions on an international code of conduct and launching bilateral talks on cyber.'[37] Later, in November 2012, India and Japan organized their first dialogue on cyber security in Tokyo.[38] In September 2014, the Indian and Japanese prime ministers acknowledged their 'shared interests' in the cyber domain.[39] Subsequently, a joint working group meeting in December 2014 launched a handful of joint projects.[40] Unlike in the space domain, India has lagged in the development of effective policies for cyber security, while Japan has invested far more resources and energy in this sector.[41] Here again, the faster the advance in India–US cyber security cooperation, the greater the scope for India–Japan collaboration.

Strategic Economic Cooperation

Manufacturing and supplying rare earth chlorides from India to Japan acquired some importance amidst a Chinese embargo on the sale of these vital materials to Japan in 2010. Japanese officials expressed their intention to import rare earth materials from India in order to 'diversify the sources of supply'.[42] This interest came after Beijing's decision to suspend the export of rare earths to Tokyo following the arrest of a Chinese fishing boat captain by the Japanese Navy not far from the disputed Senkaku/Diaoyu Islands. In 2012, Delhi and Tokyo agreed to promote bilateral cooperation on expanding the Indian production of rare earths and their export to Japan.[43] It was estimated that Japan could import over 4,000 tonnes of rare earths a year from India.[44]

During Prime Minister Modi's 2014 visit to Japan, he and Prime Minister Abe affirmed their strong support for an early finalization of a commercial contract between Indian and Japanese companies for the production of rare earths.[45] Indian Rare Earths Limited, a government corporation operating under the Department of Atomic Energy (DAE), is expected to begin supplying raw materials to a proposed new Japanese facility in Visakhapatnam for producing rare earth materials.[46] Although the economic value of the agreement is limited, it underscores the recognition in both capitals of the new imperative of strategic economic cooperation.

The strategic economic imperative has also begun to loom large as China has unveiled its ambitious plans to build so-called silk roads over land and across the waters of Asia. Although many of these initiatives had begun under earlier leaders, President Xi Jinping has lent them a new urgency and energy with his 'one belt, one road' initiatives.[47] The former refers to the silk road economic belt over land, and the latter to the maritime silk road. Xi has announced massive financial support for both projects, which involve building a variety of transport and industrial corridors connecting China to markets in Eurasia as well as Africa and the Middle East. Beijing has been pressing India to support these initiatives, especially the so-called Bangladesh–China–India–Myanmar corridor that links eastern India with south-western China.[48] Delhi has been deeply ambivalent about overland connectivity with its northern neighbours, and is even more anxious about China's maritime silk road initiative that builds on China's expanding economic activity in the Indian Ocean since the turn of the millennium. As India's neighbours welcome these initiatives, Delhi is looking for ways to cope with this challenge through its own initiatives and collaboration with other powers. Given Japan's own concerns on these issues, there is a growing recognition in both capitals on the need to partner with each other. Japan, which is building the Delhi–Mumbai industrial and freight corridors and developing the Chennai–Bengaluru corridor, has now agreed to take additional steps to promote connectivity within India's north-eastern region and between India and Southeast Asia. In the Tokyo Declaration, 'the two Prime Ministers placed special emphasis on Japan's cooperation for enhanced connectivity and development in Northeast India and linking the region to other economic corridors in India and to Southeast Asia, which would catalyse economic development and increase prosperity in the region.'[49]

The China Challenge

One of the factors drawing Japan and India closer in the twenty-first century is indisputably the rise of China, its growing military power, and its increasing assertiveness on territorial disputes. That India–Japan cooperation is growing amidst the deterioration of Sino-Japanese relations has generated the notion of a triangular dynamic between the three Asian countries. This phenomenon of course is not new. At the dawn of the twentieth century, there were strong forces in the three countries that imagined the inevitable re-emergence of Asia from the shadow of the West through intra-Asian collaboration. But the inter-war period showed how difficult it was to construct cooperation among the three Asian powers or to develop a common front against the West. The uneven development of the three countries, marked by the early and rapid rise of Japan, had dramatic consequences such as imperial Tokyo's occupation of China. As Chinese nationalists and communists fought against Japan, India was deeply divided. While the full resources of India—military and economic—were mobilized by the British to defeat Japan, a section of the Indian nationalists, led by Subhas Chandra Bose, aligned with Tokyo to defeat the British Empire in India. The Indian National Congress (INC), the major political party that led the freedom struggle, was opposed to Japan's occupation of China but was unwilling to support the British war against Japan despite requests from Chinese leader Chiang Kai-shek.[50] After the Second World War, Japan aligned with the US, India chose non-alignment, and China swung widely between collaboration and confrontation with the US. The uneven evolution of comprehensive national power in China, India, and Japan—marked by Beijing's rapid rise since the late 1970s—sets the stage for a new phase in relations between the three countries and between each one of them and the United States.

In the immediate aftermath of independence, the policies of India and Japan towards China rarely ran in parallel, let alone converged. When Japan did not have diplomatic relations with China and joined with the US in trying to isolate China in the 1950s, Delhi was at the forefront of a campaign to promote Beijing's integration into Asia and the world. By the time Japan normalized relations with China in the 1970s, Delhi was at odds with Beijing. As Japan rapidly expanded its economic cooperation with China and the two sides found some common interest in limiting the Soviet Union's power in the 1980s, India was largely seen as aligned with Moscow. It was only in the 1990s that India began to expand engagement with both China and

Japan. If Delhi was at the same time concerned about China's power, however, Tokyo seemed less interested in those concerns. It was only from the late 2000s that China's rise began to emerge as a major factor in India–Japan relations. As China–Japan relations deteriorated, Tokyo's concerns about Beijing began to mount; but Delhi appeared quite cautious and reluctant to make China the main driving force in bilateral relations with Japan.

China's emergence as a great power on its borders has triggered a significant domestic debate in India on Delhi's options in responding to this challenge.[51] Despite the expanding economic engagement with China and the long-standing tradition of expressing political solidarity with China against the West, Indian apprehensions about China's rise have steadily grown.[52] While Indian leaders have been reluctant to engage in a public debate on the China challenge, they have been quite explicit in expressing their growing concerns in private. For example, in 2010, Prime Minister Manmohan Singh affirmed, in what was meant to be an off-the-record conversation, that China was 'seeking to expand its influence in South Asia at India's expense'.[53] Meanwhile, there was no way Delhi could ignore Beijing's assertiveness in its territorial disputes with neighbours in Asia, including Vietnam, the Philippines, Japan, and India itself. Tensions on the long and contested frontier between India and China have steadily risen since the late 2000s. These tensions tended to cloud the visits of Chinese premier Li Keqiang to India in May 2013 and President Xi Jinping in September 2014, both aimed at expanding the political and economic engagement between Delhi and Beijing.

Meanwhile, Japan's anxieties about China's rise as well as new doubts about the credibility of the US–Japan alliance have complicated Asia's security environment and provided a new incentive for security cooperation between Delhi and Tokyo. Yet neither country wants to provoke China and drift into an unwanted military escalation and conflict. Japan's deep economic interdependence with China and India's growing interest in seeking Chinese cooperation in advancing its own development tend to keep both Tokyo and Delhi from making the Chinese threat the defining element of their strategic partnership with third countries. Instead, they have tended to underline the exceptional nature of their relations with China. The complexity and duality in India's approach to China was well captured by Prime Minister Manmohan Singh in a speech in Beijing in 2013. Claiming that relations between India and China were 'unique in the world', Singh declared:

> India welcomes China's emergence. Frankly, old theories of alliances and containment are no longer relevant. India and China cannot be contained and our recent history is testimony to this. Nor should we seek to contain others... . Our strategic partnerships with other countries are defined by our own economic interests, needs and aspirations. They are not directed against China or anyone else. We expect a similar approach from China.[54]

In Singh's United Progressive Alliance (UPA) government, there was considerable concern that drawing too close to Japan might create problems with China. Now, Narendra Modi's government appears to be playing Sino-Japanese tensions with greater aplomb. Modi has aggressively courted economic cooperation with both Tokyo and Beijing. He has been bolder in seeking a stronger defence partnership with Japan. He was not hesitant to indirectly refer to Chinese 'expansionism' from Japanese soil in September 2014. He said, 'We have to decide if we want to have "vikas vaad" [development] or "vistar vaad" [expansionism] which leads to disintegration. Those who follow the path of Buddha and have faith on "vikas vaad", they develop. But we see, those having ideas of the eighteenth century, engage in encroachments and enter seas [of others].'[55] Although External Affairs Minister Sushma Swaraj clarified that the prime minister was not referring to China, it was quite clear that the Modi government was hinting at India's new strategic options with Japan. At the same time, Modi has also underlined the importance of deeper economic cooperation with China as a critical element of his strategy for accelerating India's economic growth.[56]

Delhi and Tokyo will find it hard to accept China's emerging primacy in Asia. For both of them, the rapid rise of China and the growing prospects for the emergence of a Sino-centric Asia threaten to undermine their own presumed places in the region. At the same time, both need to maintain good relations with China and do not want to find themselves alone in leading the charge against Beijing. As China's rise increases the gap between its strategic capabilities and those of India and Japan, Delhi and Tokyo recognize the imperative of working with each other more closely than ever before. Deepening bilateral strategic cooperation without provoking China, then, is the greatest political challenge for both capitals.

Towards Strategic Coordination in Asia

The rise of China is also compelling India and Japan to look beyond the bilateral and seek partnerships with third countries. In the US, both the (George W.) Bush and Obama administrations have encouraged stronger bilateral security cooperation between India and Japan and have sought to develop trilateral and quadrilateral frameworks of engagement. As noted earlier, it was Abe who in 2006 called for a quadrilateral security dialogue among Japan, the US, Australia, and India. Tokyo suggested that there was 'ample room' for the four countries to work together and promote 'peace and stability' over sea lanes 'vital' to them in the Asia Pacific region.[57] The initiative did not last long and was set back when the Australian Prime Minister Kevin Rudd chose to pull out of the quad at the end of 2007. But the idea of the regional powers working together did not vanish. In 2011, India, Japan, and the US initiated a trilateral dialogue at the official level. During Modi's 2014 visit to Japan, Abe sought to elevate this dialogue to the ministerial level, but Delhi was hesitant. Nonetheless, the two sides left room for such a possibility and the potential expansion of the forum to include other countries in the future. In the Tokyo Declaration, Modi and Abe noted the progress of the trilateral dialogue, called for concrete projects to advance the shared interests of the three countries, and 'decided to explore holding this dialogue among their foreign ministers. They will also explore the possibility of expanding, at an appropriate time, their consultations to other countries in the region'.[58]

Although it has been hesitant to revive the quadrilateral grouping, the Modi government has embraced the idea of a separate trilateral grouping with Japan and Australia.[59] In June 2015, the Indian foreign secretary S. Jaishankar met with Japanese vice foreign minister Akitaka Saiki and the secretary of Australia's department of foreign affairs and trade, Peter Varghese, in New Delhi.[60] During the meeting, issues pertaining to regional security, naval exercises, and economic cooperation were discussed. Speaking in a public forum, Saiki later suggested that the discussions at the trilateral meeting focused on the challenges posed by the assertiveness of China and noted that the participants were 'on the same page'.[61] However, no announcements or joint statements were released by the Indian Ministry of External Affairs (MEA). Although the Modi government appears less inhibited on minilateral security engagements in Asia, it has no desire to needlessly provoke China.[62]

In the past, India's security dialogues and exercises with the US and its allies invited sharp criticism from China. In September 2007, when India, Japan, the US, Australia, and Singapore participated in a multilateral naval exercise in the Bay of Bengal, Beijing protested by sending official demarches to the participants. The Chinese media went a step further and censured the exercises as part of an attempt to establish an 'Asian NATO'. The Chinese reaction did have some political impact in India. Responding to the objections of the communist parties in his own ruling coalition (the UPA), Defence Minister A.K. Antony said that it was 'only an exercise' and not a 'military alignment'.[63] But there was no doubt that Antony and other leaders of the Congress party—the dominant member of the UPA—were deeply defensive about the new dynamic in India's military engagement with the US. Antony ordered the Indian Navy to stop holding trilateral and multilateral exercises in the Indian Ocean with the US and its allies. The current ruling coalition—the National Democratic Alliance (NDA), led by Modi—has, however, begun to reverse some of the UPA's defensiveness on China.

Confronted with China's rising influence in the subcontinent, India has become more welcoming of Japan's engagement in its backyard. Faced with China's assertiveness in the western Pacific, Japan is eager to see a greater Indian role in its region as well. On its part, Delhi encouraged Japan to apply for observer status in the South Asian Association for Regional Cooperation (SAARC) when India's neighbours were pressing for a similar status for China during 2005. This overture implied the possibility of greater India–Japan coordination on regional issues, especially in the subcontinent, the Indian Ocean, and East Asia, but did not go too far during the 2000s. Japan's growing activism in the subcontinent during Abe's second term and India's own focus on the subcontinent and Asia under Modi should open the possibilities for greater regional coordination.

In the Tokyo Declaration, the two leaders 'affirmed their intention to engage with other countries in the region and beyond to ... deepen regional cooperation and integration, strengthen regional economic and security forums and promote peaceful resolution of disputes. They underscored the importance of closer consultation and coordination between India and Japan in regional forums'.[64] In an indirect reference to the growing maritime tensions between China and its Asian neighbours, the two leaders also underlined 'their shared commitment to maritime security, freedom of navigation and overflight, civil aviation safety, unimpeded lawful commerce, and peaceful settlement of disputes in accordance with international law'.[65]

One of the central challenges for greater strategic coordination between India and Japan is coming to an agreed understanding on the role of the United States. For Japan, despite the emerging concerns about American steadfastness in Asia and the dangers of a potential compromise between Washington and Beijing, the alliance with the US remains the anchor of its security policy, hence the constant emphasis in Tokyo on a trilateral dialogue with the US and India. It was also Japan that had come up with the idea of a democratic quad in Asia along with Australia. India, however, put greater emphasis on bilateral security cooperation with Japan. Despite the expanding engagement with the US since the 1990s, there was considerable hesitation in Delhi to be seen as part of a US-led alliance system. This approach was not really about upholding the principle of non-alignment. After all, India had drawn close to the Soviet Union to address the consequences of Sino-US rapprochement in the 1970s, thereby demonstrating that India was no different from other countries in responding to changes in the balance of power in its neighbourhood. The sources of Indian hesitation were elsewhere.

There was nagging doubt in Delhi on whether the US was ready for a genuine strategic partnership with India. While the (George W.) Bush administration answered this question by unveiling the historic civil nuclear initiative and affirming its commitment to assisting India's rise to great power status, not everyone in the Indian political classes and the security establishment was convinced. Although it was the UPA government that presided over major breakthroughs in the India–US relationship during 2004–5, Prime Minister Manmohan Singh found it hard to convince the Congress party leadership of the logic of building a strategic partnership with the US. Party president Sonia Gandhi nearly pulled the plug on the civil nuclear initiative, citing the concerns of the communist parties who were a major partner in the UPA coalition at the time.[66] The Bharatiya Janata Party (BJP), which had launched the effort at nuclear reconciliation with the United States in the late 1990s, turned hostile to the US–India nuclear agreement. If the BJP's political opportunism was stunning, large sections of the Delhi establishment, especially in the foreign office, the defence ministry, and the scientific establishment were deeply wary of India's new warmth towards the US. But all public opinion polls in India pointed to a big shift in favour of the US and debunked the notion that there was popular opposition to a closer relationship with Washington.[67] A stronger government, a more robust political leadership, and better political and administrative management in Delhi could have pushed through the civil nuclear deal far more easily than Manmohan Singh did. After all, Indira Gandhi changed the direction of India's strategic policy in 1971 by signing a peace and friendship treaty with the Soviet Union despite vociferous opposition that the agreement violated the principles of non-alignment.

While the UPA government led by Manmohan Singh was constrained by the fears of the Congress party in consolidating his strategic initiatives towards the US and its Asian allies, the NDA government that came to power in 2014 under Modi has been bolder in advancing the bilateral and trilateral security agenda with the US and Japan. Modi's new approach was underlined by an entirely unexpected joint statement with Obama that laid out a shared strategic vision for the Indian Ocean and the Asia Pacific, when the US president visited India in January 2015 to participate in the annual Republic Day celebrations. The statement not only emphasized the importance of stronger regional security cooperation between India and the US at the bilateral level, but also called for engagement with third parties. The two leaders declared that they 'will strengthen our regional dialogues, invest in making trilateral consultations with third countries in the region more robust, deepen regional integration, strengthen regional forums, explore additional multilateral opportunities for engagement, and pursue areas where we can build capacity in the region that bolster long-term peace and prosperity for all'.[68] In a separate joint statement, they called for the strengthening of the trilateral dialogue with Japan through the 'identification of projects of common interest and their early implementation', and also 'decided to explore holding the dialogue among their Foreign Ministers'.[69]

Overcoming the Constraints

After many fumbles in the post–Cold War period, there has been a steady expansion of economic, political, and security cooperation between Delhi and Tokyo since the turn of the century. There is a new 'confidence, excitement and optimism' about the future of the bilateral partnership.[70] Yet there is no denying the many obstacles that impede the rapid growth of the India–Japan partnership. One is the inertia of the powerful national security bureaucracies in both countries.

Second is the persistence of certain attributes of strategic culture from an earlier era. Although the leaderships in both countries recognize the new imperatives for a strategic partnership amidst the rise of China, their ability to move forward is constrained by the lingering legacies of military isolationism in India and pacifism in Japan. For all the listing of shared interests in Asia and beyond and the new political will to pursue them, there is considerable resistance within the strategic communities of the two countries to embark on a strong bilateral military partnership to balance China's rise. Linked to this is the divergence between an enduring intellectual support to non-alignment in India and the centrality of the US alliance in Japan's national security calculus.

Third, while Tokyo's emphasis is on making the US an integral part of expanding security engagement with India, Delhi continues to privilege bilateralism over trilateralism in its security cooperation with Japan. This apparent tension between the Japanese preference for trilateralism and Indian bias towards bilateralism, however, has been made less germane as the Indian establishment finds it increasingly easier to deal with the US on difficult issues than with Japan. Whether it is the question of non-proliferation or the tradition of maintaining an even-handed policy towards India and Pakistan, Delhi has found Washington ready for innovation while it sees Tokyo as far more conservative. The US has had the gumption to take a strategic perspective on relations with India and to break well-established policies in pursuit of a stronger partnership. The White House has not hesitated in overruling bureaucratic concerns from powerful groups—like the non-proliferation community—within and outside the government. In contrast, the Japanese political leadership faces more entrenched internal resistance to accepting India's nuclear exceptionalism.

Fourth, the rapid accretion of China's comprehensive national power has allowed Beijing to tempt Washington with the virtues of a 'G-2' arrangement through its call for a 'new type of great power relationship'.[71] Despite Japan's close alliance with the US and India's claim to great power status, Beijing is in a position today to present itself as a more credible partner to the US in managing the global order. Despite Washington's denial of any plans for a G-2 and its active support to bilateral and trilateral cooperation with Japan and India, Beijing's leverage in Washington is growing and creating an ambivalence in the US approach to Asia.[72] This in turn sows doubts in the minds of Delhi and Tokyo about the reliability of America as a long-term partner in their emerging regional contestation with Beijing.

Fifth, on regional security cooperation and consultation, both Delhi and Tokyo see the value of their partnership in limiting the consequences of China's non-peaceful rise. Each would like the other to play a larger role in their respective regions in constraining Beijing. Yet neither side is willing to offer unambiguous support to the other in their separate quarrels with China. Equally important is the fact that the ability of one to operate effectively in the neighbourhood of the other is constrained by the tyranny of distance. While this can be overcome to some extent by an effective pooling of their strategic assets, military interoperability, greater political and military coordination, and partnerships with third parties, the two sides are some distance away from arriving there. But the journey has indeed begun.

The pace of progress and the intensity of future strategic cooperation depend to a greater degree on Indian initiative and the energy that Delhi is prepared to expend on transforming the relationship. Although it takes two hands to clap, the circumstances of India–Japan relations suggest the importance of Delhi taking the political leadership and bureaucratic initiative in building a partnership that is at once enduring and consequential. For one, the post-war political evolution of Japan has left its political leadership weak and incapable of engineering big strategic moves on the foreign policy front. Many of India's weaknesses in recent decades have been defined by enduring political coalitions that constrained the power of the prime minister and his authority over the conduct of India's economic and strategic policies. In the middle of the second decade of the twenty-first century, it is entirely fortuitous that Tokyo has one of its strongest leaders with an impressive political mandate and Delhi has the first leader in three decades with a majority in the lower house of Parliament. As it turns out, Abe and Modi also have a personal rapport and are strongly committed to taking the strategic partnership to a higher level.

But it is Modi who must take the initiative. On the economic front, many of the problems in ensuring stronger Japanese participation have been in Delhi. These problems are generic to India's broader economic management rather than directed at any particular country like Japan. Structural reforms that ease doing business in India and facilitate more substantive participation by Japan in the development of the Indian economy need changes in Delhi's economic policies and management. Modi has already promised many of these changes, and any success on the reform front will inevitably translate into greater commercial engagement with Japan. Similarly in the strategic domain, India needs significant reforms in the security sector at home, including on issues relating to defence cooperation and military diplomacy. It is equally important that Modi does not let the relationship with Japan become hostage to one issue, especially civil nuclear cooperation. Although the scale and scope of the India–Japan relationship is wide, Delhi since 2008 has put special emphasis on negotiating the civil nuclear agreement with a Japan that has been reluctant to make rapid adjustments to its nuclear policy in order to move forward with India. Unlike the US, which made many concessions on the nuclear front to get the larger relationship moving forward, Japan has been hesitant to demonstrate similar flexibility. Delhi, then, should focus on seeking forward movement wherever possible in the bilateral security relationship rather than insisting on putting the nuclear issue above all others.

India's general tradition has been to focus on the bilateral when it comes to dealing with major partners either in the neighbourhood or beyond. In dealing with Japan, Delhi will have to learn to prioritize small multilateral or minilateral engagements with third parties to advance the strategic partnership with Tokyo. Central to this is India's ability to leverage its expanding relationship with the United States in deepening ties with Japan. On a number of issues, having the US on India's side makes it easier to get Tokyo to alter its policies towards Delhi. Modi appears to have realized this by agreeing to expand and intensify trilateral engagement with the US and Japan. He has also launched a trilateral dialogue with Japan and Australia. This framework need not necessarily be limited to US allies in the region. Vietnam, Indonesia, the Philippines, and Singapore, for example, are all eager to deepen ties with both Japan and India. Developing multiple overlapping triangular dialogues will give much-needed depth to the India–Japan partnership. Of special importance is strategic economic cooperation with Japan and with third countries, which is critical for India in addressing challenges of transborder connectivity, especially in the context of China's ambitious 'silk road' initiatives. India is in no position to unilaterally match Chinese initiatives to promote connectivity in Asia, but cooperation with Japan could provide the necessary resources and expertise to develop alternative corridors within the subcontinent and between South Asia and Southeast Asia. While India has formally acknowledged the imperative, it needs to take the lead in facilitating early action on this front.

Expanded engagement with Japan is bound to generate some concerns in Beijing, given its unfolding tensions with Tokyo. If the UPA government in Delhi was careful in avoiding cooperation with the US for the fear of provoking China, the Modi government appears to be taking a more proactive approach. It is ready to do more with both Japan and China and has not been afraid of exploring the ways in which Delhi could benefit from their rivalry, as in the competition between Tokyo and Beijing in the development of high-speed railways in India. But in dealing with the tensions between China and Japan, India could well take a leaf out of Nehru's book. At the dawn of independence, Nehru departed from the conventional wisdom in Asia by insisting that both China and Japan have a large role to play in shaping the destiny of the region and that neither should be isolated. That approach in the twenty-first century translates into simultaneous and expansive engagement with both countries. But this engagement need not be symmetric. India stands to benefit from economic cooperation with both China and Japan. But India will have more to do with Japan on the security front while Delhi learns to manage the significant problems in its relationship with Beijing and finds ways to resolve them.

Notes

1. MEA, Government of India, 'Remarks by Prime Minister at the Joint Press Briefing with Prime Minister Shinzo Abe of Japan', 1 September 2014, retrieved from http://mea.gov.in/Speeches-Statements.htm?dtl/23966/ Remarks_by_Prime_Minister_at_the_Joint_Press_Briefing_with_ Prime_Minister_Shinzo_Abe_of_Japan on 11 September 2015.
2. MEA, 'Remarks by Prime Minister at the Joint Press Briefing'.
3. T.R. Sareen, 'India and Japan in Historical Perspective', in R. Panda and Y. Fukazawa (eds), *India and Japan in Search of Global Roles*, New Delhi: Promila & Co., 2007, p.46.
4. C.P. Chen, 'San Francisco Peace Conference, September 8 1951', *World War II Database*, n.d., retrieved from http://ww2db.com/battle_spec. php?battle_id=316 on 11 September 2015.
5. 'Treaty of Peace between Japan and India', 9 June 1952, retrieved from http://www.gwu.edu/~memory/data/treaties/India.pdf on 11 September 2015.
6. Parliament of India, 'Jawaharlal Nehru's Answer to Bishop Richardson's Question in the Parliament', Compensation from Japanese Government, Lok Sabha debate, Meeting no. 796, 12 June 1952.
7. H. Yamaguchi, 'Japanese Perception of India in Modern Times', in H. Yamaguchi and H. Yanagisawa (eds), *Tradition and Modernity: India and Japan towards the Twenty-First Century*, New Delhi: Munshiram Manoharlal, 1997, p. 90.
8. See U. Kei, 'Pal's "Dissentient Judgement" Reconsidered: Some Notes on Post-war Japan's Responses to the Opinion', *Japan Review*, 19, 2007, pp. 215–24.
9. L.S. Spector, 'Silent Spread', *Foreign Policy*, 58, 1985, p. 60.
10. MoFA, *Diplomatic Bluebook for 1974: Review of Recent Developments in Japan's Foreign Relations*, 1975, retrieved from http://www.mofa.go.jp/ policy/other/bluebook/1974/1974-3-1.htm on 11 September 2015.
11. MoFA, 'Comments by the Chief Cabinet Secretary on Measures in Response to the Second Nuclear Testing conducted by India',

14 May 1998, retrieved from http://www.mofa.go.jp/announce/announce/1998/5/0312-09.html on 11 September 2015.

12. MoFA, 'Comments by the Chief Cabinet Secretary'.

13. S. Jaishankar, 'India-Japan Relations after Pokhran II', *Seminar*, 487, March 2000, retrieved from http://www.india-seminar.com/2000/487/487%20jaishankar.htm on 11 September 2015; S. Kumar, 'US Measures against Pakistan's Nuclear Policies, 1990–2001', in M. Brzoska and G.A. Lopez (eds), *Putting Teeth in the Tiger: Improving the Effectiveness of Arms Embargoes*, Bingley: Emerald Press, 2009, p. 85.

14. MEA, 'India-Japan Relations', July 2014, retrieved from http://www.mea.gov.in/Portal/ForeignRelation/Japan_-_July_2014_.pdf on 11 September 2015.

15. R. Chengappa, 'Kiss and Make Up', *India Today*, 28 August 2000.

16. MEA, 'India-Japan Partnership in a New Asian Era: Strategic Orientation of India-Japan Global Partnership', 29 April 2005, retrieved from http://www.mea.gov.in/bilateral-documents.htm?dtl/2498/Joint+State ment+IndiaJapan+Partnership+in+a+New+Asian+Era+Strategic+Orien tation+of+IndiaJapan+Global+Partnership on 11 September 2015.

17. MEA, 'Joint Statement towards India-Japan Strategic and Global Partnership', 15 December 2006, retrieved from http://mea.gov.in/bilateral-documents.htm?dtl/6368/Joint+Statement+Towards+India Japan+Strategic+and+Global+Partnership on 11 September 2015.

18. MoFA, 'Prime Minister Shinzo Abe's Speech at the Indian Parliament, "Confluence of the Two Seas"', 22 August 2007, retrieved from http://www.mofa.go.jp/region/asia-paci/pmv0708/speech-2.html on 11 September 2015.

19. MEA, 'Tokyo Declaration for India-Japan Special Strategic and Global Partnership', 1 September 2014, retrieved from http://mea.gov.in/bilateral-documents.htm?dtl/23965/Tokyo_Declaration_for_India__ Japan_Special_Strategic_and_Global_Partnership on 11 September 2015.

20. MEA, 'Joint Statement, Visit of Mr. Pranab Mukherjee, Minister of Defence to Japan', 25 May 2006, retrieved from http://mea.gov.in/bilateral-documents.htm?dtl/6159/Joint+Statement+Visit+of+Mr+P ranab+Mukherjee+Minister+of+Defence+to+Japan on 11 September 2015.

21. MoFA, 'Joint Declaration on Security Cooperation between Japan and India', 22 October 2008, retrieved from http://www.mofa.go.jp/region/asia-paci/india/pmv0810/joint_d.html on 11 September 2015.

22. 'Japan, India Eye Launch of Security Dialogue Involving Foreign, Defense Chiefs', *Japan Times*, 22 August 2014; MEA, 'Tokyo Declaration'.

23. See G. Khurana, 'Security of Sea Lines: Prospects for India-Japan Cooperation', *Strategic Analysis*, 31(1), 2007, pp. 139–53.

24. Khurana, 'Security of Sea Lines'.

25. MEA, 'Action Plan to Advance Security Cooperation Based on the Joint Declaration on Security Cooperation between Japan and India', 29 December 2009, retrieved from http://www.mea.gov. in/bilateral-documents.htm?dtl/5089/Action_Plan_to_advance_ Security_Cooperation_based_on_the_Joint_Declaration_on_Security_ Cooperation_between_Japan_and_India on 24 September 2015.

26. Indian Navy, 'First Indo-Japan Bilateral Naval Exercise "JIMEX12" Underway', 9 May 2012, retrieved from http://indiannavy.nic.in/press-release/first-indo-japan-bilateral-naval-exercise-jimex12-underway   on 11 September 2015.

27. MEA, 'Tokyo Declaration'.

28. Ibid.

29. Ministry of Defence, Government of India, 'India and Japan Hold Defence Dialogue: Joint Press Release', 30 March 2015, retrieved from http://pib.nic.in/newsite/PrintRelease.aspx?relid=117830 on 11 September 2015.

30. 'Japan, India Agree to Continue Talks on Potential US-2 Exports', *Japan Times*, 31 March 2015.

31. S. Singh, 'Exercise Malabar: Japan Navy to Join India, US in Bay of Bengal', *Indian Express*, 30 June 2015.

32. Madhavan Nair, 'Towards a New Era of Space Development: International Cooperation between India and Japan', Interview with JAXA, 2003, retrieved from http://global.jaxa.jp/article/interview/ vol35/p2_e.html on 11 September 2015.

33. Embassy of India in Japan, 'Institutional Cooperation Agreements', n.d., retrieved from http://www.indembassy-tokyo.gov.in/institu-tional_cooperation.html on 11 September 2015.

34. MoFA, 'Joint Declaration on Security Cooperation'.

35. See J.C. Moltz, *Asia's Space Race: National Motivations, Regional Rivalries, and International Risks*, New York: Columbia University Press, 2013.

36. See R.P. Rajagopalan and A.K. John, 'A New Frontier: Boosting India's Military Presence in Outer Space', Occasional paper no. 50, Observer Research Foundation, New Delhi, January 2014; S.M. Pekkanen and P. Kallender-Umezu, *In Defence of Japan: From the Market to the Military in Space Policy*, Stanford: Stanford University Press, 2010.

37. MoFA, 'Sixth Japan-India Foreign Ministers' Strategic Dialogue', 30 April 2012, retrieved from http://www.mofa.go.jp/region/asia-paci/india/meeting1204_fm.html on 11 September 2015.
38. MoFA, 'The 1st Meeting of Japan-India Cyber Dialogue', 5 November 2012, retrieved from http://www.mofa.go.jp/announce/announce/2012/11/1105_01.html on 11 September 2015.
39. MEA, 'Tokyo Declaration'.
40. Press Information Bureau, Government of India, 'India Japan to Cooperate in Cyber Security', 4 December 2014, retrieved from http://pib.nic.in/newsite/PrintRelease.aspx?relid=112548 on 11 September 2015.
41. See Australian Strategic Policy Institute, *Cyber-maturity in the Asia-Pacific Region*, 2013, pp. 23–5 and 29–31.
42. MoFA, 'Press Conference by the Deputy Press Secretary, Ministry of Foreign Affairs, Japan', 4 November 2010, retrieved from http://www.mofa.go.jp/announce/press/2010/11/1104_01.html on 11 September 2015.
43. MEA, 'India and Japan Sign Two Agreements', 16 November 2012, retrieved from http://mea.gov.in/press-releases.htm?dtl/20816/India+and+Japan+Sign+Two+Agreements on 11 September 2015.
44. Japan signs pact to import rare earths from India. (2012, November 16). *Business Standard.*
45. MEA, 'Factsheet: India and Japan—Partners for Common Development', 1 September 2014, retrieved from http://pib.nic.in/newsite/PrintRelease.aspx?relid=109224 on 11 September 2015.
46. 'Japan, India to Ink Rare Earths Deal', *Business Standard*, 28 August 2014.
47. See J. Wong and L.F. Lye, 'Reviving the Ancient Silk Road: China's New Diplomatic Initiative', *East Asian Policy*, 6(3), 2014, pp. 5–15.
48. See P. Uberoi, 'The BCIM Economic Corridor: A Leap into the Unknown', Working paper, Institute of Chinese Studies, New Delhi, November 2014.
49. MEA, 'Tokyo Declaration'.
50. See G. Samarani, 'Shaping the Future of Asia: Chiang Kai-shek, Nehru and China-India Relations during the Second World War Period', Working paper no. 11, Centre for East and South-East Asian Studies, Lund University, 2005, retrieved from https://lup.lub.lu.se/search/publication/951381 on 11 September 2015.
51. M. Malik, 'Eyeing the Dragon: India's China Debate', Special assessment, Asia-Pacific Center for Security Studies, Honolulu, December 2003.

52. See R. Medcalf, 'India Poll 2013', Lowy and Australia India Institute Survey, 20 May 2013, retrieved from http://www.lowyinstitute.org/files/india_poll_2013_0.pdf on 11 September 2015.

53. 'PM Warns on China's South Asia Foothold', *Indian Express*, 7 September 2010.

54. Manmohan Singh, 'India and China in the New Era', Speech at Central Party School, Beijing, 24 October 2013, retrieved from http://pib.nic.in/newsite/PrintRelease.aspx?relid=100218 on 11 September 2015.

55. 'Modi in Japan: PM Invites Japanese Investment, Announces Special Team to Facilitate Business', *Indian Express*, 1 September 2014; V. Mallet and J. Soble, 'India's Narendra Modi Chides China as He Embraces Japan', *Financial Times*, 2 September 2014.

56. S. Raghavan, 'India-China Relations: Economic Cooperation Helps Mitigate Security Competition', *Economic Times*, 5 February 2015.

57. MoFA, 'Deputy Press Secretary Tomohiko Taniguchi's Answer to a Question on Quadrilateral Military Cooperation', 8 December 2006, retrieved from http://www.mofa.go.jp/announce/press/2006/12/1208.html on 11 September 2015.

58. MEA, 'Tokyo Declaration'.

59. H. Pant, 'Asia's New Geopolitics Takes Shape around India, Japan, and Australia', *Diplomat*, 28 July 2015.

60. M. Pubby, 'India Kicks Off Trilateral Talks with Japan and Australia; Joint Training, Naval Exercises on Agenda', *Economic Times*, 8 June 2015.

61. D. Mitra, 'India, Australia, Japan on Same Page about China', *New Indian Express*, 10 June 2015.

62. Mitra, 'India, Australia, Japan on Same Page'; E. Roche, 'Japan Keen on Regular Participation in US-India Malabar Exercises', *Mint*, 10 June 2015.

63. S. Robinson, 'A Gunboat Message to China', *Time*, 6 September 2007.

64. MEA, 'Tokyo Declaration'.

65. Ibid.

66. 'Difficulties in Operationalising N-Deal: Manmohan Tells Bush', *Business Standard*, 16 October 2007.

67. See, for example, Pew Research Centre, 'Indians Reflect on Their Country & the World', March 2014, retrieved from http://www.pew-global.org/files/2014/03/Pew_Research_Center_Global_Attitudes_Project_India_Full_Release_FINAL_March_31_2014.pdf on 11 September 2015.

68. MEA, 'U.S.-India Joint Strategic Vision for the Asia Pacific and the Indian Ocean Region', 25 January 2015, retrieved from http://www.

mea.gov.in/bilateral-documents.htm?dtl/24728/USIndia_Joint_
Strategic_Vision_for_the_AsiaPacific_and_Indian_Ocean_Region on
11 September 2015.

69. MEA, 'Joint Statement during the Visit of President of USA to India:
Shared Effort; Progress for All', 25 January 2015, retrieved from http://
mea.gov.in/bilateral-documents.htm?dtl/24726/Joint_Statement_dur-
ing_the_visit_of_President_of_USA_to_India_Shared_Effort_
Progress_for_All on 11 September 2015.

70. MEA, 'Tokyo Declaration'.

71. Y. Hongjun, 'China and the United States: Building New Relations
between Major Powers', China Institute of International Studies,
Beijing, 25 November 2013, retrieved from http://www.ciis.org.cn/
english/2013-11/25/content_6486747.htm on 11 September 2015;
C. Li and L. Xu, 'Chinese Enthusiasm and American Cynicism: The
"New Type of Great Power Relations"', China-US Focus, 25 November
2013, retrieved from http://www.chinausfocus.com/foreign-policy/
chinese-enthusiasm-and-american-cynicism-over-the-new-type-of-
great-power-relations/ on 11 September 2015.

72. See L. Mingjiang and K. Kemburi (eds), *New Dynamics in U.S.-China
Relations*, New York: Routledge, 2015.

Part IV

GLOBAL GOVERNANCE

7

Japan–India Relations from the Perspectives of Global Governance and International Institutions

Shinichi Kitaoka and Naoko Kumagai

This chapter examines Japan's cooperation with India from the perspectives of Japan's national interests, bilateral cooperation, and regional and global governance. We focus on four areas of potential cooperation. First, Japan and India should see beyond the existing governance framework of the Non-Proliferation Treaty (NPT) and International Atomic Energy Agency (IAEA) to prevent nuclear terrorism. Second, in the United Nations Security Council (UNSC), Japan and India can propose the option of establishing semi-permanent seats in order to create a more democratic and effective body that is capable of more substantial deliberation. Third, Japan and India can cooperate for freer trade in regional arenas and cooperate bilaterally on India's food security, which would eventually lead to further trade liberalization in the sensitive issue area of agriculture. Finally, Japan and India should seek complementarity of the new China-led financial institutions with existing institutions such as the International Monetary Fund (IMF) and the World Bank.

This chapter explores whether individual efforts in pursuit of the national interests of Japan and India, respectively, might lead to mutual interests or even serve global governance, thus enhancing the common good of the world. Our findings demonstrate the presence of significant differences in national interests between Japan and India, particularly in the short term, as well as the possibilities of both bilateral and multilateral cooperation in light of Japan's continuous and India's growing presence in the world economy, their aspirations to be leaders in the changing global governance framework, their status as Asian democracies embracing the common values of the rule of law and tolerance, and the geopolitical challenge from the rise of China. Cooperation could be bilateral, regional, multilateral, or transnational in a multi-layered way, such that partnership is mutually enhancing and complementary, and often with the involvement of other major powers such as the US and China. In assessing the success or failure of cooperation, we take a look at not only the achievement of any stated policies but also the institutional side effects.

Nuclear Non-proliferation and International Peace and Security

Japan, as the only country to have been the victim of atomic bombs, has had national interests in the facilitation of nuclear disarmament, non-proliferation, and nuclear security agreements. However, the revival of the Russian–American rivalry, particularly over Ukraine; delays in disarmament; the rise of new nuclear powers such as North Korea, Pakistan, and India outside of the framework of the Treaty on the Non-Proliferation of Nuclear Weapons (NPT); and ongoing terror threats, particularly since the 9/11 terrorist attacks, all pose significant challenges to the security of Japan.

Japan has been one of the most ardent actors in the movement for nuclear disarmament and non-proliferation. It has participated in and promoted the functions of the International Atomic Energy Agency (IAEA) since 1957 and the NPT since 1970. In 1967, Japan created its 'three non-nuclear principles', which stated that the country would not manufacture, possess, or introduce nuclear weapons into its territory.[1] Behind Japan's commitment to the NPT has been a deep-seated political dilemma. Needless to say, the tragedies of Hiroshima and Nagasaki in 1945 had a decisive impact in creating a strong anti-nuclear sentiment in Japan. However, the country was not in a position to demand that the US remove its nuclear weapons because post-war Japan, surrounded by heavily militarized countries, owed its security to the US military, including the extended deterrence of the American nuclear umbrella.

Japan's position toward the US's nuclear weapons has always been ambiguous. When the US–Japan security treaty was revised in 1960, it was agreed that the US had to engage in prior consultations with Japan regarding facilities and areas and the status of US armed forces.[2] However, there was a secret pact between Japan and the US to allow the transit of vessels loaded with nuclear weapons.[3] In 1969, President Richard Nixon and Prime Minister Eisaku Sato agreed to return administrative rights over Okinawa to Japan without nuclear weapons, but there was again a secret pact (whose existence was disclosed in the 2000s) under which the US could request that Japan reintroduce nuclear weapons in Okinawa in case of an emergency.[4]

In spite of such facts, it is fair to say that Japan showed great restraint in not seeking nuclear weapons. Public opinion in Japan was fully aware of the dilemma—the continuing contradictory governmental policies of the American nuclear umbrella on the one hand and the three non-nuclear principles on the other—to the extent that it was very critical of Sato's Nobel Peace Prize in 1974. Also, in light of the international context in East Asia, the fact that France and China developed nuclear weapons—in 1960 and in 1964 respectively, before the NPT came into force in 1970—and the attempts by many other countries to develop their own nuclear weapons, Japan's effort not to develop or possess nuclear weapons was quite serious. In practice, Japan has followed the spirit of the NPT by developing nuclear energy technology for peaceful use without developing nuclear weapons. In the face of North Korea's nuclear tests between 2006 and 2013, which posed a more serious threat to Japan than India's test in 1974 and India's and Pakistan's tests in 1998 due to the unpredictability of the North Korean regime and the country's geographical proximity to Japan, it has been the American nuclear umbrella that has effectively protected Japan from potential nuclear threats. Consequently, no serious argument for the possession of nuclear weapons has arisen in Japan.

A major problem for the non-proliferation movement comes from the double standard operating between the recognized nuclear possessors and non-nuclear powers, which is embedded in the NPT. The treaty obliges non-nuclear powers not to produce, develop, or possess nuclear weapons, while it calls on the five nuclear possessors—China, France, Russia, the United Kingdom, and the United States—to disarm and eventually abolish their nuclear weapons. Non-nuclear powers complain about the de facto legalization of these five countries' nuclear arsenals. In practice, since 2000, at least two NPT review conferences (in 2005 and in 2015) have failed to reach consensus, mainly over issues of disarmament. Furthermore, nuclear disarmament has been making little progress through the Conference on Disarmament, while regulations and restrictions on nuclear proliferation are becoming stronger through the IAEA safeguards system. India, while supporting nuclear abolition in the long term, has consistently protested the NPT by opposing the United Nations General Assembly (UNGA) annual resolutions calling for India's accession to the NPT as a non-nuclear-weapons state.

In order to achieve both their nuclear interests, Japan and India should jointly provide moral support to any initiative for total nuclear disarmament, such as the call for global nuclear zero by the Four Wise Men from the United States in 2008, another call from Russia in 2010,[5] and President Barack Obama's stated policy of nuclear abolition as first articulated in Prague in 2009 and subsequently in Berlin in June 2013. The potential for such efforts to eventually enhance the accountability of the US can be seen in Washington's participation in the most recent Non-Proliferation and Disarmament Initiative meeting in 2014 and in Obama's creation of the Nuclear Security Summit, which acted as the institutionalization of the commitments made in his 2009 speech. Also, Japan and India can urge the new framing of the issue of nuclear weapons, which emphasizes their inhumane nature. In practice, states impatient with the lack of progress towards disarmament called for the Conference on the Humanitarian Impact of Nuclear Weapons, first held in Norway in March 2013 in response to the 2010 NPT review conference's final document, which expressed concern about this issue.[6] The 2013 conference continues to attract many more state participants and NGOs, and Japan has also continued to address the importance of the humanitarian impact of nuclear weapons.[7] Japan, with its tradition of pacifism based on the experiences of Hiroshima and Nagasaki, can cooperate with India and its tradition of non-violence to strengthen this new framework for promoting future nuclear disarmament. The experience of landmine disarmament success through discourse change, from the framework of military utility to that of humanitarianism, might help in this regard.[8]

Power-based nuclear disarmament negotiations among the nuclear powers are unrealistic, though theoretically speaking gradual disarmament based on the balance of power could be started once the nuclear arsenals of Russia and the United States are reduced from their current size of 7,000–8,000 warheads to a level closer to 300. The success of the 2001 Strategic Arms Reduction Treaty (START) between Russia and the United States is largely attributed to the two powers' attention to cost–benefit calculations. Now with the renewal of rivalry between the United States and Russia, further disarmament efforts might not be as easy. In the recent and ongoing case of the crisis in Ukraine since 2014, Russian President Vladimir Putin mentioned that he was ready for a nuclear alert if necessary,[9] even though this is considered a diplomatic ruse that did not involve the serious intention to use such weapons.

Despite having different understandings of non-proliferation, Japan and India can overcome the difference by understanding the defensive nature of India's nuclear possession and the importance of efforts toward counter–nuclear terrorism, the real and most urgent threat in the contemporary world. There might not be a short-term solution to the root cause of India's possession of nuclear weapons, which is its perceived threat from Pakistan and China. Although India's relationship with China has improved over time, tensions with Pakistan remain high. Confidence building between Delhi and Islamabad could be promoted through practical and technical cooperation, particularly on counter-terrorism measures, but India is deeply sceptical because of Pakistan's involvement in a series of terrorist activities in India in the 2000s.[10] Nonetheless, India's defensive nuclear posture has been persistent, even institutionalized in the doctrine of 'no first use' by former Bharatiya Janata Party (BJP) Prime Minister Atal Bihari Vajpayee in 1998, and maintained by Prime Minister Narendra Modi, who went so far as to say that no first use is a reflection of the nation's cultural inheritance.[11] India's somewhat contradictory endorsement of the illegalization of the use of nuclear weapons combined with its adamant persistence in retaining the right to conduct nuclear tests also testifies to the defensive nature of India's nuclear possession. Similarly, India has been against the Comprehensive Nuclear-Test-Ban Treaty (CTBT), but has in place a voluntary moratorium on nuclear tests.

As for counter-nuclear terrorism, frameworks outside of the NPT and CTBT can serve the pragmatic function of addressing nuclear threats particularly from non-state actors. The CTBT's overly strict condition for its entry into force—requiring the ratification of 44 states with nuclear technology, including the recalcitrant states of Israel and Pakistan—leaves it legally ineffective (not to mention that neither China nor the US has ratified the treaty). Traditional military management at the state level through measures such as deterrence and non-proliferation cannot fully guarantee security from nuclear terrorist threats. Counter-nuclear terrorism measures require cooperation from non-NPT nuclear possessors India and Pakistan, particularly in countering illicit nuclear trade. For instance, India has been targeted as a source or route of would-be proliferators' supplies.[12] This means that India could be a target of non-state actors as well as of states with nuclear ambition. Illicit nuclear trade countermeasures should cover the management, control, and handling of fissile materials; the transparency of these processes; the development of a complete registry of fissile materials usable for weapons; enhanced security response capabilities; and radiation detection at airports, seaports, and border crossings. Furthermore, legislative and executive efforts towards these actions require comprehensive governance and cooperation from diverse actors such as scientists, border guard services, marine policing units, nuclear engineers, and commercial transportation services.

As a universal effort, United Nations Security Council (UNSC) Resolution 1540 obliges states to refrain from supporting non-state actors in developing, acquiring, manufacturing, transporting, and transferring nuclear weapons as well as chemical and biological weapons and their delivery systems.[13] This effort could be facilitated more effectively through the gradual strengthening of existing export control regimes by states with advanced nuclear technologies, particularly including India. Existent regimes—such as the Nuclear Suppliers Group (NSG), which regulates the transfer of fissile materials for peaceful purposes, the Missile Technology Control Regime (MTCR), and the Wassenaar Arrangement to promote transparency and responsibility of state actors in transfers of dual-use goods and technologies—are composed mainly of developed democratic states.

In line with this argument, Japan can emphasize what makes India unique among the non-NPT nuclear powers, that is, its high spirit of responsibility for nuclear safety and security. India's policy of no first use has not been adopted by Pakistan. India participated in the 2005 Amendment to the Convention on the Physical Protection of Nuclear Material, the IAEA Amended Protocol, and the 2005 International Convention on the Suppression of Acts of Nuclear Terrorism, which neither Pakistan nor North Korea has joined. These actions testify to India's focus on nuclear safety and security, and thus on counter–nuclear terrorism.

On a bilateral basis, Japan can move toward a nuclear agreement with India on the export of nuclear technology by imposing rigorous regulations for nuclear safety and security. Japan's civil nuclear agreement with India, which is currently under negotiation, would be the first case of such a deal between Japan and any non-NPT country. It would symbolize Japan's trust in India's commitment to the peaceful use of nuclear technology and counter-nuclear terrorism, and would also serve the growth of the Japanese economy. The agreement would also benefit India, which is planning a 10-fold increase in its nuclear power generation by 2032 (in order to maintain continuous economic growth),[14] which would require a stable supply of fissile materials.

A bilateral nuclear agreement between Japan and India could be a good complement to the Convention for the Suppression of Acts of Nuclear Terrorism and the Global Initiative to Combat Nuclear Terrorism, which aim to improve national and international capacities for prevention, detection, and response to a nuclear terrorist act. Confidence in India would set a realistic precedent of de facto enhancement of nuclear security regardless of the cleavage between NPT and non-NPT countries.

For the peaceful and safe use of nuclear power, Japan can contribute its lessons learned from the Fukushima nuclear accident in March 2011. The Japanese government expressed its determination to cooperate with the international community for the decommissioning of the Fukushima power plant and to disseminate any relevant information in a transparent manner.[15]

In conclusion, Japan and India are sharply divided in their respective stances toward the NPT. Japan is a strong supporter of the non-proliferation principle, while India is an adamant opponent of it. Still, both share the ultimate goal of nuclear abolition in the long term. In view of both countries' pragmatism, seen in their contradictory policy mixtures of realism and idealism, they can share the current common threat perception of nuclear terrorism and cooperate to address the problem through efforts toward nuclear security and safety in both bilateral and multilateral arenas beyond the existing framework of non-proliferation. On a bilateral basis, Japan could extend nuclear power cooperation with India based on the lessons of Fukushima. On a multilateral basis, they could fully utilize the IAEA, the CTBT, and any other arenas of nuclear control and management that India could join.

The UN: Security Council and General Assembly Reform

As soon as Japan concluded the San Francisco Peace Treaty in 1951, it started its bid for membership in the UN. Tokyo was blocked by Moscow's veto twice, but was eventually accepted in December 1956. When Japan published its first Diplomatic Bluebook in 1957, 'diplomacy centred on the UN' was given the highest priority together with 'cooperation with the Free World' and 'diplomacy as an Asian country'.[16] In reality, Japan has centred its foreign policy on the US–Japan alliance for decades, but the alliance itself is premised on promoting the UN's diverse functions for the maintenance of international peace and security.[17]

Japan has long been the second largest donor to the UN's regular and peacekeeping operations (PKO) budgets (10.83 per cent of the UN peacekeeping budget as of March 2014) and has served as a non-permanent member of the UNSC 10 times, the highest number along with Brazil.[18] Japan is expected to be elected an 11th time in

October 2015 as a non-permanent member for 2016 and 2017. In 2014, in the regional group of Asia, a consensus was reached that the one non-permanent seat to be renewed for the next term would go to Japan. Between 1992 and February 2015, Japan participated in 13 United Nations Peacekeeping Operations (UNPKOs), contributing to the stabilization of war-torn societies in many parts of the world. Although Japan's participation in UNPKOs started only in 1992, much later than India, Japan has tried significantly to enhance its contribution, particularly in terms of the range of activities of the Japan Self-Defense Forces (JSDF). These efforts have been constrained in many ways because of Article 9 of the Japanese constitution.[19] Nonetheless, the Japanese Diet recently passed the so-called security bills to expand the scope of the JSDF's contribution to UNPKOs to include protection of civilians, units, and personnel under attack.

As a former permanent member of the League of Nations Council, the Ministry of Foreign Affairs (MoFA) of Japan began to express its desire to be a permanent member of the UNSC in the latter half of the 1960s, when Japan's economic power surpassed that of three permanent members of the UNSC: the Republic of China, the United Kingdom, and France. Tokyo's effort to become a permanent member began in earnest with Japan's rapidly growing personnel and financial contribution to UNPKOs starting in 1992 after the end of the Cold War. While Japan is currently the second largest financial contributor to PKOs, this budget is decided at the UNSC in the absence of Japan.

The most serious effort to reform the UNSC took place in 2004–5 when the High-Level Panel (HLP) on Threats, Challenges and Change proposed two possible plans to reform the council. Model A proposed an increase of six permanent seats without veto and three non-permanent seats, while Model B proposed an increase of eight semi-permanent seats (for four-year re-electable terms) and one ordinary non-permanent seat.[20] In both models, non-permanent and semi-permanent seats would be divided among the four regional categories of Africa, Asia Pacific, Europe, and the Americas.

Japan, India, Germany, and Brazil—also known as the G-4—supported an increase of both permanent and non-permanent seats and tabled a draft resolution based on Model A of the HLP report in May 2005. On the other hand, Pakistan, Italy, South Korea, Argentina, Mexico, and others created a group called Uniting for Consensus

(UFC) and prepared a draft resolution based on Model B of the HLP report. It was estimated that the G-4 had the support of more than 100 out of 191 member countries.[21] However, in order to adopt a resolution to amend the composition of the UNSC, the support of more than two-thirds of the member countries—then 128 votes—was needed. The G-4 tried to obtain the support of African countries in order to reach this number, but failed to do so. This failure marked the end of the 2005 UNSC reform movement.[22]

There were three reasons why the G-4 failed. First, the US supported Japan and India but was reluctant to expand the total number of UNSC members. Washington stressed that too great an expansion of the UNSC would make it less effective.[23] Second, China strongly opposed Japan's aspiration. At the time, Sino-Japanese relations were worsening as a result of Prime Minister Junichiro Koizumi's visit to the controversial Yasukuni Shrine in August 2005.[24] Third, though they were willing to receive two permanent seats, African countries failed to reach an agreement as to who would occupy them. No particular African countries were nominated as strong potential candidates.

Ten years later, the difficulties remain the same. China has strengthened its opposition to Japan's candidacy, African countries are as undecided as before, and, to make the situation worse, Russia is now more assertive and moving against the UN principles of territorial integrity, the rule of law, and peaceful settlement of conflicts, as seen in its annexation of Crimea in March 2014 and the ongoing tension with Ukraine. The power and influence of the US have become relatively weaker and Japan's relative economic power has waned considerably, though it is still the second biggest donor to the UN.[25] It is now widely recognized that the UNSC is not serving its purpose. It could not take effective action in the crises in Georgia, Ukraine, and Syria, or against the Islamic State. The US attitude used to be 'if it ain't broke, don't fix it',[26] but the institution is now broken.

One positive change with regard to UNSC reform might be the policy of the US, which is becoming less unilateral and hegemonic and more flexible and cooperative. Over the past few years, the US has reversed its policy of isolating Myanmar and Cuba, which had been the cause of anti-US sentiments among some countries at the UN. The recent nuclear deal between Iran and the P5+1 (the permanent UNSC members and Germany) has also been a sign that greater international cooperation could be possible. The overall shift from unilateralism toward multilateralism is a positive sign for UNSC reform.

It is time to seriously consider the possibility of an intermediate UNSC reform plan, starting with the idea of Model B for a complete reform plan. If the plan were to be proposed by the G-4 with cooperation from at least some of the UFC countries, there is a possibility of success. If it is realized, Japan and India will certainly occupy the two semi-permanent seats from Asia for the first term. Then, Japan could be elected for the second term, or possibly be replaced by South Korea. In any case, the two semi-permanent seats for Asia would be occupied mainly by Japan and India and occasionally by South Korea, Indonesia, and Pakistan. Middle-income and developing countries are unlikely to have the required diplomatic and financial resources to stand for re-election for a semi-permanent seat every four years. Therefore, there would be a two-thirds or half permanent seat without veto power for Japan and India. Considering the increasing difficulty and competitiveness involved in being elected as a non-permanent member of the UNSC (partly due to the absence of strict adherence to the rotation system within each region),[27] the classification of semi-permanent and non-permanent seats is a wise choice to avoid wasting energy on election campaigning.[28] Also, in practice, to perform effectively as a semi-permanent member for four years at the UNSC would require an adequate diplomatic network and sources of information. Eligible countries with such capabilities might be G-4 or UFC members. Furthermore, it is reasonable that a resolution on UNSC reform should trigger a review 10 or 12 years later so that some countries that have demonstrated excellent performance as semi-permanent members might have a chance to become permanent members.

Even if reform is possible, it would be unrealistic to insist on new permanent or semi-permanent members receiving veto power. In the 2005 G-4 resolution, the veto was designed to be given to new permanent members 15 years later, which means substantially that the veto was given up, though it was not totally denied.[29] This time, it would be impossible to immediately give a veto to any new member. Rather, there should be an effort to limit the use of the veto. The first step (that failed in May 2012) was a resolution proposed by the Small

Five Group (S5) of Costa Rica, Jordan, Liechtenstein, Singapore, and Switzerland demanding that the P5 explain their reasons if they cast a veto.[30] Japan and India should push this cause again. There are other ideas such as half a veto (in which two states share one veto), the creation of a vote of 'no' without veto for the P5, or the prohibition of a veto in the case of a humanitarian crisis.[31]

Another way to confine the prerogative of the P5 is to create a new power dynamic in the UNGA. First, the process of selecting the Secretary-General could be modified. According to Article 97 of the UN Charter, the UNGA is to appoint the Secretary-General upon the recommendation of the UNSC. However, in practice, the UNSC usually nominates only one candidate (with permanent members having veto power over this process). The UNGA is virtually forced to accept this choice. Therefore, a UNGA resolution could be passed requiring the UNSC to nominate more than one candidate for Secretary-General so that the UNGA can choose from multiple candidates.[32] Michael Doyle has recently proposed that the UNSC nominate at least three candidates.[33] This would be a change from the long-held position of the UNGA that it was 'desirable for the Security Council to proffer one candidate only for the consideration of the General Assembly, and for debate on the nomination in the General Assembly to be avoided'.[34]

Second, in addition to reforming the UNSC, Japan and India should cooperate to strengthen the League of Democracies at the UN. The most important line of cleavage at the UN has been between advanced countries and underdeveloped countries, with the latter group being dominated by the G-77 and China. This division used to be roughly equivalent to the line between democratic and non-democratic countries, with only a few exceptions like India. This is not the case any more. China, for example, now has the second largest economy in the world, but remains undemocratic. On the other hand, there are many countries that are not as rich as China but are governed more democratically. Strengthening the League of Democracies may weaken the power of the G-77 and China, apply pressure on Russia and China to behave more democratically (through focused criticisms of their undemocratic polities and policies), and contribute to the democratization of the UN as a whole. India, with its leading status and role in the G-77, might not be willing to split the group along the democratic/non-democratic line. However, we expect India to be a leader of the world beyond its leadership of the G-77.

Realizing meaningful reform of the UNSC is crucial, but the effort and cooperation towards reform is important in itself. During the G-4 process in 2004–5, there was a remarkable growth of mutual trust and effective cooperation not only among G-4 countries but also among co-sponsoring countries such as France in other areas besides UNSC reform. As a whole, an effort toward radical reform of the UNSC would be a great contribution to the renewed effectiveness of the UN.

International Trade: WTO and Regional Arrangements

Due to Japan's scarcity of natural resources, international trade has been crucial to the survival and growth of the economy. The country mostly imports natural resources and exports manufactured goods such as automobiles and electronics. Although Japan has benefited from the General Agreement on Tariffs and Trade's (GATT's) principles of non-discrimination and most favoured nations, the agreement could not always guarantee a multilateral free-trade framework for Japan. Particularly since the 1970s, Japan has been under US pressure to accept trade policies to further lower tariff levels on certain agricultural products and on automobiles.[35] However, the establishment of the World Trade Organization (WTO) in 1995 with dispute settlement mechanisms has guaranteed fairer trade among states, and the organization's regulations pertaining to investment, services, and the protection of intellectual property have benefited Japan. The shift of Japan's exports to more competitive and fast-growing technology-oriented products has enhanced the importance of the protection of intellectual property, guidelines for which are contained in the WTO.

In parallel with the WTO, Japan also utilizes a regional free trade framework. Particularly since 2013, Japan has participated in talks on the Trans-Pacific Partnership (TPP), an economic agreement under negotiation between 12 countries in the Asia Pacific region.[36] While the automobile industry has been a strong proponent of trade liberalization, the agricultural industry has advocated for protectionist policies. The TPP has at least two merits for Japan. First, from the political and strategic points of view, the TPP would guarantee stable efforts towards freer trade in the Asia Pacific region under the hegemony of the United States, which also guarantees US engagement in order to reduce geopolitical insecurity in the region. Japan can incorporate the growth of vibrant economies in the Asia Pacific region through further trade liberalization under the TPP. The TPP is more ambitious than the WTO since it seeks not only to eliminate trade barriers but also to standardize production and business rules across borders, thus serving as a pioneer for further, freer multilateral trade in the future. Second, the TPP could apply the necessary *gaiatsu* (external pressure) on the protectionist sectors of Japan's economy, particularly the agricultural sector. Free trade, whether multilateral or regional, has the potential to further innovation and growth in the Japanese agricultural sector. Though Japan has been traditionally known for agricultural protectionism, with a tariff of 778 per cent on rice,[37] this policy is unlikely to last. The political initiative towards liberalization of the agricultural sector has just started, as seen in Prime Minister Shinzo Abe's initiative to promote a more private-sector-oriented competitive agricultural industry, encourage large-scale farming for efficient production, and reduce trade regulations on agricultural imports.[38] A representative case is the February 2015 decision to dissolve the Japan Agricultural Cooperatives,[39] a nationwide organization of farm cooperatives controlling the distribution and pricing of staple foods.

The idea behind current reforms is not only that the protectionist agricultural sector has slowed down the growth of agricultural and other business,[40] but also that Japan can actually benefit from free trade in agriculture. It is important to reduce protectionism and rationalize the production system to facilitate a more effective market-oriented agricultural system. It is, however, difficult to reduce protectionism due to the vested interests of the majority of farming families, who tend to be involved in side businesses as well. Many protected rice farmers are small-sized farming families with other businesses, and they have strong voting power. Such farmers have deep vested interests in protection in terms of relatively high and stable rice prices and subsidies (direct payments of the difference between the standard cost of rice production and the sales price of rice under

Japan's Individual-Household Income Compensation Programme). Therefore, it is natural for them not to agree with the rationalization of rice agriculture. With a large number of small-scale rice farmers running side businesses,[41] it is difficult to find large-scale, full-time rice farmers with the required area of farm land to increase the overall amount of rice cultivation. Small-scale farmers constitute a strong voice against agricultural reform, to the extent that they contributed to the electoral defeat of the Liberal Democratic Party (LDP), which had suggested a subsidy plan to support only relatively large-scale farmers, in the 2009 general election.

External pressure or *gaiatsu* from foreign countries for trade liberalization is thus the best way to counter the political weight of small- and medium-sized farmers and thereby facilitate the rationalization of Japanese rice agriculture. The TPP could be a useful source of external pressure against the wall of domestic vested interests in favour of protectionism in Japan. The reduction of rice agriculture's protectionism is even more important since it has negative effects in other issue areas as well, particularly automobiles, whose manufacturers face difficulties in enjoying freer trade in their foreign markets due to Japan's protectionist agricultural policy.

There are arguments that the liberalization of Japanese agriculture will prevent it from competing against the low agricultural prices of developing countries in world markets, and that this might harm Japan's food security. However, these arguments lack merit for a number of reasons. First, the liberalization of beef and oranges in 1988 did not bring about the bankruptcy of beef and orange farmers in Japan. Instead, these farmers transformed their products into high-value-added brands. Second, Japan can be competitive in high-value-added agricultural products in foreign markets, particularly in emerging Asian economies such as China, Indonesia, and Thailand as their living standards rise. Finally, the growing business of agricultural technology transfer and foreign investment can enable the local production of high-quality Japanese food. In this context, the WTO's protection of intellectual property rights and regulation of service trade and investment would further benefit Japan's agricultural sector.

The flawed argument also prevails that freer agricultural trade puts the food security of Japan, whose total food self-sufficiency ratio on a calorie supply basis is almost 39 per cent,[42] at risk. However, it is not trade protectionism but rather a stable supply that can enhance food security. A stable supply depends on higher efficiency in agricultural production and freer food trade. Constant agricultural imports up to a certain level would allow for room to reduce the vulnerability of Japan's food security, particularly in case of an unexpected sharp decline in domestic food production due to a natural or man-made disaster. Furthermore, a combination of the import of cheaper rice and the export of high-quality rice abroad would guarantee both food security and profit.[43] Therefore, the approaching agreement at the TPP is an important moment of good *gaiatsu* for Japan.

Also, the TPP is an ideal arena for Japan strategically due to the country's relatively more influential position within it than at the WTO, thus allowing Japan to shape the former's rules to its advantage. Japan should also compete for initiative and influence in the WTO, not only with major powers such as the US and the EU, but also with the emerging economies of China and India. But in the TPP, Japan enjoys a strong position second only to the US.

The TPP has the further merit of influencing China to move towards freer trade. A solidly constructed TPP would guarantee the further enhancement of free trade under the Free Trade Area of the Asia Pacific (FTAAP), which includes China and TPP members. This step is crucial because the presence of China, which has the second largest economy in the world, might slow down the level of liberalization in the region if Beijing were not compelled to meet TPP standards. As things stand, China still imposes heavy restrictive regulations on foreign investment and business practices and has been reluctant to stringently protect intellectual property rights. China's further trade liberalization also matters for both Japan and India since China is the biggest trading partner of both countries.[44]

In terms of Japan–India cooperation in freer trade, multilateral cooperation in a blanket manner might not be so effective, particularly in view of the increasing tension between developed and developing states in the WTO. Japan and India, due to their different stages of economic development and social conditions, have different interests in free trade. While Japan pursues further liberalization of industrial goods and protection of the environment and intellectual property in free trade, India prefers a slower pace of free trade in terms of tariff reduction in limited types of commodities.

Still, Japan and India can and should identify their common interests and mutual complementarities. First, both have interests in the promotion of free trade in the long run, albeit at different paces of liberalization. India has surely benefited from free trade, particularly in light of its long economic stagnation and de facto failure due to Delhi's import substitution policy, and the slow pace of economic liberalization in the 1980s. After India switched to a freer economy in the early 1990s, its economic growth has been significant.[45] Also, from the late 1950s, the relative weight of Japan's economic relations shifted from India to Southeast Asia due to Japan's policies of war reparation toward Southeast Asian countries, which included economic assistance agreements, and due to India's non-alignment and socialist policies particularly in the 1960s and 1970s.[46]

Second, Japan can enjoy complementarity in trade with India.[47] Along with financial and economic support as promised by Prime Minister Abe in his bilateral summit with Prime Minister Modi in September 2014,[48] Japan's technology transfers to India will facilitate India's continuous economic development. This would help India avoid the middle-income trap, whereby a hitherto rapidly growing economy becomes stuck after reaching a certain income level and fails to rise up to the ranks of high-income countries.[49] In turn, expanded trade with India, with its population of 1.2 billion and rich mineral resources, particularly iron ore, will provide Japan and its declining population with natural resources and a potentially huge market. On a bilateral basis, Japan and India have started institutionalized cooperation with the entry into force of the Japan–India Comprehensive Economic Partnership Agreement (CEPA) in 2011. However, the effect of this very ambitious agreement remains to be seen. As of July 2015, the bilateral economic relationship, albeit growing overall, remains very small in comparison with each state's economic relations with other states, particularly China. For example, the total amount of bilateral trade between Japan and India during the 2014 fiscal year was ¥1.62 trillion, while that between Japan and China was ¥32.58 trillion.[50]

Still, a longer-term view is necessary. Both India and Japan share the common value of democracy, which creates mutual confidence, thus leaving room for in-depth societal-level cooperation. Following the successful model of Suzuki, Japanese companies have undertaken further business and market exploration in India, and there has grown a good foundation in Japan and India for human development cooperation for Indian managers, elites, and engineers. A case in point is the Visionary Leaders for Manufacturing (VLFM) project between August 2007 and March 2013, which trained almost 900 management leaders. This project was incorporated as part of India's growth strategy. Subsequently, the Champions for Societal Manufacturing (CSM) project has been training those who can manage the VLFM programme with a view to creating an eco-friendly production system. Both the VLFM and CSM involve cooperation between governments, academia, and businesses in both countries.[51] This demonstrates that the India–Japan relationship is not just a competition between a developing and developed country. The two countries can be characterized as complementary partners based on their firmly embedded values of democracy. In an even longer perspective, Japan–India trade cooperation will contribute to the continuous growth of world trade.

Japan also has the advantage in addressing the root cause of India's resistance to freer food trade, which is the issue of food security for the poor. Japan can particularly assist India's efforts in poverty reduction. In this regard, Japan's official development assistance (ODA) to India, particularly the Grant Aid for Grassroots Human Security since 1989,[52] should also strengthen the framework of human security in India, which had a 29.5 per cent poverty rate in 2014.[53]

Multilateral attempts at the WTO have so far been unsuccessful in addressing the food security problem in India. India's food security issue touches upon the WTO's growing dilemma regarding the relationship between developing and developed countries. India's food security problems are in the areas of food accessibility, sufficiency and consistency of food supply, and ensuring sufficient financial resources for households to obtain appropriate foods for a nutritious diet.[54] Disputes over the balance between free trade and food security, particularly food accessibility, are prevalent in many developing countries, causing a sharp divide among countries as already seen in the unsuccessful Doha round of WTO negotiations. India's abrupt withdrawal of its support for the WTO's hard-won Trade Facilitation Agreement in October 2014 (which would have simplified global customs procedures) as a protest against the slow movement of discussions on public stockholding for food security purposes in developing countries represents the irritation of developing countries at the unfair treatment of food security in favour of trade facilitation. Although the India–US agreement in November 2014 resolved the impasse, a permanent solution for the issue of public stockholding for food security purposes remains a subject for the WTO to deal with.

Aside from the particular issue of food security, the proposed Regional Comprehensive Economic Partnership (RCEP) might be a good arena in which to enhance India's free trade. The RCEP, launched in 2012, has great economic potential. Combined with the Association of Southeast Asian Nations' (ASEAN's) free trade agreements with Japan, China, South Korea, India, Australia, and New Zealand, the RCEP includes 3.4 billion people, 29.7 per cent of global gross domestic product (nominal), and 27.4 per cent of world merchandise trade.[55] The RCEP would provide a good opportunity for India to enhance its economic growth through integration in the Asia Pacific's regional production networks. In comparison with the TPP, which addresses state-owned enterprises, labour, environmental issues, intellectual property rights, government procurement, rules of origin, and services, the RCEP's liberalization agenda is moderate, though it will also touch upon services, investment, and intellectual property.[56] Thus, the RCEP is an ideal arena for India, with the latter's long history of an inward-looking economic policy of import substitution and relatively short history of economic cooperation with the Asia Pacific region, in that the RCEP is not as ambitious as the TPP in trade liberalization in terms of coverage and standards, but allows India—not a member of the Asia-Pacific Economic Cooperation (APEC) forum or of the TPP—to strengthen economic ties with countries in the Asia Pacific region. Japan, with its long history of economic cooperation with ASEAN, could be a good link between ASEAN and India in RCEP negotiations. The RCEP's ASEAN-led, consensus-based decision-making format might also work better for India, accommodating the latter's moderate liberalization process in comparison with other more liberalized developed countries.[57] Importantly, India has shown interest in strengthening trade relations with ASEAN as seen in its Look East policy since 1991,[58] in Prime Minister Manmohan Singh's 2006 proposal to create an Asian Economic Community for trade and investment liberalization,[59] and in the Act East policy announced by Indian external affairs minister Sushma Swaraj in 2014.[60]

Whether on the bilateral or regional level, Japan should adopt a careful approach in encouraging Prime Minister Modi's pro-business policies, taking into account the strong protectionist tendencies of the Indian textile and footwear lobbies. India's cautious approach can be seen in the cancellation of plans to participate in RCEP talks in Naypyidaw in late August 2014, and in the fact that India is relatively less open to trade liberalization within the RCEP.[61] Against this backdrop, Japan and India can set the policy direction and speed of liberalization with an emphasis on its long-term benefits for India in terms of growth and employment.

All in all, in trade, while Japan has benefited a lot from the WTO and multilateral cooperation, in terms of Japan–India cooperation for freer trade, the bilateral route is better. Japan and India, at different stages of economic development and with different comparative advantages, can find room for complementary cooperation for mutual benefit in trade, including human development and technology transfer. Newly emerging regional trade arenas (instead of the WTO), with their more moderate pace and sphere of trade liberalization, could be a good platform for India's trade liberalization, providing a multilateral arena for trade cooperation between Japan and India.

International Financial Institutions

The multilateral financial mechanisms of the IMF and the World Bank have shaped the post–Second World War management of international monetary cooperation. Japan joined the management of these institutions along with the United States and the European powers through their weighted voting systems, and has also significantly benefited from the system. The steady and open flow of capital and a stable exchange system contribute to trade and economic growth for participants and the world as a whole.

The IMF, with its 188 member countries, works as the de facto international lender of last resort, with the main role of providing surveillance and loans to help members maintain their respective balances of payments, and ensuring the stability of the international financial system. As of 2015, Japan participates in the management of the IMF with almost 6 per cent voting power, second only to the United States with 15 per cent.[62] During times of economic disturbance, such as the suspension of the gold standard in 1971 and the series of financial crises in the 1980s, 1990s, and 2000s, Japan has contributed to the management of a stable exchange rate and to macroeconomic policy adjustments as a principal financial power in the IMF and in multilateral summit meetings of the G-7, G-8, and later the G-20. Recent cases of Japan's contributions to the IMF are its voluntary commitment of US$100 billion in 2009 after the G-20's decision to increase IMF capital three-fold from US$380 billion, and its US$60 billion contribution to the IMF in April 2012 to address the financial crises in Europe.

During the early post-war years, Japan benefited from loans from the World Bank, which provides longer-term loans to pay for specific projects in developing countries such as transportation, electric power, and water supply projects. In the 1970s, Japan transitioned from being a borrower to being an important lender of the World Bank.[63] Since 1984, Japan has been the second largest contributor to the World Bank,[64] thus contributing to the enhancement of economic growth in developing countries.

Japan has had a significant interest in taking bilateral and regional leadership in the management of regional finances in Southeast Asia, both for the region's stable economic growth and for Japan's own national interests. The region serves as a source of natural resources and as the main destination for investments and the export of steel and transportation products from Japan. Tokyo has been the main ODA provider to the region and has taken regional initiatives through the Asian Development Bank (ADB), where it has held the top position since the bank's establishment in 1966. As of 2013, Japan held the largest portion of ADB shares at 15.7 per cent, slightly larger than the share of the United States at 15.6 per cent.[65]

Japan faces the challenge of China's economic, financial, and political rise, which has also affected the overall architecture of the governance system of international finance. In response, on a bilateral basis, Japan has changed its strategic tone by introducing a new charter for Japanese ODA in February 2015. The new charter permits aid to foreign militaries and sets the principles of democracy and rule of law as ODA goals, in addition to the original goals of economic and social development and poverty alleviation.[66] This change also has security implications: for example, potential candidates for ODA under the new charter would be Indonesia and Oman, both important for the protection of sea lanes.

Some perceive the rise of China as posing a new challenge to the global systems of managing international finance for open economic and business transactions, balance of payments, and international loans for economic growth. The New Development Bank (NDB), established in July 2014, and the Asian Infrastructure Investment Bank (AIIB), established in June 2015, both emerged under China's strong initiative. Both banks' headquarters will be located in China, with the NDB in Beijing and the AIIB in Shanghai. The West might view the launch of the NDB warily, as a symbolic move to form a new international regime—reflecting a shifting power balance led by China's rise—against the existing regimes of the IMF and the World Bank. The NDB will compete with the IMF's short-term loans and with the World Bank's long-term infrastructure loans to developing countries.

India's recent participation in the launch of the NDB and the AIIB is worth close examination. As the number two economic power within the BRICS (Brazil, Russia, India, China, and South Africa)—the grouping that operates the NDB—India's cooperation with China would significantly affect the current system of international financial governance. India and China have both been concerned by the United States Congress's failure so far to ratify a new IMF agreement that would address the discrepancy between members' economic size and influence in the organization.[67] Under the new agreement, China would be the third largest quota-holder at the IMF (second only to the US and Japan). India, along with China, is expected to have greater influence in the IMF with an increase in its quota from 2.44 per cent to 2.75 per cent, and an enhanced voting rate from 2.34 per cent to 2.63 per cent.[68] However, despite these common voices of frustration against the Bretton Woods system, the growth potential of the NDB remains to be seen. Due to their diverse domestic regimes and economic capabilities, the founder countries of these new institutions—the members of BRICS—are united but without any concrete common vision to replace the existing undemocratic financial system.

The establishment of the AIIB, with 57 prospective founding members from South and Central Asia, including India, Europe, and Africa as of September 2015, seems to address another issue in the existing international financial system. With an initial capital of US$100 billion, the AIIB is expected to complement the shortage of infrastructure investments for sustainable development in Asia. The ADB estimates that continual economic growth in the region requires US$7.5 trillion for infrastructure investment between 2010 and 2020 (US$750 billion per year), whereas the ADB's estimated annual lending approval is only about US$13 billion.[69] Beijing's motivation to increase its political influence in the Asian region is also evident from China's US$40 billion commitment to a new Silk Road Fund to improve transportation infrastructure in Asia.

The US's wariness with regard to the AIIB was expressed in its alleged pressure on Australia and South Korea not to participate as founding members of the bank.[70] Evidently, Washington does not want the AIIB to gain the prestige and respectability that Beijing seeks.[71] The US's concern is understandable in light of China's dominance in the AIIB—China's almost 30 per cent shareholding in the AIIB planned as of June 2015 is exceptionally high in comparison with the United States' 15 per cent IMF shareholding. China's ambitions in this regard are not hard to understand. The AIIB would allow Beijing to invest part of its huge foreign reserves of roughly US$3.9 trillion on commercial terms with expected return on capital. It would also internationalize the yuan, secure contracts for Chinese firms, and depoliticize China's bilateral funding in infrastructure projects, particularly by the Chinese Development Bank and the Export-Import Bank of China, which have faced local resentment especially in Africa.

In practice, Japan should not overreact to these new regional institutions. For one thing, the NDB and the AIIB are not as large as the existing global financial institutions. The NDB and the AIIB have capital worth US$50 billion and US$100 billion respectively, compared to the ADB's US$160 billion,[72] the World Bank's US$223 billion,[73] and the IMF's US$334 billion, which is expected to increase to US$1 trillion.[74] Furthermore, the Contingent Reserve Arrangement under the BRICS, with an emergency lending agreement, is estimated to be inadequate for Brazil and Russia based on their respective borrowing histories from the IMF during financial crises.[75] What Japan needs to do is to help improve the management of the new Asian financial institutions. Their potential failure and corresponding negative effects on members would further affect the operation of the existing financial institutions, thus intensifying any crisis generated from the mismanagement of the new ones. Whether China's economic growth is sustainable remains to be seen, particularly in view of the recent Chinese stock market tumble since mid-June 2015.

India and Japan need to continue dialogue in order to arrive at a common view on effective international financial regimes and governance, particularly in order to create a mutually reinforcing coexistence between the existing Bretton Woods regimes and the newly formed NDB and AIIB, especially in the areas of management, transparency, and representation. It should also be emphasized that the World Bank and the ADB have functional complementarity with the AIIB, in that the AIIB, unlike the World Bank and the ADB, focuses only on hard infrastructure, not on soft infrastructure such as education and health.

Tokyo is not concerned about the AIIB and the NDB working negatively or positively for Japan's national interests or for the interests of existing financial institutions such as the ADB, the IMF, and the World Bank. Japan has never expressed any opposition to the increasing number of international financial institutions. Rather, it seeks the establishment of fair and healthy organizational management practices and functions in any international financial institution.[76] Thus, Japan hopes that India will participate in these institutions with the same philosophy and stance. Japan can employ strong communication with India to keep India's policies consistent with the IMF and to deter China from the unilateral exercise of power, particularly any actions that would disturb the existing international monetary and financial order. Japan's smooth implementation of its ¥3.5 trillion (approximately US$35 billion) pledge for public and private investment and financing to India, as promised by Prime Minister Abe in September 2014, will help maintain mutual trust between Japan and India, especially because the latter is in need of increased infrastructure investment. Japan, with rich experiences of global and regional financial governance at the ADB, IMF, and World Bank, can assist India in managing effective and fair institutional frameworks with rigorous management structures and transparency in lending processes with appropriate lending quality controls, risk management, and environmental and social regulations in the NDB and AIIB, so that the locus of responsibility is clear. In practice, the president of the ADB, Takehiko Nakao, has also officially signalled the ADB's willingness to cooperate with the AIIB.[77] One of the problems in the AIIB and NDB is incomplete institutionalization; an executive council, a board of directors, and a management team have not been formed, and they are highly likely to be formed with the influence of the president, represented by China.[78] The voting rights of China in the AIIB would be 26.06 per cent, which would give China veto power in crucial issues requiring a super majority of 75 per cent, among which are the choosing of the president of the bank, funding projects outside the region, and the allocation of the bank's income.[79] Reckless loans could not only damage the recipient country's economic growth but also the global economy as a whole. Investment projects could be hugely affected by unexpected exchange rate changes, as happened in the suspended Chinese investment in monorail construction in Indonesia.[80]

On a bilateral basis, Japan can also encourage India, as a democratic country, to take the initiative in enhancing transparency and fairness in the negotiation and decision-making systems of the AIIB and the NDB. In order for Tokyo to increase its influence, enhancing its common interests with Delhi in international finance is important. One option is the use of Japan's strong ties with the ADB to promote bilateral interests. Another is for Japan and India to collaboratively assist South–South cooperation, particularly in Africa. The combination of India's rich financial experience in Africa and Japan's relatively stronger financial capabilities would enhance the bilateral relationship and enable knowledge sharing. Furthermore, the joint effort could constitute a strong joint financial competitor against China in the African continent.

At the same time, Japan should actively work towards the reform of the ADB, as well as the IMF and the World Bank, so that effective and efficient infrastructure loans in Asia can be disbursed with minimal waste and corruption. Japan could assist ADB members to eliminate corruption, guarantee private property rights for further investment, improve tax systems, and strengthen banking systems and independent rating agencies. With regard to the IMF, Japan should encourage the United States to implement the proposed new regulations with higher voting weights for India and China. Japan went through a similar experience in its effort to increase its subscription and voting weight in the IMF, facing US hesitation. To facilitate a more democratic setup, Japan could propose the appointment of an officer from a developing country to serve alternately as the IMF managing director and the Bank president. Japan could also link the voices of both developed and developing democratic countries on diverse global issues. Japan should actively engage in dialogue between existing and new financial institutions so that any implications of the rise of China in this field can be meaningfully translated into international cooperation, not into the unnecessary escalation of hegemonic rivalry in the ongoing power-balance shift in the Asia Pacific region.

To conclude, in the issue area of international finance, Japan and India are likely better off pursuing individual efforts in their respective interests rather than cooperating in a multilateral governance setting. Bilateral cooperation between Japan and India has some scope for enhancing mutual benefits and the global public good of financial stability through both existing and new financial institutions.

* * *

The current systems of global governance face challenges in the areas of nuclear security, UNSC reform, international trade, and international finance in terms of their ineffectiveness in facing new threats, addressing the negative side effects of existing procedures, and reflecting the new global balance of power. It is correct to say that global governance and international institutions are on the threshold of a new era, albeit in diverse ways. Any fracture or malfunctioning of these institutions would jeopardize national and global interests. Depending on the issue area, Japan and India can make selective use of or participate in these institutions and governance structures while making greater unilateral or bilateral efforts to achieve their respective national interests.

This chapter has explored whether Japan, in its pursuit of national interests, can find common ground with India on both a bilateral and multilateral basis. It finds that there is some room for bilateral cooperation, particularly based on complementarity, though Japan and India have different national interests and economic structures.

Thus, cooperation should assume the form of natural harmony or functional cooperation relying on common interests. Such bilateral cooperation can be based on their mutual trust as democracies in Asia espousing norms of tolerance (represented in the countries' cultural diversity and their forward-looking, rather than backward-looking, perspectives on international relations), and through procedural, technical, and incremental reforms in global governance in pursuit of the best mix of representation, effectiveness, flexibility, and agility. The possibilities of Japan–India cooperation are wide-ranging and promising, with a wide array of diplomatic, economic, and institutional tools at hand.

Having said that, Japan and India could cooperate more proactively to tackle current diverse new challenges for the common global good. Overall, such challenges suggest that there are limitations to Western-dominated and state-centric global governance. As leading Asian powers that seek to uphold the basic principles of human rights, rule of law, and democracy, Japan and India could serve as a practical bridge in this transitional period. Japan's unique, deep-rooted tradition of religious tolerance and India's achievement of democratic stability amidst ethnic diversity demonstrate the possibility of any pragmatic bilateral cooperation for the management of global governance evolving into a multi-civilizational framework that could be translated into a new institutional design of global governance. The two states should consciously share this unique common identity when undertaking any mutual cooperation.

Notes

1. MoFA, 'Statement by Prime Minister Eisaku Sato at the Budget Committee in the House of Representatives', 11 December 1967, retrieved from http://www.mofa.go.jp/policy/un/disarmament/nnp/ on 14 September 2015.
2. MoFA, 'Exchange of Notes concerning Article XII, Paragraph 6(d) of the Agreement regarding Facilities and Areas and the Status of United States Armed Forces in Japan', 19 January 1969, retrieved from http://www.mofa.go.jp/region/n-america/us/q&a/ref/2.html on 4 October 2015.
3. 'Secret Pact between Japan and the United States Disclosed: No Prior Consultation on the Transits of the Vessels with Nuclear Weapons',

Asahi Shimbun, 30 August 2000; 'Acceptance of the Transits of the Vessels with Nuclear Weapons in the 1963 Ohira-Reischauer Meeting', *Asahi Shimbun*, 1 August 1999.

4. For more detailed information, see MoFA, 'Report of Expert Committee on the So-Called Mitsuyaku (Secret Agreements)', 9 March 2010, retrieved from http://www.mofa.go.jp/mofaj/gaiko/mitsuyaku/pdfs/hokoku_yushiki.pdf on 14 September 2015.

5. P. Shultz, W. Perry, G. Kissinger, and S. Nunn, 'Toward a Nuclear Free World', *Wall Street Journal*, 15 January 2008; E. Primakov, I. Ivanov, E. Velikhov, and M. Moiseyev, 'From Nuclear Deterrence to Common Security', *Izvestiya*, 15 October 2010.

6. UN, '2010 Review Conference of the Parties to the Treaty on the Non-proliferation of Nuclear Weapons Final Document', vol. 1, p. 19, retrieved from http://www.un.org/ga/search/view_doc.asp?symbol=NPT/CONF.2010/50%20(VOL.I) on 4 October 2015.

7. MoFA, 'Foreign Minister Fumio Kishida's Nuclear Disarmament and Non-proliferation Policy Speech at Nagasaki University on 20 January 2014', retrieved from www.mofa.go.jp/dns/ac_d/page18e_000041.html on 14 September 2015.

8. R. Price, 'Reversing the Gun Sights: Transnational Civil Society Targets Land Mines', *International Organization*, 52(3), 1998, pp. 613–44.

9. 'Ukraine Conflict: Vladimir Putin "Was Ready for Nuclear Alert"', *Guardian*, 16 March 2015, retrieved from http://www.theguardian.com/world/2015/mar/16/putin-ukraine-conflict-ready-nuclear-alert on 4 October 2015.

10. See K.A. Kronstadt, 'Pakistan-U.S. Relations', Congressional Research Service, 24 May 2012, retrieved from http://fpc.state.gov/documents/organization/193708.pdf on 14 September 2015.

11. D. Busvine, 'India's Modi Says Committed to No First Use of Nuclear Weapons', Reuters, 16 April 2014, retrieved from http://www.reuters.com/article/2014/04/16/us-india-election-nuclear-idUSBRE-A3F15H20140416 on 14 September 2015.

12. 'India Can't Be Target of Regime Restrictions: Mathai', *Hindu*, 19 April 2012, retrieved from http://www.thehindu.com/news/national/india-cant-be-target-of-regime-restrictions-mathai/article3332934.ece on 4 October 2015.

13. UNSC Resolution 1540, retrieved from http://www.un.org/en/ga/search/view_doc.asp?symbol=S/RES/1540%20(2004) on 4 October 2015.

14. Enerdata, 'Nuclear Power Corporation of India Limited (NPCIL) Plans to Generate 60 GW of Nuclear Power in India by 2032', 9

September 2013, retrieved from http://www.enerdata.net/enerdatauk/press-and-publication/energy-news-001/npcil-plans-generate-60-gw-nuclear-power-india-2032_22106.html on 14 September 2015. As of 2013, India had a largely indigenous nuclear power programme, which represents 4.4 GWe of generation capacity. See World Nuclear Association, 'Nuclear Power in India', 2013, retrieved from http://www.world-nuclear.org/info/inf53.html on 14 September 2015.

15. Delegation of Japan to the Conference on Disarmament, 'Statement by H.E. Mr. Toshio Sano, Ambassador Extraordinary and Plenipotentiary, Delegation of Japan to the Conference on Disarmament, Geneva', 5 May 2014, retrieved from http://www.disarm.emb-japan.go.jp/Statements/140505%20NPT.pdf on 14 September 2015.

16. MoFA, *Waga gaikou no kinkyou* (Diplomatic Bluebook), 1957.

17. The Preamble and Article 1 of the Treaty of Mutual Cooperation and Security between Japan and the United States of America read: 'Japan and the United States of America, … reaffirming their faith in the purposes and principles of the Charter of the United Nations, … will endeavor in concert with other peace-loving countries to strengthen the United Nations so that its mission of maintaining international peace and security may be discharged more effectively.' See MoFA, 'Japan-U.S. Security Treaty', 19 January 1960, retrieved from http://www.mofa.go.jp/region/n-america/us/q&a/ref/1.html on 4 October 2015.

18. MoFA, 'Japan's Contribution to United Nations Peacekeeping Operations as of March 2014', n.d., retrieved from http://www.mofa.go.jp/policy/un/pko/pdfs/contribution.pdf on 14 September 2015.

19. Article 9 reads: 'Aspiring sincerely to an international peace based on justice and order, the Japanese people forever renounce war as a sovereign right of the nation and the threat or use of force as means of settling international disputes. In order to accomplish the aim of the preceding paragraph, land, sea, and air forces, as well as other war potential, will never be maintained. The right of belligerency of the state will not be recognized.' See Kantei, 'The Constitution of Japan', n.d., retrieved from http://japan.kantei.go.jp/constitution_and_government_of_japan/constitution_e.html on 4 October 2015.

20. UN, *A More Secure World: Our Shared Responsibility*, 2004, retrieved from http://www.un.org/en/peacebuilding/pdf/historical/hlp_more_secure_world.pdf on 14 September 2015.

21. S. Kitaoka, *Kokuren no seiji rikigaku: Nihon ha doko ni irunoka* (Power Politics at the United Nations: Where Japan Is Situated), Tokyo: Chuko Shinsho, 2007, p. 243.

22. For a detailed on-site observation and analysis of the whole process of UNSC reform in 2004–5, see Kitaoka, *Kokuren no seiji rikigaku*.

23. Global Policy, 'Statement by Ambassador Shirin Tahir-Kheli, Senior Advisor to the Secretary of State for UN Reform', 12 July 2005, retrieved from https://www.globalpolicy.org/security-council/security-council-reform/41376.html?itemid=915 on 14 September 2015.

24. After the enshrinement of Class A war criminals in the Yasukuni Shrine in 1978, China began to criticize Japanese prime ministers' official visits there, starting with Prime Minister Yasuhiro Nakasone in 1985.

25. UN Secretariat, 'Assessment of Member States' Contributions to the United Nations Regular Budget for the Year 2015', 29 December 2014, retrieved from http://www.un.org/ga/search/view_doc.asp?symbol=ST/ADM/SER.B/910 on 14 September 2015.

26. T.G. Weiss, *Thinking about Global Governance: Why People and Ideas Matter*, New York: Taylor and Francis, 2012.

27. Security Council Report, 'Security Council Elections 2014', 16 September 2014, retrieved from http://www.securitycouncilreport.org/atf/cf/%7B65BFCF9B-6D27-4E9C-8CD3-CF6E4FF96FF9%7D/srr_unsc_elections_2014.pdf on 14 September 2015.

28. Japan had to persuade Papua New Guinea to withdraw its candidacy to be elected as a non-permanent member in 2004; persuade Mongolia to withdraw its candidacy and to defeat Iran in an election in 2008; and persuade Bangladesh to be elected in 2015. Securing a non-permanent seat on the UNSC is becoming more and more competitive and difficult even for Japan.

29. UNGA, 'Question of Equitable Representation on and Increase in the Membership of the Security Council and Related Matters', UN Document No. A/59/L.64, 6 July 2005.

30. International Coalition for the Responsibility to Protect, 'A "Responsibility Not to Veto"? The S5, the Security Council, and Mass Atrocities', 18 May 2012, retrieved from http://icrtopblog.org/2012/05/18/a-responsibility-not-to-veto-the-s5-the-security-council-and-mass-atrocities/ on 14 September 2015; Center for UN Reform, 'Presentation of the 2-5 Draft Resolution L.42 on the Improvement of the Working Methods of the Security Council', 4 April 2012, retrieved from http://www.centerforunreform.org/sites/default/files/S5%20Presentation%20of%20draft%20resolution%2004.04.2012.pdf on 14 September 2015.

31. General Assembly, 'Follow-Up to the Outcome of the Millennium Summit', UN Document No. A/59/565, Paragraph 256, 2 December 2004; Center for UN Reform, 'Presentation of the 2-5 Draft Resolution'.

32. The Elders, 'Strengthening the United Nations', 7 February 2015, retrieved from http://theelders.org/sites/default/files/2015-04-22_elders-statement-strengthening-the-un.pdf on 14 September 2015.

33. 'Interview with Michael Doyle', *Nihon Keizai Shimbun*, 26 September 2015.

34. UNGA, Resolution 11(I) 4 (d), 1946, retrieved from http://www.un.org/en/ga/search/view_doc.asp?symbol=A/RES/11(I) on 14 September 2015.

35. Also, under the Super 301 section of the US Trade Act of 1974, the US named Japan as an unfair trading partner particularly in supercomputers and satellites. This sustained intensive bilateral trade negotiations with possible retaliation threats from the United States in the 1980s and the 1990s.

36. As of February 2015, Australia, Brunei, Canada, Chile, Japan, Malaysia, Mexico, New Zealand, Peru, Singapore, the United States, and Vietnam were the TPP's negotiating members.

37. W. Pesek, 'Japan Needs to Cut Its Rice Farmers Down to Size', *Japan Times*, 27 April 2015, retrieved from http://www.japantimes.co.jp/opinion/2015/04/27/commentary/japan-commentary/japan-needs-to-cut-its-rice-farmers-down-to-size/ on 14 September 2015.

38. Government of Japan, '"Abenomics" Is Progressing! Making the Impossible Possible', n.d., retrieved from http://www.japan.go.jp/tomodachi/Features/Abenomics.html on 4 October 2015.

39. Kantei, 'Headquarters on Creating Dynamism through Agriculture, Forestry and Fishery Industries and Local Communities', 13 February 2015, retrieved from http://japan.kantei.go.jp/97_abe/actions/201502/13article1.html on 14 September 2015; Kantei, 'Cabinet Decision', 3 April 2015, retrieved from http://www.kantei.go.jp/jp/kakugi/2015/kakugi-2015040301.html on 4 October 2015; 'Cabinet Approves JA-Zenchu Reform Bill', *Japan Times*, 3 April 2015, retrieved from http://www.japantimes.co.jp/news/2015/04/03/national/politics-diplomacy/cabinet-approves-ja-zenchu-reform-bill/ on 4 October 2015.

40. The TPP is expected to benefit not only large-scale corporations but also medium- and small-scale corporations. See, for example, 'Japan-US Reaching a TPP Agreement', *Yomiuri Shimbun*, 2 August 2015, p. 9.

41. The ratio of large-scale rice farmers is less than 40 per cent. See S. Tadashi, 'Destroy "Part-Time Farmers" in Japan', *Nikkei Business*, 20 February 2009, retrieved from business.nikkeibp.co.jp/article/manage/20090218/186539/?rt=nocnt on 4 October 2015.

42. Ministry of Agriculture, Forestry and Fisheries, 'Status of Agriculture and Food Self-Sufficiency Ratio', n.d., retrieved from www.maff.go.jp/e/tokei/kikaku/monthly_e/other/g096b.xls on 14 September 2015.

43. K. Yamashita, *Nihon nougyou ha sekai ni kateru* (Japanese Agriculture Can Beat the World), Tokyo: Nihon Keizai Shinbun Shuppansha, 2015, p. 116.

44. MoFA, 'China's Economic Conditions and Japan-China Economic Relations', 2015, retrieved from http://www.mofa.go.jp/mofaj/files/000007735.pdf on 14 September 2015.

45. V.K. Aggarwal and R. Mukherji, 'India's Shifting Trade Policy: South Asia and Beyond', in V.K. Aggarwal and M.G. Koo (eds), *Asia's New Institutional Architecture: Evolving Structures for Managing Trade and Security Relations*, Heidelberg: Springer Verlag, 2008, pp. 215–58; A. Panagariya, 'India's Trade Reform: Progress, Impact and Future Strategy', 4 March 2004, retrieved from http://www.columbia.edu/~ap2231/Policy%20Papers/IPF_India.pdf on 14 September 2015.

46. Japan's textile industry during the pre-war period relied on cotton imported from India, and Japan's heavy industry development during the early post-war period in the 1950s depended upon cheap iron ore imported from India. Japan's normalization of diplomatic relations with India, Pakistan, and Sri Lanka took place in 1952, much earlier than with Southeast Asian countries.

47. India is the 24th largest trading partner for Japan, and Japan is the 16th largest trading partner for India. See MOFA, 'Current Indian Affairs and Japan-India Relations', 2015, retrieved from http://www.mofa.go.jp/mofaj/files/000020898.pdf on 14 September 2015.

48. MoFA, 'Tokyo Declaration for Japan-India Special Strategic and Global Partnership', 1 September 2014, retrieved from http://www.mofa.go.jp/files/000050532.pdf on 14 September 2015.

49. S. Aiyar, R. Duval, D. Puy, Y. Wu, and L. Zhang, 'Growth Slowdowns and the Middle-Income Trap', International Monetary Fund Working Paper WP/13/71, 2013, retrieved from https://www.imf.org/external/pubs/ft/wp/2013/wp1371.pdf on 14 September 2015.

50. MoFA, 'Recent Developments in India and Japan-India Relations', 2015, retrieved from http://www.mofa.go.jp/mofaj/files/000020898.pdf on 14 September 2015.

51. For more information on VLFM and CSM, see JICA, 'Activities in India', n.d., retrieved from http://www.jica.go.jp/india/english/activities/activity19.html on 14 September 2015; JICA, '"Champions for Societal Manufacturing" Project Launched: Focus towards Sustainable and Inclusive Development of India through Manufacturing

Perspective', 18 March 2013, retrieved from http://www.jica.go.jp/india/english/office/topics/130318.html on 14 September 2015.

52. Funding is for small projects for local governments, medical and educational institutions, and non-governmental organizations in developing countries. For each case, the maximum amount of aid is less than ¥10 million. There were 20 cases in the 2010 fiscal year. See MoFA, 'Japan's Economic Aid to India', 2011, retrieved from http://www.in.emb-japan.go.jp/Japan-India-Relations/ODA_Jpn_Jun2011.pdf on 14 September 2015.

53. M.K. Singh, 'New Poverty Line: Rs 32 in Villages, Rs 47 in Cities', *Times of India*, 7 July 2014, retrieved from http://timesofindia.indiatimes.com/india/New-poverty-line-Rs-32-in-villages-Rs-47-in-cities/articleshow/37920441.cms on 4 October 2015.

54. WHO, 'Trade, Foreign Policy, Diplomacy and Health: Food Security', n.d., retrieved from www.who.int/trade/glossary/story028/en on 14 September 2015.

55. A. Palit, 'Mega Trading Blocs and New Regional Trade Architectures: Implications for Small States and LDCs', *Trade Hot Topics*, 107, 2014, pp. 1–8.

56. A. Palit, 'The RCEP Negotiations and India', *ISAS Brief*, 334, 24 June 2014, pp. 1–5; Palit, 'Mega Trading Blocs'.

57. S.B. Das, 'RCEP and TPP: Next Stage in Asian Regionalism', *Asia Pathways*, 3 July 2013, retrieved from http://www.asiapathways-adbi.org/2013/07/rcep-and-tpp-next-stage-in-asian-regionalism/#sthash.Nks2olQi.dpuf on 14 September 2015.

58. T. Haokip, 'India's Look East Policy: Its Evolution and Approach', *South Asian Survey*, 18(2), 2011, pp. 239–57.

59. C. Ma, 'Chuin boeki no kakudai to chuin FTA keikaku' (The Expansion of China–India Trade and the China–India FTA Plan), *Ajiken World Trends* (Institute of Developing Economies World Trends), 131, 2006, retrieved from http://d-arch.ide.go.jp/idedp/ZWT/ZWT200608_010.pdf on 14 September 2015.

60. 'Sushma Swaraj Tells Indian Envoys to Act East and Not Just Look East', *Economic Times*, 24 August 2014, retrieved from http://articles.economictimes.indiatimes.com/2014-08-26/news/53243802_1_india-and-asean-countries-east-asia-strategically-important-region on 4 October 2015.

61. Palit, 'The RCEP Negotiations and India'.

62. IMF, 'IMF Members' Quotas and Voting Power, and IMF Board of Governors', 20 August 2015, retrieved from http://www.imf.org/external/np/sec/memdir/members.aspx on 14 September 2015.

63. World Bank, '40 Years of World Bank Bonds in Japan', n.d., retrieved from http://treasury.worldbank.org/cmd/htm/40YearsofWorldBankBo ndsinJapan.html on 14 September 2015.

64. World Bank, 'Japan, Overview', n.d., retrieved from http://www.worldbank.org/en/country/japan/overview on 14 September 2015.

65. ADB, 'Shareholders', n.d., retrieved from http://www.adb.org/site/investors/credit-fundamentals/shareholders on 14 September 2015.

66. MoFA, 'Cabinet Decision on the Development Cooperation Charter', 10 February 2015, retrieved from http://www.mofa.go.jp/files/000067701.pdf on 14 September 2015.

67. P. Hill, 'China Presses Congress for Action on Stalled IMF Reforms', *Washington Times*, 8 October 2014, retrieved from http://www.washingtontimes.com/news/2014/oct/8/china-presses-congress-for-action-on-stalled-imf-r/?page=all on 14 September 2015; Bretton Woods Project, 'Calls for IMF Quota Reform Implementation', 2 December 2013, retrieved from http://www.brettonwoodsproject.org/2013/12/developing-countries-demand-2010-quota-reform-implementation/ on 14 September 2015.

68. IMF, 'Quota and Voting Shares Before and After Implementation of Reforms Agreed in 2008 and 2010', n.d., retrieved from https://www.imf.org/external/np/sec/pr/2011/pdfs/quota_tbl.pdf on 4 October 2015.

69. D.R.O. Junio, 'Asian Infrastructure Investment Bank: An Idea Whose Time Has Come?', *Diplomat*, 14 December 2014, retrieved from http://thediplomat.com/2014/12/asian-infrastructure-investment-bank-an-idea-whose-time-has-come/ on 14 September 2015.

70. Z. Keck, 'Under US Pressure, Major Countries Snub China's New Regional Bank', *Diplomat*, 23 October 2014, retrieved from http://thediplomat.com/2014/10/under-us-pressure-major-countries-snub-chinas-new-regional-bank/ on 14 September 2015.

71. J. Perlez, 'US Opposing China's Answer to World Bank', *New York Times*, 9 October 2014, retrieved from http://www.nytimes.com/2014/10/10/world/asia/chinas-plan-for-regional-development-bank-runs-into-us-opposition.html?_r=0 on 14 September 2015.

72. S.B. Das, 'China's Three-Pronged Strategy on Regional Connectivity', *Kyoto Review of Southeast Asia*, 2015, retrieved from http://kyotoreview.org/yav/chinas-three-pronged-strategy-on-regional-connectivity/ on 14 September 2015.

73. Liquid Investments, 'Raising the Stakes in Global Development Banking', 16 July 2015, retrieved from http://liquid-investments.com/raising-stakes-global-development-banking/ on 14 September 2015.

74. IMF, 'The IMF at a Glance', 16 September 2015, retrieved from http://www.imf.org/external/np/exr/facts/glance.htm on 5 October 2015.
75. While Brazil and Russia can borrow up to US$5.4 billion under the Contingent Reserve Arrangement, Russia borrowed US$38 billion from the IMF during the 1990s, and Brazil, in 2002 alone, borrowed US$30 billion during the financial crisis. See B. Steil, 'Is the BRICS Contingent Reserve Arrangement a Substitute for the IMF?', Council on Foreign Affairs, 6 August 2014, retrieved from http://blogs.cfr.org/geographics/2014/08/06/bricscra/ on 14 September 2015.
76. 'Possibility of Participation Negotiation if Conditions Are Met', *Nikkei Shimbun*, 20 March 2015, retrieved from http://www.nikkei.com/article/DGXLASFS20H0S_Q5A320C1EAF000/ on 5 October 2015.
77. ADB, 'Statement by ADB President Takehiko Nakao on the Signing of AIIB Articles of Agreement', 29 June 2015, retrieved from http://www.adb.org/news/statement-adb-president-takehiko-nakao-signing-aiib-articles-agreement on 5 October 2015.
78. H. Lockett, 'China's New Infrastructure Bank May Prove a Regional Boon if Beijing Can Put Politics Aside', *China Economic Review*, 11 May 2015, retrieved from http://www.chinaeconomicreview.com/AIIB-contentious-contender on 14 September 2015.
79. K.G. Qing and B. Blanchard, 'China to Hold Some Veto Powers in New Asian Bank', Reuters, 30 June 2015, retrieved from http://in.reuters.com/article/2015/06/29/asia-aiib-china-stake-idINKC-N0P907Z20150629 on 5 October 2015.
80. 'Weak Rupiah Delays Bandung Monorail Project's June Construction', *Jakarta Globe*, 12 January 2015, retrieved from http://jakartaglobe.beritasatu.com/business/weak-rupiah-delays-bandung-monorail-projects-start-construction/ on 5 October 2015.

8

India and Japan

Partnering to Shape Multilateral Rules and Institutions?

Waheguru Pal Singh Sidhu and Karthik Nachiappan

This chapter looks at India's interests, record, and achievements vis-à-vis global governance and international institutions to outline possible areas of cooperation with Japan to further their mutual interests. It argues that India has extensive economic, normative, and security interests across the global governance landscape, but has not had a stellar record in achieving them. Despite this state of affairs, there exist opportunities for Japan and India to enhance their cooperation in areas such as international development, maritime security, civil nuclear issues, United Nations peacekeeping, and reform of the UN Security Council (UNSC) and international financial institutions (IFIs). To deepen cooperation, however, both countries have to contend with certain institutional, normative, and political constraints on the issues being considered. Nonetheless, opportunities exist, with the leadership in both countries infusing new vigour into the bilateral relationship. The chapter concludes with some policy recommendations for the Indian government on the issue areas examined.

India–Japan relations have entered a new phase with the election of Indian Prime Minister Narendra Modi and the political revival of Japanese prime minister Shinzo Abe. Delhi has signalled its desire to boost cooperation with Tokyo on a range of important international issues such as climate change, maritime security, and nuclear cooperation, among others. This chapter looks at the global governance structure and multilateral institutions and considers those issues in which both countries have opportunities to deepen their cooperation.

The chapter commences by providing an extensive overview of India's interests across the global governance landscape and the range of strategies it has used to achieve them. In the next section, we argue that India has had significant triumphs but also pronounced failures in achieving these goals insofar as global governance is concerned. The third section surveys the opportunities to strengthen cooperation—specifically, the areas of maritime security, nuclear cooperation, international development, global governance reform, and UN peacekeeping. The fourth section looks at the challenges and opportunities confronting both nations in deepening cooperation. Finally, the chapter concludes with a number of policy recommendations to boost cooperation on global governance issues.

India's Extensive Multilateral Interests

India's interests in the global governance landscape are wide-ranging—from normative issues (maintenance of a democratic, liberal model and rule-based global order) to development (receiving and providing assistance) and peace and security issues (addressing transnational threats). Broadly, India's interests in global governance can be classified into four categories.

First, India's principal interest is to harness the international order to drive its development trajectory. To realize this goal, Delhi has extensively tapped the expertise and resources of international financial institutions (IFIs) and worked to shape trends in international development cooperation. India has been the World Bank's single largest borrower since the institution's founding in 1945. As of 2014, the total amount borrowed by India from the World Bank Group, including the International Bank for Reconstruction and Development and the International Development Association, stood at roughly US$78 billion.[1] This source of funding was crucial in the first two decades of India's post-independence existence when it lacked alternative capital options to fund its development. As options grew, the proportion of annual assistance drawn from the bank, in turn, decreased. Since 1986, the Asian Development Bank (ADB)— of which India is a founding member—has allocated approximately US$32 billion to India for mostly infrastructure-related projects.[2] A key aspect of the ADB's engagement with India has been its capacity-building support to enable Indian agencies to plan and implement development projects. To this end, the ADB has established a capacity development resource centre at its resident mission in New Delhi.[3]

Second, to protect its development trajectory, India has worked to effect a benign international security environment. To this end, India has relied on several strategies. During the Cold War, India used non-alignment to stay out of the bipolar superpower confrontation. Since then, Delhi has remained normatively ambiguous in order to avoid making commitments on major international crises (except through UN peacekeeping missions), especially those concerning non-UN multilateral intervention in other countries, where India invariably takes a 'middle path'.[4] As Western powers test the resolve of rising powers in joining or contributing to interventions, India has expressed deep reservations. It has resisted getting entangled in conflicts that it has no control over and has safeguarded its own interests in regions where crises unfold. Moreover, the selective choices underpinning multilateral interventions and the arbitrary nature in which they unfurl have long irked Indian diplomats. In 2011, during its tenure on the United Nations Security Council (UNSC), for instance, India (along with Brazil and South Africa) for the first time invoked the 'responsibility to protect' (R2P), but subsequently abstained from voting on a resolution authorizing military intervention in Libya to enforce R2P.[5] Economic concerns factored in India's decision, given its extensive commercial interests in Libya's oil fields that stood to be liquidated by intervention.[6] In Syria a similar scenario unfolded. India's calculus, resistant at the outset, shifted in the wake of American and Saudi pressure that warned Delhi of loss of access to its oil reserves should war break out in the region. Although Delhi supported the resolution, it still managed to lay out conditions that effectively kept India out of the conflict.[7]

India's opposition to non-UN interventions is in contrast to its participation in UN peacekeeping operations (UNPKOs). For decades Delhi has deployed military forces in UN missions for peacekeeping as well as humanitarian and relief purposes. Between 1950 and 2013, India committed more than 165,000 soldiers, military observers, and civilian police officers in over 45 UN missions.[8] India's commitments have sustained through the decades, before and after the Cold War; in fact, India's highest level of participation was during 1990–4 when it committed troops to operations in Angola, Cambodia, El Salvador, Iraq, Mozambique, Nicaragua, Somalia, and Rwanda.[9] More recently, India has been deploying its forces in operations outside of the UN framework. In 2002 the Indian Navy escorted high-value US vessels through the Strait of Malacca during the US-led war effort in Afghanistan.[10] Alongside other rising powers, the Indian Navy participated in the Combined Task Force 151 counter-piracy mission in the Gulf of Aden.[11] The Indian military was also deployed for humanitarian and relief missions in Indonesia, the Maldives, and Sri Lanka following the 2004 Indian Ocean tsunami, when India coordinated relief operations with Australia, Japan, and the US.[12] Of late, India has participated in various bilateral and multilateral security frameworks and dialogues such as the East Asia Summit, Indian Ocean Rim Association (IORA), Association of Southeast Asian Nations (ASEAN) Regional Forum, Shanghai Cooperation Organization (SCO), and the Shangri-La dialogue with major powers and other regional actors to enhance regional security.

Third, India has worked to shape international rules that affect its security and development. Since independence, India has played a key role within the UN, the Non-Aligned Movement (NAM), and the Commonwealth. Through this involvement, Delhi sought to generate opportunities and advance ideas on behalf of developing countries.[13] On climate change, India's agency and positions have been consistent for two decades. Since developing countries like India had historically contributed very little to the growing problem, the Indian position has been that it has no special burden when it comes to mitigating climate change unless it is given sufficient financial and technological assistance by the West. This position was key as 'India took the lead in constructing a southern coalition to develop a common developing country strategy on this issue' at the Conference of Select Developing Countries on Global Environmental Issues in April 1990 that split responsibility for reducing greenhouse gas emissions between developed and developing countries; the principle of 'common but differentiated responsibilities' has since functioned as the bedrock in international climate negotiations.[14]

India's efforts on maritime security have been equally forthright. In 1971, India pushed for a resolution to declare the Indian Ocean as a 'zone of peace' in reaction to various incidents, most notably the deployment of the *USS Enterprise* in the Bay of Bengal during the India–Pakistan standoff over East Pakistan (later Bangladesh).[15] With the adoption of the United Nations Convention on the Law of the Sea (UNCLOS) in 1982, sea lanes and the country's exclusive economic zone assumed importance as vital pathways of commerce and development. In response, India has been keen to shape the multilateral discourse around the law of the sea, given interests in its own maritime domain—the Indian Ocean. India ratified UNCLOS in 1995 and has engaged with several UN maritime bodies, including the International Maritime Organization, the International Tribunal for the Law of the Sea, and the International Seabed Authority.[16] However, in areas where Indian interests clash with existing international rules and norms, resistance invariably follows.

On a number of issues, India has sought to evade and contest institutional constraints that undermine its core interests. Nuclear armament is one example. India took part in the Treaty on the Non-Proliferation of Nuclear Weapons (NPT) negotiations but chose not to be a signatory; since then it has been a vocal critic of the treaty. Similarly, despite pushing for a nuclear test ban treaty for decades and initially joining the negotiations for the Comprehensive Nuclear-Test-Ban Treaty (CTBT), India eventually rejected it. National security considerations have, more often than not, trumped normative justifications when it came to India's will to develop nuclear weapons.[17] However, since 1998, when India conducted several nuclear tests and declared itself to be a nuclear weapon state, it has been more receptive to non-proliferation efforts in order to counter the threat of nuclear terrorism and illicit nuclear commerce, including the regimes that govern nuclear trade.[18]

Fourth, India has sought to reform the existing international order and its principal institutions, the UNSC and IFIs, such that they become more representative of international political realities and more receptive to India's concerns. With respect to the UNSC, India has been in the running for a permanent seat for decades. Grounds for inclusion have been based on India's sheer size in demographic and economic terms coupled with its sustained contributions to the UN. This argument has featured heavily in India's approach as a part of the G-4 (Brazil, Germany, Japan, and India) that has sought expansion of the council by six permanent and four non-permanent members to a total of 25 members.[19] India also pushed this cause through the L-69, a group of developing countries that has engaged intensively with the committee of 10 (C-10)—a group of 10 African countries seeking UNSC reform—to coordinate a joint position on expansion.[20] Concurrently, India has endeavoured to make the UNSC more 'transparent, responsive, and constrained' in its functioning relative to the UN General Assembly (UNGA) by scrutinizing the working methods of the UNSC.[21] India has also pushed to make council operations more responsive by requiring the five permanent members (P-5) to engage with member states should the latter have a stake in an issue being considered by the council.[22] Similarly, India has realized the need to improve its institutional standing and weight within the World Bank and the International Monetary Fund (IMF) just as its reliance on them as a recipient has lessened. India's efforts have manifested through intermittent calls to reform the leadership of both institutions and by pushing internal restructuring such that developing countries would become greater shareholders within these institutions.[23]

As reform efforts lag in these international institutions and space opens up for rising power cooperation, newer multilateral permutations are emerging across the international landscape. On a series of issues including trade, climate change, public health, and development cooperation, India is opting to pursue gains through plurilateral and South–South vehicles such as the Group of 20 Countries (G-20), BRICS (Brazil, Russia, India, China, and South Africa), BASIC (Brazil, South Africa, India, and China), IBSA (India, Brazil, and South Africa), the SCO, and others. India's affinity for the G-20 stems from the mechanism's lithe nature; it largely functions as an institutional committee convened as an experience- and information-sharing platform on economic and financial issues. India's G-20 approach has been rather cautious: participate, restrict the grouping's remit to economic issues, resist proposals that encroach on India's domestic interests (especially with respect to climate change), and endorse matters where Delhi sees a clear interest, like the tax avoidance agreement that allows governments to curb tax evasion.[24]

Concurrently, India's participation in other groupings such as IBSA, BRICS, and BASIC has grown. Broadly, this can be attributed to converging economic and political interests with other rising powers on matters of growth, development, and management of the international order. The unifying feature, of course, is their economic strength as large emerging economies that give them collective weight in the international system. Normatively, these South–South groupings tend to extol the primacy of state sovereignty and national political and economic agendas against purported global norms and global governance concerns.[25] Finally, extra-regional bodies are becoming more relevant for India due to deepening cross-continental connections. In 2015, India gained membership in the SCO, which seeks to enhance regional stability across the Eurasian landmass. The Asia-Pacific Economic Cooperation (APEC) forum has also made space for India as an observer since 2011, given India's maturing economic ties across the Pacific. And finally, the Arctic Council granted India observer status in May 2013 in response to India's scientific research and contributions; this happened at an opportune juncture considering that the withering of the Arctic ice cap has engendered commercial opportunities.[26]

Assessing India's Performance in the Multilateral Arena

Given its wide range of interests, how successful has India been in securing them? At best, India's record relative to its efforts in the multilateral arena has been mixed, punctuated by some significant triumphs and rather pronounced failures.

In terms of its own development, India has been prolific at securing the necessary financial and technical assistance. India has been the World Bank's single largest borrower since the institution's inception. Despite the large volumes of funding it has received, India has followed its own development trajectory without much undue interference.[27] In fact, Delhi has made the bank more receptive to its preferred priorities and modalities vis-à-vis development financing (for example, partnering the bank with various states).[28] As a leading developing country, India's profile and determined efforts to tackle poverty after independence catalysed global debates on international development; in the 1950s and 1960s, growing awareness of India's economic situation not only generated more resources to assist developing countries confronting poverty, but also influenced the modalities used to channel them. In the early days of international development lending, donors preferred to channel financing through specific projects and hoped to deploy them through the private sector, but these preferences clashed with the realities of development across the global South that privileged state-led industrialization. To engender a more recipient-friendly assistance approach, Indian efforts were crucial; using India as the weathervane, donors—especially the World Bank—grew to appreciate the conditions of developing countries and sought to fashion assistance more flexibly. India's efforts were also significant in the establishment of the International Development Association in 1960, given the inability of many developing countries to access capital markets due to their lack of creditworthiness. For more than a decade, India 'pressed with unrelenting zeal for an institution which could grant or otherwise transfer purchasing power to poor countries on extremely concessional terms'.[29]

While still an aid recipient, India has evolved to become a budding international development donor. This partly springs from geopolitical exigencies, being ensconced in a region littered with complex political and economic deficits. Economic interests have also mattered. Within South Asia, India has been providing some form of development assistance to its neighbours since 1950. During the Cold War, India furthered its commitment to various multilateral economic development initiatives such as the Commonwealth Fund for Technical Cooperation, the Special Commonwealth Assistance for Africa Programme, the United Nations Conference on Trade and Development,[30] the United Nations Industrial Development Organization, and the ADB. India worked assiduously to increase the capital options available to nations as they sought to develop; to this end, India's aid programme was situated within NAM and the G-77 at the UN, incorporating aid activities into India's multilateral agenda.[31] But it equally did so with a measure of self-interest;

strategic and economic considerations coupled with normative concerns have long factored in the determination of India's foreign aid.[32] Disbursals by the Ministry of External Affairs (MEA) for development purposes have grown over the decades. In 2013–14, it is estimated that roughly US$1.3 billion was channelled principally through small-scale development projects, lines of credit, and technical assistance and training.[33]

Of late, assistance has also functioned as a gateway for the Indian private sector, pushing it into uncharted markets.[34] However, it is questionable if India's efforts have yielded tangible gains in countries where aid is disbursed, or if India has gained commensurate diplomatic backing in return. One yardstick that can be used to measure the efficacy of Indian aid is the level of support it receives from recipients for a seat at the UNSC. Analyses over the recent past indicate that India has not garnered the requisite support.[35] This is at least partly due to the way aid is formulated and disbursed within the MEA, which leaves little room for recipient desires to be effectively considered. As Fuchs and Vadlamannati argue, 'India's aid allocation is partially in line with our expectations of the behaviour of a needy donor' that is dominated by commercial and political self-interest, not recipient needs and concerns.[36] Moreover, India's development assistance has not been able to add to its influence within South Asia and Sub-Saharan Africa, its leading aid targets. Public opinion surveys gathered from citizens across 25 countries in 2013, including South Asia and Africa, indicate that with regard to international influence, only 33 per cent of respondents rated India positively, while about 35 per cent viewed it negatively.[37]

Another notable failure has been India's inability to secure a permanent seat at the UNSC and make meaningful institutional gains within the IFIs. In its most recent stint in the UNSC in 2011–12, India repeatedly raised the issue of UNSC expansion, to no avail. The politics of translating this desire into reality have proven insuperable, not least due to the reluctance, if not opposition, of the P-5. An attempt in February 2011 to pass a resolution in the UNGA endorsing the G-4's claim to permanent membership also fell short of the required two-thirds majority.

Reform of IFIs appears equally difficult, though here there is a gap between India's intentions and ability to achieve change. In principle, India aims to change the process through which leaders of these institutions are picked, but in practice it has opted not to reject candidates on the basis of nationality given its weak political leverage on the matter. Instead, Delhi has examined the merits of the candidate's impact on its interests within each institution, but in most instances, India's options are foreclosed by convention. In the most recent leadership contest at the IMF, India (alongside China, Brazil, and Europe) backed Christine Lagarde's candidacy. Although Lagarde had an eminent and arguably more experienced competitor—Agustín Carstens, Mexico's Central Bank governor— who explicitly campaigned on a platform of 'diversity' and greater representation, India had to accept Lagarde once the United States formally endorsed her candidacy.[38] As has been the case, India's imprimatur was given alongside staid pontifications that these 'institutions need to be reformed'.[39] Similarly, India baulked when it came to the World Bank presidency that opened up in 2012. Jim Yong Kim, US president Barack Obama's favoured candidate, faced tough competition from Ngozi Okonjo-Iweala of Nigeria and José Antonio Ocampo of Colombia—both officials from developing countries, with formidable financial acumen and experience. Again, India voted for Kim once it became clear he was going to prevail. As the issue of IFI leadership becomes a matter of debate within other South–South forums, Delhi needs to synchronize its desires and actions as the next leadership contest arrives. Within the IMF, however, India has pushed to amend the institution's share of quotas for developing countries, but the resulting change has ultimately not added much to their institutional weight.[40]

One area where India has made a visible global contribution has been in UN peacekeeping. Since the 1950s, more than 160,000 Indian military and police personnel have been deployed under the UN's authority. As Varun Vira observes, Indian soldiers 'fall into the very narrow bracket of troop contributing countries willing and able to act kinetically'.[41] India also holds the rather unfortunate distinction of losing more officers on UN missions than any other nation.[42] However, there has been a lingering charge that Indian contributions have been overwhelmingly narrow, tactical, and cautious in nature. Despite braving hostile conditions and forces, Thierry Tardy avers, India has 'not acquired political influence commensurate with massive field presence, nor has it given any indication that it intends to do so'.[43] Richard Gowan and Sushant K. Singh argue that this inconsistent and increasingly problematic legacy stems from India's early enthusiasm for PKOs, driven by decolonization, that left it vulnerable to blowback when missions went awry under its command as they frequently did, as in the United Nations Operation in the Congo (UNOC) in 1960. In the Congo, India's robust approach was neutered by France and Britain in the UNSC due to fears of possible reverberations in their African colonies.[44] This experience left India with a deep preoccupation over how missions are managed. Discussions to this end take place, amongst several venues, in the Committee of 34 (C-34), a UN special committee convened to review PKO missions and offer recommendations for policy changes; here, troop contributors have great latitude insofar as determining the tactical nature of PKOs is concerned.[45] As a result, India has had to become more defensive, functioning as a bulwark against the United States, Japan, and European countries that appear to be pushing for more robust peace operations. Consequently, India has seldom been involved in conceptually shaping the strategic contours of international peacekeeping.

With respect to its nuclear armament agenda, India's record has been less successful. Though successful in terms of acquiring nuclear weapons capabilities and instituting the necessary doctrines to govern their use, India has so far been unable to gain access to the web of nuclear power frameworks and institutions that manage nuclear commerce and trade, despite its strong non-proliferation credentials. Informally organized, these four regimes—the Nuclear Suppliers Group (NSG), the Missile Technology Control Regime (MTCR), the Australia Group, and the Wassenaar Arrangement—include major suppliers of advanced and sensitive technologies. For decades, India had a contemptuous attitude towards export controls, viewing them as nothing less than putative roadblocks to the development of civil nuclear energy. As a leading member of NAM, India vigorously protested against the discriminatory characteristics of these regimes. The nuclear tests at Pokhran only served to distance India further. Gradually, through determined diplomacy, the wide chasm between the United States and India has narrowed on the issue of export controls, but the US lacks the authority to give India membership in these groups. To acquire membership, India must obtain consent from all four regimes by convincing them at the very least that Indian laws and practices are consonant with incumbent guidelines. In other words, India must demonstrate that it has the infrastructure for export controls replete with a sound legal and regulatory framework and institutions to govern the trade of sensitive technologies. After the United States endorsed India's membership in the four export controls regimes in November 2010 (and again in January 2015), a number of other key countries such as Russia, France, and the United Kingdom followed suit by supporting India's candidacy. Since then, support for India's membership has progressively increased but the eventual goal has not been reached yet.[46]

On maritime issues, India has been adept at shaping norms and safeguarding its interests in the Indian Ocean. Prime Minister Manmohan Singh expressed this interest succinctly during his tenure, stating that 'India's strategic calculus has long encompassed the waters from the Gulf of Aden to the Strait of Malacca', which effectively places India at the centre of activities on matters such as piracy and maritime terrorism, and as an important player across a raft of maritime frameworks.[47] Evidence of India's maritime leadership is seen through the IORA, which aims to enhance maritime security through sustained dialogue.[48] Delhi organized the inaugural Indian Ocean Naval Symposium, providing a forum 'for discussion for all littoral navies of the Indian Ocean, through a series of seminars and workshops on issues of common concern such as piracy or the effects of climate change'.[49] Delhi's role as a net security provider has also risen. India has been working with many ASEAN nations to police sea lanes from the Indian Ocean to the Malacca Strait; part of this effort involves a bevy of regional exercises conducted by the Indian Navy with over 40 different countries. The Indian Navy's Milan programme, a biennial naval exercise involving several other Asia Pacific countries, concluded another iteration in 2014 with some African countries taking part as well.

The outbreak of piracy in 2007 shifted India's maritime attention westward, given the importance and volume of commerce flowing through the Gulf of Aden and the increasing number of Indian ships transiting that route. Complementing its independent anti-piracy patrols that have foiled several attempts, India has coordinated with other navies multilaterally through the Shared Awareness and De-confliction mechanism and the Regional Cooperation Agreement on Combating Piracy and Armed Robbery against Ships in Asia.[50] India also used its stint at the UNSC in 2011–12 to produce a joint statement to coordinate inter-state efforts to criminalize piracy domestically and to chair the 13th plenary session of the Contact Group on Piracy off the Coast of Somalia at the UN in December 2012, which endorsed collaboration between affected navies through capacity building, information sharing, and deeper links.[51]

Partnering to Shape Rules

In light of this gap between India's aspirations and achievements in various multilateral and global governance institutions, are there areas where India and Japan could work together to their mutual advantage?

In terms of development cooperation, opportunities exist as India evolves as a donor. Currently, India's approach to development cooperation is ostensibly centred on a demand-driven, consultative model of engagement with recipient nations. A sizeable portion of aid flows are directed towards the energy sector, away from areas such as health, education, agriculture, and livelihood creation. Moreover, it is not the lower-income countries that receive a greater share of India's assistance; in fact, countries at a similar developmental stage to India are more likely to be aid recipients and not those that 'need' the aid more, which belies India's claims of being a needs-based donor.[52] It is not unprecedented that nations deploy assistance in areas and for purposes that are in their interest, but when it is done without adequate internal oversight, it undercuts aid's utility as an instrument of foreign policy. Here, Japan's decades of experience as a donor can help India institute effective aid practices as it progresses in that role. For instance, Japanese experiences can help spur greater dialogue between Indian development officials, research institutes, non-governmental organizations, and the private sector to assist in policy-making functions. There is currently a notable absence of external stakeholders playing a role in India's official development assistance policy as noted in a 2013 report.[53]

On global governance reform, it is clear that both countries would benefit from the reform of major international institutions—

particularly the UNSC and IFIs—but the route to this outcome appears complex, partly due to differences within India and partly on account of external factors. Besides, even though Delhi and Tokyo might share the same goal of reforming the UNSC and IFIs, their challenges and approaches to reform are divergent. While China looms large in their calculations, their respective positions as leaders of the North (given Japan's membership of the G-7) and the South (given India's role in G-77 and IBSA) make it difficult to create a common appealing narrative. Moreover, both have very different perspectives of their role in these reformed institutions. For instance, in a reformed UNSC that includes India and Japan, the two are unlikely to be on the same side on most peace and security issues, as is evident from their different positions on R2P, Libya, and Syria.

While political leadership has been evident, with both Prime Ministers Abe and Modi calling to upgrade bilateral efforts alongside G-4 consultations during their August–September 2014 summit, it will not be enough. For their bilateral efforts to be taken seriously, both countries will have to highlight how they can individually and jointly further the cause of the UN and its member states. This might include, for example, a common programme for the priorities of a reformed UNSC and steps to enhance UN peacekeeping strategically and tactically. The latter is a particularly ripe area for cooperation given the recent dust-ups within the C-34 between troop contributors and funders and the need to operationalize the high-level panel report on UN peacekeeping, *Uniting Our Strengths for Peace—Politics, Partnership and People.*[54]

Both India and Japan are key supporters of UNPKOs, the former as a troop contributor and the latter as a funder. For both, however, issues pertaining to the focus and effectiveness of their efforts have been recurring. Indian misgivings on the expanding role and raison d'être of recent PKOs have only increased. Despite its extensive contribution to UN peacekeeping, richly measured in blood and treasure, India has not made a mark through leadership or by contributing new ideas.[55] This fact is puzzling given that several high-ranking Indians have headed UN peace missions over the decades.[56]

Here, Japan's record and contributions in leveraging its limited peacekeeping role on the ground into greater political support within the UN might be instructive. Tokyo's contribution to UN peacekeeping commenced in 1992 following the enactment of Japan's international peace cooperation law, which allowed limited participation in standard peacekeeping activities such as separating combatants, monitoring combatants, and patrolling buffer zones.[57] Hamstrung by domestic legal constraints on the use of force, Japan focused its contributions on the financial and intellectual aspects. Tokyo has played an important role within various peacekeeping working groups including the C-34, the Security Council Working Group on Peacekeeping Operations, and the Peacebuilding Commission. It has also led the UN Military Units Manuals project, contributing to the development of manuals that provide systematic support for peacekeepers, and has been hosting seminars and symposiums on UN peacekeeping. In 2007, the Japanese foreign ministry established a peacebuilding training facility at the UN that provides conceptual and practical training before trainees find positions as UN peacekeepers.[58] A clear synergy therefore exists for India–Japan cooperation on this issue.

On nuclear issues, there is scope to boost cooperation, provided that profound differences in nuclear values can be overcome. However, this caveat applies more to Japan, given long-standing domestic constraints that include constitutional impediments, resilient anti-nuclear public perceptions, and painful historical legacies. Japan has long evinced discomfort over India's nuclear policies, but the George W. Bush administration's strategic embrace of India culminating in the 2008 India–US nuclear deal shifted Tokyo's calculus, resulting in civil nuclear discussions between Japan and India. This change suggests that the domain of engagement on this issue has widened despite Indian reservations on the NPT and CTBT. But normative differences fester. Tokyo has tacitly accepted India as a de facto nuclear weapons state through its conditional approval of the India–US deal in the NSG, but continues to insist that civil nuclear relations can only take hold when India becomes a party to the CTBT and begins negotiations on the Fissile Material Cut-off Treaty (FMCT).[59] During recent negotiations, both sides could not bridge existing differences over Japan's insistence on a tougher safeguards regime and a 'no nuclear test' clause in a potential bilateral civil nuclear deal. However, Tokyo has recently given in to India's demand to reprocess spent nuclear fuel from Japanese-made reactors—the first time that

Japan has relaxed this provision for another country.[60] India has also been insisting on a self-imposed moratorium on its tests, objecting to Tokyo's insistence on the clause in the text of the bilateral agreement under discussion that provides for automatic termination of nuclear ties if India conducts tests in future. Unless this particular gulf is bridged, civil nuclear cooperation is unlikely to be realized.

The Road Ahead: Challenges and Opportunities

To nudge cooperation forward on these crucial global governance issues, both countries need to confront and overcome certain roadblocks. However, these obstacles sit beside opportunities that, if capitalized upon, can advance mutual interests within the international order.

The first key challenge is state capacity. Lately, scholars have lamented the raft of institutional inadequacies limiting Indian foreign policy.[61] For these critics, the limited number of foreign service officers manning South Block (the offices of the MEA), the disregard of specialists and their expertise to make sense of 'wicked problems' like climate change,[62] the lack of opportunities for external policy advice, and the consequently reactive nature of foreign policy making do not bode well for a rising power like India. While the issue of institutional deficits and their impact on foreign policy has not been demonstrated empirically, it is evident that the Indian Foreign Service faces constraints that could limit its ability to achieve India's multilateral interests. Above this, a larger problem exists. At least on multilateral matters, there does not appear to be an overarching political strategy influencing the range of India's international diplomatic activities. In some areas such as peacekeeping, international development cooperation and development assistance, and reform of IFIs and the UNSC, India's behaviour appears to be driven by historical legacies that place it as a developing country striving for autonomy to manage its development and security. However, that moment has passed. With economic liberalization and robust growth trajectories, India's material and geopolitical clout has risen and its interests have widened. To better protect and advance them in a fluid international order, India needs to dispense with its schizophrenic character and settle on a political strategy through which its positions and contributions on multilateral issues are coordinated. Doing so would also help when it collaborates with Japan (and other countries) to achieve mutual interests in the international order.

The second challenge is geopolitics. For the United States and Japan, India appears as a bulwark against a rising China. The budding entente between Japan and India generates opportunities for both countries, but it can also distance both nations from China, breeding resentment in Beijing of a putative anti-China alliance. This would hurt India's interests not only due to China's economic importance (Sino-Indian trade hit US$67 billion in 2012 as compared to US$18 billion of India–Japan trade),[63] but also because, according to Kumar and Malhotra, 'India has made common cause with China on critical multilateral issues, such as reform of international financial institutions, climate change, and the Responsibility to Protect. Both countries prefer a UN mandate to coalitions of the willing for peacekeeping and humanitarian actions.'[64] Moreover, China's role as a P-5 member is crucial when it comes to India's (and Japan's) possible entry as a permanent member in the UNSC. Beijing and Delhi's collaboration within frameworks such as BRICS, BASIC, and the newly created New Development Bank (NDB) will assume greater importance as these groupings develop. India therefore needs to balance its relations with Japan and China wisely.

Third, domestic politics could hinder progress. Both countries have strong leaders now, but partisan wrangling on specific matters could impede progress. Civil nuclear cooperation between the two nations and acquiring Japanese consent for India's entry into the broader non-proliferation regime—though not the NPT—is contingent on domestic political forces within Japan that forcefully exert their anti-nuclear credentials. Similarly, in India, any concessions that might be made on the CTBT to assuage Japanese nuclear fears rile up critics who bemoan the loss of strategic autonomy. With respect to UN peacekeeping, the potential of Indo-Japanese cooperation in field operations if any crises break out in Asia is limited given legal restrictions that bar the deployment of the Japan Self-Defense Forces (JSDF) overseas. This constraint seems 'unlikely to change in the near future', despite recent moves by Tokyo to increase rapid deployment operations in the wake of 9/11.[65] A heavy focus on domestic issues over the next few years, especially in India, could divert attention away from bilateral engagement on key multilateral issues.

At the same time, opportunities exist to boost cooperation on the multilateral front. Both countries now have strong executive leadership, a critical feature that has been largely absent in Delhi and Tokyo for the last two decades. Expectations are high, given that the leaders have elevated the India–Japan relationship to the level of a Special Strategic and Global Partnership. On the development side, fruitful progress was made during the August–September 2014 visit of Modi to Tokyo and during subsequent bilateral encounters between the two sides. Tokyo has promised US$35 billion for infrastructural investment alone over the next five years in India.[66]

Both Modi and Abe are right-of-centre politicians who ostensibly have more space to make policy choices—notably on the security side—in order to clear snags that hold the relationship back. Nuclear cooperation continues to be strained, despite both leaders reaffirming their commitments to ensure that India becomes a full member of international export control regimes. However, the two leaders have directed their interlocutors to speed up negotiations on this and other issues in the proposed bilateral agreement for cooperation in the peaceful uses of nuclear energy.[67]

With both navies modernizing, there is scope to enhance maritime cooperation around the Indian Ocean. In 2014, Japan, the United States, and India conducted the Malabar joint naval exercise after concerted prodding from the Japanese leadership to allow its forces to participate.[68] India's security concerns have risen, given Beijing's growing port presence and access, its airfields and gas pipelines, and its investments in infrastructure development used by its ever-expanding and modernizing navy across the Indian Ocean. This growing Chinese presence doubles as a concern for resource-strained Japan, which relies greatly on oil imported through that particular route. Notwithstanding the US–Japan alliance and its constitutional restrictions, Japan is evincing interest in maritime multilateralism, reposing faith in these mechanisms to ease tensions. Admiral Katsutoshi Kawano, chief of staff of the Japan Maritime Self-Defense Force (JMSDF), reiterated his desire in 2014 to deepen multilateral maritime exercises with India as tensions rise across the South and East Asian oceanic fronts.[69] Given the absence of a solid regional organization to secure the Indian Ocean, such naval exercises provide a real opportunity to advance maritime multilateralism between nations.

Policy Recommendations

India's role as an aid donor has grown over the past decade. Beyond its neighbourhood, India now extends assistance to several African and Asian countries. Recognizing this change, the MEA created the Development Partnership Administration (DPA) to centralize and coordinate the implementation of India's development assistance. Although the unit is further divided into three divisions, there appears to be no explicit, overarching strategy or framework governing policy formulation.[70] The DPA, however, is not involved in the political decision making around India's foreign aid, which is left to other country desks in the MEA, whose decisions the DPA then implements.[71] Moreover, it appears that there are very few oversight mechanisms and safeguards for the monies disbursed. Also, there seems to be a greater emphasis on engagement with the private sector within the aid apparatus without understanding the implications for foreign policy writ large.[72] To institutionalize robust practices and bolster the nascent apparatus, India should heed the practices and philosophy of the Japan International Cooperation Agency (JICA), which functions in accordance with a clearly defined charter through which assistance is disbursed.[73] Importantly, JICA's charter privileges the participation of non-state actors (non-governmental organizations, universities, and so on) in the aid policy process, which produces two key benefits: it brings key ideas and expertise into the policy process from local development experts, and it strengthens the relationship between the donor and recipient by showing them that assistance is formulated with their interests at heart. This would be an essential first step before India and Japan might consider joint development assistance in other countries.

On maritime security, after a brief interregnum, the Indian Navy has deepened joint multilateral exercises with the JMSDF through the Malabar exercises, which also include the United States. Going further, as a logical extension of their peacekeeping responsibilities, India and Japan can contribute to maritime forces at the UN's International Maritime Organization, which regulates and protects international shipping lanes. Another possible area of cooperation across the Indian Ocean littoral is in disaster management. As naval drills and exercises between the two nations grow, a clear interest and opportunity exists in focusing some of this attention on managing disasters by enhancing search and rescue capabilities. Finally, Japan currently attends IORA meetings as a dialogue partner but, as the organization matures, India can encourage Japan to join and nudge Tokyo to provide resources for the group's activities on disaster risk reduction, maritime transport, and fisheries. On the diplomatic front, India and Japan might also work towards developing an institutional mechanism by which they can contribute to the peaceful resolution of territorial disputes in the South and East China Seas (which is something Southeast Asian countries have been calling for).

On the UNSC, the inability of the council to respond to crises across the Middle East (ISIS), Eastern Europe (Crimea), and Asia (South China Sea) has renewed questions about the relevance and responsiveness of the unreformed body, particularly in India and Japan. Yet there is recognition that reforms are unlikely in the foreseeable future. This was starkly evident in the caveats posed by China, Russia, and the US to the text of the Intergovernmental Negotiations on Security Council Reform in 2015.[74] Given this prospect, it perhaps makes more sense in the interim for India and Japan to focus on the procedural side, working to regulate the council's agenda and operations in the near future. Leaving UNSC membership aside, there exists scope to work on other issues within the council such as counterterrorism. Both nations support the proposed Comprehensive Convention on International Terrorism that has intermittently stalled, but adopting a joint declaration on counterterrorism could reinvigorate this initiative.

On peacekeeping, Japan and India can promote exchanges on UNPKOs between the Centre for UN Peacekeeping of the Indian Army and the Japan Peacekeeping Training and Research Center (JPC). In the past, the JPC's training had been reserved for the JSDF, but since 2014 officers from foreign militaries have been accepted for specialized courses on the decision-making processes surrounding troop detachment.[75] Both Japan and India have also expressed support for the 'responsibility while protecting' (RWP) principle introduced by Brazil in 2012, which calls for establishing criteria to ensure that interventions by force only occur as a last resort and do not cause major damage as they unfold.[76] Since then, the concept has largely been in oblivion. This gives Japan and India a chance to reintroduce the concept, consider its validity and pertinence, and bring those views to the attention of the P-5 at the UNSC. The Indian MEA should also become more involved in the international politics of UN peacekeeping by dispatching more Indian nationals to serve at UN headquarters. Here, it can draw from Japan's history in peacekeeping that has been marked, amongst other things, by a robust presence in New York. Richard Gowan argues that UN peacekeeping over the last 15 years has been deployed 'in support of peace agreements, mandated to extend the authority of state authorities in parallel with host governments, and been tasked with protecting civilians, in addition to the promotion of human rights'.[77] This paradigm shift represents a distinct political departure from peacekeeping experiences before 9/11. Clearly, the political sands have shifted and if India and Japan hope to influence the future of this trajectory, they need to be in a position to shape the political contours of UN peacekeeping in the future.

* * *

It is to the mutual benefit of India and Japan to work together to shape the existing and evolving multilateral rules and institutions related to international peace and security, development, and the nuclear order. The present leadership in Delhi and Tokyo has provided the necessary political impetus by establishing the Special Strategic and Global Partnership between the two countries. This pronouncement notwithstanding, the prospects of an India–Japan partnership to effectively shape global governance norms and institutions will depend on two conditions. First, the ability of India and Japan to build on areas of convergence, such as reform of the UNSC, maritime security, and development assistance; and second, to manage their areas of divergence, particularly related to the nuclear order and peacekeeping. Their ability to strengthen the former and narrow the latter will determine their ability to shape the global order.

Notes

1. World Bank, 'Country Summary—India', n.d., retrieved from https:// finances.worldbank.org/countries/India on 16 September 2015.

2. ADB, 'Asian Development Bank and India: Fact Sheet', n.d., retrieved from http://www.adb.org/sites/default/files/publication/27768/ind.pdf on 16 September 2015.

3. ADB, 'Asian Development Bank and India'.

4. N. Pai, 'India and International Norms: R2P, Genocide Prevention, Human Rights and Democracy', in W.P.S. Sidhu, P.B. Mehta, and B. Jones (eds), *Shaping the Emerging World: India and the Multilateral Order*, Washington, D.C.: The Brookings Institution Press, 2013, pp. 303–18.

5. B. Jones, *Still Ours to Lead: America, Rising Powers and the Tension between Rivalry and Restraint*, Washington, D.C.: The Brookings Institution Press, 2014.

6. Jones, *Still Ours to Lead*, p. 139.

7. Ibid.

8. C. Ogden, *Indian Foreign Policy: Ambition and Transition*, Cambridge, UK: Polity, 2014.

9. K. Krishnasamy, 'A Case for India's Leadership in United Nations Peacekeeping', *International Studies*, 47, 2010, pp. 225–46; United Nations Peacekeeping, 'Troop and Police Contributors Archive', n.d., retrieved from http://www.un.org/en/peacekeeping/resources/statistics/contributors_archive.shtml on 16 September 2015.

10. C. R. Mohan, 'India and International Peace Operations', *SIPRI Insights on Peace and Security 2013/3*, Stockholm International Peace Research Institute, 2013.

11. Jones, *Still Ours to Lead*, p. 86.

12. Mohan, 'India and International Peace Operations', p. 6.

13. Ogden, *Indian Foreign Policy*, p. 104.

14. S. Sengupta, 'International Climate Negotiations and India's Role', in N. Dubash (ed.), *Handbook on Climate Change and India: Development, Politics and Governance*, London: Oxford University Press, 2012, pp. 101–17.

15. I.L. Rehman, 'From an Ocean of Peace to a Sea of Friends', in W.P. S. Sidhu, P.B. Mehta, and B. Jones (eds), *Shaping the Emerging World: India and the Multilateral Order*, Washington, D.C.: The Brookings Institution Press, 2013, pp. 131–56.

16. V. Sakhuja, *Asian Maritime Power in the 21st Century: Strategic Transactions in China, India and Southeast Asia*, Singapore: Institute of Southeast Asian Studies, 2011.

17. R. Rajagopalan, 'From Defensive to Pragmatic Multilateralism and Back: India's Approach to Multilateral Arms Control and Disarmament', in W.P.S. Sidhu, P.B. Mehta, and B. Jones (eds), *Shaping the Emerging*

World: India and the Multilateral Order, Washington, D.C.: The Brookings Institution Press, 2013, pp. 197–216.

18. A. Tellis, *India as a New Global Power: An Action Agenda for the United States*, Washington, D.C.: Carnegie Endowment for International Peace, 2005.

19. The seed for the G-4 plan initially rose out of the 2004 Panel on Threats, Challenges and Change that proposed UNSC expansion for new permanent members without veto powers. Criteria for inclusion included commitment to democracy and human rights, economic size, population size, military strength, financial contributions to the UN, and a successful record on non-proliferation and counterterrorism. The G-4 countries united to pursue reforms on these grounds. See Ogden, *Indian Foreign Policy*, p. 104; O. Stuenkel, *Responding to Global Development Challenges: Views from Brazil and India*, Bonn: German Development Institute, 2010.

20. The C-10 group includes Algeria, Libya, Senegal, Sierra Leone, Namibia, Zambia, Kenya, Uganda, Equatorial Guinea, and the Republic of Congo.

21. R. Mukherjee and D.M. Malone, 'India and the UN Security Council: An Ambiguous Tale', *Economic And Political Weekly*, 48(29), 2013, pp. 110–17.

22. Mukherjee and Malone, 'India and the UN Security Council', p. 113.

23. D. Kapur, 'India and International Financial Institutions and Arrangements', in W.P.S. Sidhu, P.B. Mehta, and B. Jones (eds), *Shaping the Emerging World: India and the Multilateral Order*, Washington, D.C.: The Brookings Institution Press, 2013, pp. 237–60.

24. Kapur, 'India and International Financial Institutions', pp. 247–9.

25. C. Jaffrelot and W.P.S. Sidhu, 'From Pluralism to Multilateralism: G-20, IBSA, BRICS and BASIC', in W.P.S. Sidhu, P.B. Mehta, and B. Jones (eds), *Shaping the Emerging World: India and the Multilateral Order*, Washington, D.C.: The Brookings Institution Press, 2013, pp. 319–40.

26. R. Kumar and A. Malhotra, *Back to Reality: India's National Interests and Multilateralism*, Policy analysis brief, Stanley Foundation, 2014.

27. J. Kirk, *India and the World Bank: The Politics of Aid and Influence*, New York: Anthem Press, 2010, p. 5.

28. Kirk, *India and the World Bank*, p. 6.

29. L. Veit, *India's Second Revolution*, New York: McGraw Hill, 1976.

30. In 1964, India helped establish the UN Conference on Trade and Development, from which emerged the larger G-77 (Group of 77) that brought developing states into one forum.

31. I. Taylor, 'India's Rise in Africa', *International Affairs*, 88(4), 2012, pp. 779–98.
32. R. Mukherjee, 'India's International Development Program', in D. M. Malone, C.R. Mohan, and S. Raghavan (eds), *Oxford Handbook of Indian Foreign Policy*, Oxford: Oxford University Press, 2015, pp. 173–87.
33. V. Sharan, I. Campell, and D. Rubin, *India's Development Cooperation: Charting New Approaches in a Changing World*, Special report, Observer Research Foundation (New Delhi) and Saferworld (London), 2013; S. Chaturvedi, A.M. Chenoy, D. Chopra, A. Joshi, and K.H.S. Lagdhyan, *Indian Development Cooperation: The State of the Debate*, Evidence Report No. 95, Brighton: Institute of Development Studies, 2014; P. Srinath, 'Infographics: Foreign Aid Going Out of India', *Pragati—The Indian National Interest Review*, December 2013, retrieved from http://pragati.nationalinterest.in/2013/12/infographic-foreign-aid-going-out-of-india/ on 16 September 2015. See also Global Humanitarian Assistance, 'India', n.d., retrieved from http://www.globalhumanitarianassistance.org/countryprofile/india on 16 September 2015.
34. A. Fuchs and K.C. Vadlamannati, 'The Needy Donor: An Empirical Analysis of India's Aid Motives', *World Development*, 44, 2013, pp. 110–28.
35. R. Mukherjee, 'Can't Buy Me Love: India's Foreign Aid and Soft Power', *Seminar*, 658, 2014, pp. 55–9.
36. Fuchs and Vadlamannati, 'The Needy Donor', p. 125.
37. Mukherjee, 'Can't Buy Me Love', p. 57.
38. 'Mexico's Carstens Makes Case for IMF Job', Reuters, 22 June 2011.
39. Press Trust of India, 'Pranab Mukherjee Congratulates New IMF MD Christine Lagarde', *Economic Times*, 29 June 2011.
40. Kapur, 'India and International Financial Institutions', p. 245.
41. V. Vira, 'India and UN Peacekeeping: Declining Interest with Grave Implications', *Small Wars Journal*, July 2013, pp. 1–8.
42. R. Gowan and S. Singh, 'India and UN Peacekeeping: The Weight of History and Lack of Strategy', in W.P.S. Sidhu, P.B. Mehta, and B. Jones (eds), *Shaping the Emerging World: India and the Multilateral Order*, Washington, D.C.: The Brookings Institution Press, 2013, pp. 177–96.
43. T. Tardy, 'Peace Operations: The Fragile Consensus', *SIPRI Yearbook*, Stockholm International Peace Research Institute, 2011.
44. Gowan and Singh, 'India and UN Peacekeeping', p. 181.
45. Ibid., p. 188.
46. R. Nayan and I. Stewart, 'Export Controls and India', Occasional paper, Centre for Science and Security Studies, King's College London, 2012.

47. Government of India Press Information Bureau, 'Prime Minister's Address to the Combined Commander's Conference', 19 October 2012, retrieved from http://pib.nic.in/newsite/PrintRelease.aspx?relid=88528 on 16 September 2015.

48. V. Sakhuja, 'Increasing Maritime Cooperation: IORA, IONS, Milan and the Indian Ocean Network', *IPCS Special Focus*, New Delhi: Institute of Peace and Conflict Studies, 2013.

49. Rehman, 'From an Ocean of Peace', p. 140.

50. Kumar and Malhotra, *Back to Reality*, p. 7.

51. US Department of State, 'Thirteenth Plenary Session of the Contact Group on Piracy off the Coast of Somalia', n.d., retrieved from http://www.state.gov/t/pm/rls/othr/misc/202270.htm on 16 September 2015.

52. Fuchs and Vadlamannati, 'The Needy Donor', p. 116.

53. Sharan *et al.*, *India's Development Cooperation*, p. 12.

54. United Nations Peacekeeping, 'Information Note on High-Level Independent Panel on Peace Operations', 16 June 2015, retrieved from http://www.un.org/en/peacekeeping/documents/High-Level-Independent-Panel.pdf on 16 September 2015.

55. Gowan and Singh, 'India and UN Peacekeeping', p. 178.

56. For instance, India sent its top-ranking officer, General Satish Nambiar, to head the mission as the force commander of the United Nations Protection Force in former Yugoslavia (1992), and General Vijay Jetley was charged to lead peace operations in Sierra Leone. In 2010, the UN appointed India's Lt General Chander Prakash as the Force Commander for the peacekeeping force in the Democratic Republic of Congo. See Krishnasamy, 'A Case for India's Leadership', pp. 236–7.

57. D.M. Kliman, *Japan's Security Strategy in the Post 9-11 World: Embracing a New Realpolitik*, Washington, D.C.: Centre for Strategic and International Studies, 2006.

58. K. Ishizuka, 'Japan', in A. Bellamy and P.D. Williams (eds), *Providing Peacekeepers: The Politics, Challenges and Future of UN Peacekeeping Contributions*, Oxford: Oxford University Press, 2013, pp. 396–416.

59. D. Brewster, *India as an Asia Pacific Power*, London: Routledge, 2010.

60. 'Japan Eases Rules for Indian Nuclear Deal', *Japan Times*, 19 June 2015.

61. D. Markey, 'Developing India's Foreign Policy Software', *Asia Survey*, 8, July 2009, pp. 73–96; S. Tharoor, *Pax Indica*, New Delhi: Penguin, 2012.

62. H.W.J. Rittel and M.M. Webber, 'Dilemmas in a General Theory of Planning', *Policy Sciences*, 4(2), June 1973, pp. 155–69.

63. Embassy of India in China, 'India-China: Trade and Commercial Relations', n.d., retrieved from http://www.indianembassy.org.cn/DynamicContent.aspx?MenuId=3&SubMenuId=0 on 16 September 2015.

64. Kumar and Malhotra, *Back to Reality*, p. 2.

65. Ishizuka, 'Japan', p. 414.
66. N. Basu, 'Abe's $35 Billion Promise to Modi Has Riders', *Business Standard*, 16 September 2014.
67. Press Trust of India, 'India, Japan to Accelerate Civil Nuclear Deal', *Hindu*, 1 September 2014.
68. J.B. Miller, 'Japan and India's Mutual Courtship', *Al Jazeera America*, 3 October 2014.
69. A. Krishnan, 'Japan Navy Chief's Message for the Indian Govt', *Hindu*, 24 April 2014.
70. MEA, Government of India, 'The Development Partnership Administration', n.d., retrieved from http://www.mea.gov.in/development-partnership-administration.htm on 16 September 2015.
71. E. Sridharan, 'The Emerging Foreign Assistance Policies of India and China: India as a Development Partner', Center for the Advanced Study of India, University of Pennsylvania, 2014.
72. Sharan *et al.*, *India's Development Cooperation*, p. 5.
73. See MoFA, 'Japan's Official Development Assistance Charter', 29 August 2003, retrieved from http://www.mofa.go.jp/policy/oda/reform/revision0308.pdf on 16 September 2015.
74. I. Bagchi, 'US Backs China & Russia, Blow to Desi UNSC Dream', *Times of India*, 11 August 2015. See also W.P.S. Sidhu, 'UNSC: Misreading an Opportunity', *Mint*, 17 August 2015, retrieved from http://www.livemint.com/Opinion/dpiKVSV7XD6cRDqrlQvWzK/UNSC-Misreading-an-opportunity.html on 16 September 2015.
75. Ministry of Defense of Japan, 'Japan Peacekeeping and Training Center', n.d., retrieved from http://www.mod.go.jp/js/jsc/jpc/english/about/message.html on 16 September 2015.
76. O. Stuenkel, 'BRICS and the Responsibility while Protecting Concept', *Hindu*, 12 March 2012. In September 2012, Japan's permanent representative to the UN, Tsuneo Nishida, publicly welcomed the RWP principle at an informal dialogue session on the R2P. See International Coalition for the Responsibility to Protect, 'Remarks by H.E. Tsuneo Nishida Ambassador Extraordinary and Plenipotentiary and Permanent Representative of Japan on the Occasion of an Informal Interactive Dialogue on the Responsibility to Protect', 5 September 2012, retrieved from http://responsibilitytoprotect.org/Japan.pdf on 16 September 2015.
77. R. Gowan, 'Peacekeeping at the Precipice: Is Everything Going Wrong for the UN?', Background paper, International Forum for the Challenges of Peace Operations, Beijing, 2014.

Conclusion

Overcoming a History of Missed Opportunities

Anthony Yazaki and Rohan Mukherjee

With the global balance of power gradually shifting towards Asia, a strengthened India–Japan partnership is poised to have a major impact on the twenty-first century.[1] Unlike some of Asia's other major powers, the two countries are unburdened by a historically difficult relationship, and they have numerous areas of common or complementary interests where they can engage in mutually beneficial cooperation. These sectors span from economics to energy, security, and global governance. However, in order to make deeper cooperation a reality, the two countries will have to overcome their differences, which are apparent across many areas of their societies including national ethos, business, and government bureaucracy. Taking all of this into consideration, the two countries would have much to gain if they were able to channel their resources into a strengthened partnership.

To many, Asia's ongoing rise to greater global prominence does not come as a surprise. The fact that the term 'Asian Century' has been used to describe the twenty-first century since at least the 1980s attests to the potential that has existed for economic development to help the continent grow in primacy.[2] Keeping in mind the 30-plus years of rapid economic growth in China, 20-plus in India, and a range of positive performances in Southeast Asia picking up where the original Asian 'tigers' had left off, a former American official has described the US 'pivot' or strategic rebalance toward Asia since 2012 as flowing from an acknowledgement that the 'lion's share of the political and economic history of the twenty-first century will be written in the Asia-Pacific region'.[3]

China will play a major role in writing this history, but so will others. As the centre of geopolitical gravity gradually shifts towards Asia, India and Japan will need to ensure that they play a significant part in shaping the contours of the twenty-first century, if only to advance their interests in this increasingly competitive region. As the preceding chapters make clear, if the two countries can make good on the commitments made by their leaders, the Japan–India relationship is primed to play a major role in shaping the Asian Century. However, both societies are democracies with complex, somewhat opaque linkages between government and private sector, at times obscuring which is principal and which is agent. As China grows richer, its own society and the allocation of power between its various actors is bound to grow more complex as well, if an outright fracture at some stage is to be avoided. Thus, generalizations and predictions rooted in the current performance of Asia and its principal powers need to be advanced and assessed with caution.

History's Clean Slate

As has been mentioned, working in favour of Japan and India is the fact that the relationship between the two countries is not bogged down by adverse historical factors. In the First World War, colonial India was allied with Japan through London. During the Second World War, Japan's armed forces reached India's most easterly borders in 1944, culminating in grim fighting at Imphal and Kohima between exhausted, semi-starving Japanese troops and pick-up forces assembled in haste by Delhi, while India's substantial army fought on other fronts beyond South Asia for the British Empire. Japan's defeat in these battles in part marks the moment of retreat of its remarkable, over-ambitious conquest of much of Asia that self-destructed in slow motion following the catastrophic decision to attack Pearl Harbor in late 1941.

Since the Second World War, Tokyo's relationships with both China and South Korea have been coloured by their forced subordination to Japan in the 1930s and from 1910, respectively, with both ending in 1945. Despite providing considerable development assistance and a partial model for China's modernization and development, the shadow of Japan's former occupation of China has hung heavily over bilateral ties, increasingly so of late. Japan's model of post-war economic development was adopted by South Korea after the immediate consequences of Korean War were addressed, and it served the country well. Indeed, in some respects the student has outstripped the master today, with self-confident, entrepreneurial, and risk-taking South Korean firms bestriding the globe, often pipping Japanese competition at the post. These circumstances have not made Koreans any more forgiving for the experiences of their ancestors at the hands of Japan. Thus, although South Korea and Japan are both closely allied to the United States, the two have signally failed to yield to the entreaties of Washington to improve their ties. And as China's geopolitical weight grows, Beijing has been investing heavily in armed forces (even though Washington remains far ahead), which is perceived as a much greater threat in Tokyo than in Seoul. In fact, the South Korean public feels more militarily threatened by Japan than China.[4]

Notwithstanding Japan's substantial trade connections with these two countries, economic links alone have distinctly failed to construct anything that could be characterized as a partnership, let alone an alliance. This regional dysfunction was highlighted in 2012, when an intelligence-sharing deal between Japan and South Korea was put on hold due to historical concerns even though the cooperation would have pertained to North Korea, a country of obvious mutual concern.[5] Japan's relationship with the US—its protector and principal ally—is also refracted through the stained glass of history, which perpetuates a degree of resentment among some segments of the Japanese public and fuels occasional mild friction between Washington and Tokyo over matters of historical interpretation.

Like Japan, India has complicated historical relations with a number of countries in its own neighbourhood. The country's enduring enmity with Pakistan since the two nations were partitioned in 1947 has waned somewhat as India has pulled away from its rival in terms of economic and global significance, but the relationship remains pregnant with the risk of misunderstanding, possible reckless behaviour, or official complicity with sometimes very dangerous acts by non-state third parties. India has often been tarred with an overbearing attitude towards other smaller neighbours. And its relations with China, while economically vibrant, if unbalanced (in China's favour), are hamstrung to a degree by ongoing border disputes and a bruising war in 1962 that China comprehensively won and that India has still not fully overcome.

In his recent book, Pankaj Mishra evokes the powerful two-way influence of Japanese and Indian intellectual leaders early in the last century, after Japan's victory over Russia's fleet in 1905 made clear that Asian powers could defeat colonial ones.[6] Nevertheless, beyond a shared attachment to Buddhism, the two countries struggled to find natural connections after India's independence in 1947, in spite of Prime Minister Jawaharlal Nehru's welcoming hand to the defeated Japanese government during the first two decades of Delhi's foreign policy autonomy.

Due to all of these factors, Japan and India can start with a virtually clean slate. India has benefited from considerable Japanese assistance, directly through Japan's own programmes and through those of the Asian Development Bank (ADB), of which Japan is a major shareholder and arguably the dominant member. Japan's aid programme, focused in large part on helping to develop India's physical infrastructure, has contributed to making Japan consistently one of the two most favoured foreign countries in surveys of Indian public opinion.[7] Of course, Delhi and Tokyo have clashed often and somewhat ritualistically over India's nuclear policy (and, while seeking to engage each other on this terrain, still do). But this disagreement does not overwhelm the relationship as a whole and, barring unforeseen developments, is unlikely to threaten it much in the future, particularly if nuclear cooperation between them—today a prospect actively being negotiated—becomes a reality.

Thus, without being burdened by their past, Japan and India have the opportunity to forge a new kind of partnership that could help reshape inter-Asian relations and meet new global challenges of the twenty-first century. The research project that culminated in this volume was posited on the belief that—while clearly requiring careful tending—this bilateral relationship holds great promise for the two countries, their continent, and the world.

Cultural Differences

Nevertheless, we do not want to dismiss what is sometimes referred to as the 'cultural divide' between the two countries.[8] This factor relates to the national characteristics of the two countries and their inhabitants. Japan is admirably cohesive and orderly, populated by often self-sacrificing citizens who frequently endure without much complaint what is considered 'unavoidable'—for example, the absence of a more diverse set of political parties and positions to choose from. These characteristics may help explain how Japanese citizens, perplexed as they may be by the country's economic plight, have soldiered on during two decades of virtual economic stagnation while the country's demographics have become increasingly unfavourable. Hard work, an uncomplaining nature, respect for elders, tradition, and the 'Japanese way' are all admired and widely adopted throughout the country.

India, on the other hand, a country on the scale of a continent and with a population as large as that of several continents, is hugely diverse though distinctively Indian under the national umbrella. The country is raucous, at times chaotic, and has for several decades now been quite optimistic about its future, given its potential in spite of the grinding poverty still affecting too many lives. Politics is a national contact sport nearly as pervasive as cricket, drawing not just on two major national parties, but also a plethora of regional and other smaller but often influential political formations. Contestation of every sort can degenerate suddenly into violence, and several spasms of communal violence have stretched India's social fabric, generally unfolding within a local or state setting, such as in Delhi after Prime Minister Indira Gandhi's murder in 1984 and in Gujarat in 2002. To a varying degree, the sum and mix of these characteristics puzzle and alarm many Japanese observers and residents of the country, while an enthusiastic minority in Japan is strongly attracted to India precisely because of them.

Beyond these traits, Indians admire Japan's economic success, its pristine cities and countryside, and its emphasis on hygiene and a healthy diet. Virtually all Indians who have an opportunity to do so greatly enjoy visiting Japan. But a significant gulf exists between the outlook of Indians and Japanese, reflected even in their negotiating styles, with Indians rarely knowing when to stop negotiating and declare victory (or at least a truce), and the Japanese always wanting every last detail settled before anything can be agreed, while also seeking to build in as much control over outcomes as possible. Both countries, as elsewhere around the world, display forms of what others might consider corruption and self-dealing—including between business and political actors—but in forms that are very different from each other's and are therefore difficult for the citizens of one country to decode when looking at the other.

The recipe for mutual misunderstanding (amidst general sentiments of mutual goodwill) is thus clear and will require a greater willingness by each side to understand the other more than superficially.

Opportunities and Challenges

As has been suggested throughout this volume, the potential areas of cooperation can be broadly broken down into the categories of economics, energy, security, and global governance. Considering the either common or complementary interests between the two countries across these fields, it makes abundant sense that they should simultaneously work towards their own and each other's goals.

Economic Cooperation

The complementarity of interests is particularly clear in the field of economics. Japan excels at technological innovation and thrives on constantly reinventing both its urban fabric and national infrastructure. India has done very well in the services sector for the past two decades, although it is increasingly clear that services alone cannot lift the whole country out of underdevelopment. As Prime Minister Narendra Modi has emphasized, rapid urbanization will best be driven in India by a growing manufacturing sector, while smaller populations in rural areas may favour a degree of consolidation of agriculture that could drive up productivity well beyond what the Green Revolution achieved in the late 1960s and early 1970s (with its potential now largely exhausted by mismanagement of water resources and overuse of chemical and other fertilizers in excessive and toxic quantities since then).

One complementarity between the two countries, despite having significant social and cultural undercurrents in Japan, receives too little attention: demographics. As is evident in the contribution of Shujiro Urata and Mitsuyo Ando, contemporary theories addressing the phenomenon of stagnation in Japan increasingly draw on demographic decline as the central and not merely contributing factor. To rectify these circumstances, Japan's fantasies often turn to scenarios in which robotics rescues the country from economic decline and abandonment of its aged populations, suggesting how difficult it will be to promote large-scale immigration within the country—but necessity may yet do the trick where reason has failed.[9]

Japan's demographic decline (a shrinking population with a growing share of the elderly) is not a new phenomenon and is virtually certain to continue unless there is a significant change in the country's immigration policies. On the other hand, India is home to a burgeoning youth population keen on opportunities to pursue its own economic advancement. These facts alone make it clear that labour market cooperation between the two countries would simultaneously help each side meet its national economic objectives. As Devesh Kapur and Rohit Lamba note in this volume, a relaxation of visa restrictions or the creation of a visa allowing Indian nationals to work in Japan would provide indirect but tangible help to intensify and accelerate India's development and could also help to get the Japanese economy back on track.

The major obstacle in achieving a mutually beneficial agreement of this nature is clearly on the Japanese side. As an island nation on the far eastern fringe of Asia and the far western edge of the Pacific, the country has historically had an inward-looking ethos and a sense of national identity that is largely built upon its ethnic and cultural homogeneity. However, this seemingly unshakeable national identity was recently called into question following the March 2011 Fukushima nuclear disaster, when the seminal post-disaster report stated that the disaster was largely 'Made in Japan' due to 'our reflexive obedience; our reluctance to question authority; our devotion to "sticking with the program"; our groupism; and our insularity'.[10]

It would be highly beneficial to make the most of this moment of self-examination and attempt to overcome the country's aversion to the acceptance of greater numbers of foreign workers (if not permanent immigrants). In fact, Japan already has more of them than is commonly imagined, not least in agriculture where Chinese 'trainees' spend stints of up to three years tending to farms and boosting production that can no longer be managed exclusively by Japan's rapidly ageing farming community.[11] While widely resisted, at least in principle, it is clear that nursing and elder care will provide much employment to citizens of the Philippines and Indonesia, and possibly of other countries including India.

Of course, any policy change is subject to electoral politics and debate, meaning that reversing Japan's restrictive approaches to migration will be no easy task. What is needed is strong political leadership, something that Prime Minister Shinzo Abe can bring to the table after years of political uncertainty, perhaps explicitly as part of the structural 'third arrow' of Abenomics. His current tenure affords him the opportunity to make clear that Japan stands to gain more from the economic benefits of increased immigration than what it perceives it will lose in terms of its national identity and cohesion. If the decision is indeed between continued prosperity, which underpins today's social harmony, and homogeneity, Japan must quickly wake up to the full implications of what should be an active choice rather than defaulting to the path of least resistance.

Less controversial is the proposition that Japan has much to gain in the aggregate (whatever the risks on a case-by-case basis) from increased investments in India's growing economy and market. As Kapur and Lamba note, Japan boasts a capital-rich economy, while India requires increased capital inputs to continue pushing its economic development forward. In making this objective come to fruition, there will have to be changes on both sides. India will need to create an environment that is friendlier to Japanese investment, while the Japanese business community will have to overcome its risk aversion and move beyond the comfort zone of 'Japan Inc.', which has produced bulging corporate coffers but not the national prosperity and new high-quality jobs that greater global engagement should bring. In comparison, South Korea has repeatedly demonstrated how East Asian countries can operate profitably within the vast Indian market. At the other end of the equation, it will be important for Prime Minister Modi to make good on his pledge made during his 2014 visit to Japan to cut red tape for Japanese foreign direct investment (FDI). Both prime ministers can only encourage their private sectors and the executives of state companies, and thus promises like those of Prime Minister Abe that Japan will provide US$35 billion of FDI to India need to be advanced by enabling conditions on the ground, a challenge that India needs to meet not only to attract Japanese investors, but also those of other major economic powers.

Further, the Regional Comprehensive Economic Partnership (RCEP), as discussed by Urata and Ando, would help to increase trade and investment between Japan, India, and a plethora of other countries in the region, including China. Considering the countries that would be involved in the RCEP, it would have the potential to impact the lives of nearly half of the world's population, many of whom still live in poverty. Given that this kind of mega-regional free trade agreement is being more widely attempted at the moment (for example, in both the trans-Atlantic and trans-Pacific spheres, the latter perhaps eventually overlapping with the RCEP), it may be prudent for both Japan and India to ensure that they are not left behind. Each should be a forward player rather than a reluctant participant.

Energy and Climate Change

In the sphere of energy security, Japan and India can both make strides in moving towards a more sustainable future, especially in terms of climate change. Although Delhi has understandably adopted the position that it cannot sacrifice its economic development for the sake of global sustainability, especially in light of the fact that developed countries are responsible for the overwhelming majority of historical greenhouse gas emissions, there must also be a recognition that India has much to lose if the growth of global carbon emissions is not substantially contained and reduced in the near future. In that sense, Japan and India both have a shared interest (if distinct roles to play) in maintaining a liveable planet conducive to greater prosperity in both the global North and South.

As the two chapters by Shyam Saran and Radhika Khosla, and Nobuo Tanaka and Anthony Yazaki, respectively argue, India should keep this long-term view in mind and follow through on its commit-ment to increase the proportion of renewables in its energy portfolio as the country strives to offer energy access for the first time to a large proportion of its population. This step likely will not be enough: India must also introduce mitigation strategies over time to make sure that as it develops, it is contributing to a healthier environment for a population that increasingly will be demanding one. In view of recent downward shifts in the costs of alternative energy sources, mitigation strategies will probably become significantly more afford-able in the decades ahead.

While the recent increase in Japan's fossil fuel consumption was inevitable in the short term due to the sudden and unforeseen elimi-nation of nuclear power from its energy portfolio after the nuclear disaster at Fukushima in 2011, this moment of national challenge should also be seized as an opportunity to fundamentally shift energy consumption towards a more sustainable course involving an increased use of renewables, including Japan's abundant geothermal resources. Thus, bilateral cooperation on research and development as well as the deployment of renewables should be a priority in the energy sector that will reap benefits in the long term and new employment opportunities in the meanwhile. The sharp decline of oil prices in 2014 and 2015—even if not indefinitely sustained at their current low levels—provides an opportunity to use the related savings to invest in clean energy in both countries, rather than merely doubling down on the ability to consume cheap fossil fuels, tempting as that may be for fiscally strapped governments.

Aside from renewable energy, an important facet of securing India's energy future will be to improve its capacity to engineer clean coal energy due to the latter's growing feasibility and potentially large impact, a priority that was also raised by the chapters on energy and climate change in this volume. Given the current high cost of the relevant technologies, the ongoing negotiations on a joint crediting mechanism (JCM) between India and Japan will be particularly important. Expeditiously completing this agreement should remain high on the bilateral agenda, not least as the JCM could be applied in many energy-related projects aside from clean coal technology.

Both countries can also contribute to the safer and more sustain-able use of nuclear energy by engaging in joint research towards a new generation of nuclear energy reactors. Despite the global back-lash against nuclear power following the Fukushima disaster, nuclear energy will continue to have a role to play in a future marked by climate change, which could accelerate beyond current (already worrying) projections. If Japan and India can contribute to the development of new nuclear energy generation capacities that can substantially reduce the risk of another disaster, they would have made an impressive contribution to a global shift away from fossil fuel consumption. Such cooperation is contingent upon the two countries finally completing their civil nuclear agreement after years of negotiation, which requires each side to move beyond its hidebound positions. In order to do so, Japan will have to make efforts to overcome its normative aversion to India's nuclear policies, while India will also have to work to reassure Japan on this front, including through concrete rather than merely rhetorical steps. India's still somewhat unconvincing arrangements with the US relative to nuclear supplier liability in the event of an accident[12]—agreed during President Obama's 2015 visit to India—aim to cover Prime Minister Modi's embarrassment over his own party's role while in opposition in crippling the practical viability of the India–US nuclear agreement of 2008. The scheme will need to be modified, expanded, or articulated more clearly if India wishes to satisfy legitimate Japanese worries, while Japan needs to prioritize its concerns with respect to India, where no course of action for Tokyo is risk-free, particularly in the nuclear sphere. The greatest risk doubtless arises from a failure to engage with each other meaningfully, but recent reports that Japan will allow India to reprocess spent fuel suggest that compromises could be possible.[13]

Security Cooperation

In the security sphere, there is one overwhelming and overarching factor that drives Japan and India together—anxiety over the rise of China. Both countries have a need to engage positively with China while also ensuring that Chinese assertiveness does not trample on their own national interests, a task that has proved to be exceedingly difficult for Japan of late. Thus, the rise of China has created a convergence of interests between Japan and India, which is pushing them together. But at the same time, China is viscerally opposed to a Japan–India partnership, especially with American involvement. This produces a dynamic that could potentially keep these three democracies from entering into an overly tight embrace. As analysed by Noboru Yamaguchi and Shutaro Sano, and C. Raja Mohan and Rishika Chauhan in this volume, this state of play will necessitate a delicate balancing act on the parts of both Delhi and Tokyo. The sensitivity of a closer Japan–India strategic relationship—at a time when the Modi government is also trying to engage positively with Beijing—was highlighted when India refused to upgrade the Defence and Foreign Ministries' dialogue with Japan to the ministerial level in September 2014.

For the strategic thinkers of Japan and India, this conundrum raises the need to avoid framing their partnership in terms of the negative aim of containing China, instead placing emphasis on what their relationship can positively contribute to bilateral, regional, and potentially global peace and security. Thus, Japan and India may find it beneficial to work together on maritime security, especially anti-piracy, an area in which cooperation has already begun in the form of naval exercises. W.P.S. Sidhu and Karthik Nachiappan address this cooperation as a matter of global governance that could prove to be of substantial importance for both countries, considering their heavy dependence on imported energy sources, but also potentially valuable for other countries in Asia, Africa, and the Middle East. Given India's location between the straits of Hormuz and Malacca—two of the most important shipping lanes in the world—this effort is a natural one for Delhi, and one on which it shares clear interests with both Tokyo and Beijing. Maritime security thus lends itself to a degree of potentially useful trilateral confidence building if the two East Asian countries could navigate their way to actual cooperation.

As Noboru Yamaguchi and Shutaro Sano argue, cooperation on humanitarian assistance and disaster relief can also provide avenues to strengthen ties between Japan and India without creating unwanted and unnecessary controversy. Given that the two countries are the bookends of a region highly susceptible to natural disasters, cooperation in this field could be particularly meaningful for their bilateral relationship and for other partners along the Indian and Pacific Ocean littorals. This is especially true as climate change is likely to increase extreme weather events, which are already frequent in the region.[14]

United Nations Peacekeeping Operations (UNPKOs) are relevant both to global security and global governance, and increased cooperation on them would dovetail well with both countries' desires to play a more prominent role in the UN. India's experience with UN peacekeeping is vast and impressive, while Japan has engaged with it only gingerly so far, on a learning curve and testing domestic tolerance for participation in riskier peacekeeping operations than those it had subscribed to hitherto. Public opinion in Japan is fairly allergic to Japanese casualties of violence abroad, although this could change somewhat over time.

There has been a drastic increase in the number of peacekeepers deployed throughout the world over the past two decades, with the overwhelming majority of them coming from developing countries like India, while funding has been provided mostly by developed countries like Japan. The UN urgently needs the type of high-tech and logistical capabilities that the well-trained Japan Self-Defense Forces (JSDF) could offer in abundance. These capabilities would prove particularly valuable in niche roles at a time when not only the number of peacekeepers but also the nature and variety of their responsibilities have been growing. Indeed, these responsibilities now routinely encompass deployment to countries still experiencing conflict and 'with no peace to keep', which has meant that UN peacekeepers face greater risks in the field and require greater technical, logistical, and other capacities.[15] Building on Prime Minister Abe's interest in strengthening Japan's policy of 'proactive contribution to peace', either as a means to reinterpret Japan's constitutional provisions touching on its defence roles or as an end in itself, Japan will need to update its restrictive 1992 regulations on peacekeeping, which prevent Japanese troops from serving in many settings and under the most frequently prevailing circumstances of today.[16] If this task can be accomplished, Japanese forces would be poised to play a greater role in the maintenance of international peace and security, frequently alongside their more experienced Indian counterparts. The training opportunities for the Japanese personnel involved would doubtless prove useful. Overcoming the Japanese public's strong aversion to the use of force will take time and continued persuasion by the country's leaders.

Global Governance

The convergence of Japanese and Indian interests is also clear in terms of global governance. Both countries wish to see the United Nations Security Council (UNSC) reformed to provide them with enhanced roles commensurate with their international stature, at a time when the council's composition seems ever more anachronistic, still reflecting the power equations of the immediate post–Second World War period. As noted in the chapter by Shinichi Kitaoka and Naoko Kumagai, seeking permanent membership in the UNSC for either or both countries appears to be a futile goal at the moment, especially for Tokyo due to China's strong opposition to any upgrade of Japan's international status. Therefore, intermediate steps might be considered. These could relate to the council's modus operandi, including its approach to the use of the veto, given the council's recent and frequent paralysis on major crises in Syria and Ukraine. Several proposals have been floated to qualify or restrict the use of the veto by permanent members on a voluntary basis or through suasion by other member states. If there were a way to overcome Chinese opposition to an enhanced role for Japan in the UNSC, it might also be possible to create a class of semi-permanent seats that would be open to frequent—or in practice even permanent—occupancy by Japan and India, albeit without a veto. Still, it will be necessary to balance the potential benefits of council reform with the slim chances in the immediate future of making it a reality. If UNSC reform appears to be too difficult to achieve, it would be sensible to prioritize other potential areas of cooperation such as strengthening the authority of the UN General Assembly (UNGA) relative to the UNSC.

One facet of global governance on which Japan and India would benefit from coordinating their positions relates to international financial institutions (IFIs). Japan is on firm footing in terms of its voting power in the Bretton Woods institutions of the World Bank and International Monetary Fund (IMF), thus not standing to gain much from reforms that would strengthen the position of developing countries like India in these institutions. But such zero-sum calculations will hardly breed wider cooperation between the two countries. India's claim to a greater role in the IFIs can be seen as analogous to Japan's in the UNSC. Meanwhile, India has participated in the formation of new challengers to the Bretton Woods system such as the BRICS' New Development Bank (NDB) and the Asian Infrastructure Investment Bank (AIIB), which both draw support from developing countries dissatisfied with their lack of influence within existing institutions that are dominated by developed countries like Japan. And recent developments have shown that Australia, New Zealand, and European Union members are open to supporting these new institutions when invited to join.

Japan will need to consider its position carefully in this regard, as even the US may move towards participation, having failed to contain European break-out from what the US may have assumed would be a Western consensus against these new bodies. Sticking to tried and true institutional settings such as the ADB—where Tokyo's leadership has increasingly grated at least China among that institution's stakeholders—could leave Japan somewhat marooned in a fast-changing world of flexible diplomatic and international financial architecture in which nimble political and diplomatic manoeuvres will likely be rewarded. Thus, in this particular sphere, Japan may need to rethink its strategy somewhat, while India experiments with its own possibilities in what is for Delhi an exciting new realm. Expecting Delhi and Tokyo to align with each other may be over-optimistic, but they could certainly learn a great deal from each other in the years ahead, Japan having contributed so significantly to the achievements of the ADB—the most successful among the regional development banks to date—through its commitment to stringent lending practices and wider management and financial probity.

Overarching Issues

Looking at overarching issues, one of the imperatives for strengthening the Japan–India relationship will be to increase societal exchanges between the two countries and to create more opportunities for person-to-person interactions. This would be helpful in overcoming the cultural divide between the two countries discussed previously. Creating better mutual understanding between the countries beyond political, governmental, and business elites would be particularly helpful in the private sector, and also in encouraging more sophisticated media coverage of each other's evolving accomplishments, deficits, and concerns. In their chapter, Shujiro Urata and Mitsuyo

Ando cite statistics showing that only 727 Indian students were studying in Japan in 2014, as compared to over 94,000 Chinese students. Considering that India and Japan are democracies, without greater bottom-up interaction between the two populations and key sectors shaping their perceptions of each other, it will be difficult to forge a much deeper bilateral relationship. It bears remembering that one of the reasons why many Indian elites feel warmly towards the United States is because their children study, work, or live there, and because American culture has gradually permeated the entertainment industry and the arts in India.

Cultural exchange is also vital in providing the necessary language and skills training to young Indians who aspire to work in Japan, and to workers in Japan's sizeable small and medium-sized enterprise (SME) sector, which is inwardly focused at present and stands to gain a great deal by expanding to countries such as India. The private sector vehicles for facilitating the necessary training and exposure already exist—the Confederation of Indian Industry (CII) and the Federation of Indian Chambers of Commerce and Industry (FICCI) already have cells devoted to improving business ties with Japan. Similarly, the India–Japan SME Business Council is ideally placed to provide the kind of language and soft skills training necessary for Indians and Japanese to thrive in each other's business environments.

The need for greater exchange is true at the level of governments as well. The two countries frequently experience difficulty understanding each other's idiosyncrasies in terms of government structure and operating methods, which has hampered the ability to follow through on some desired areas of cooperation. For example, Japanese officials from the Ministry of Economy, Trade and Industry (METI) have indicated that an obstacle in completing the bilateral JCM agreement has been the plethora of Indian ministries involved in the process, which has made it difficult to understand which individual or agency will be making the final decision on any count.[17]

Although it will ultimately be up to the policy makers to decide which courses of action are most feasible and practical to pursue, a number of considerations should be kept in mind if the relationship is to be meaningfully deepened. First and foremost, the two countries must genuinely view each other as equal partners, unlike, for example, the American alliance model in which the US generally dominates the terms of engagement. This means that Japan and India should attempt to forge an innovative kind of partnership that eschews the classic donor–recipient model long characterizing their relations. Each needs to fully appreciate the standing of the other in the wider world and on the latter's own merits, with both sides working towards each other's interests whenever possible. Excessively self-centred agendas make for a paltry menu of bilateral cooperation. Each country will have to leverage its areas of comparative advantage to build a relationship that is both synergistic and self-reinforcing, bearing in mind their very different economic and demographic trajectories. Ringing statements by national leaders, no matter how sincere, will not suffice. Action on a broad range of fronts is required, not necessarily simultaneously but in a logical sequence, with sufficient conviction as to register within the two countries and internationally. We are not there yet.

* * *

A strong Japan–India partnership has immense potential. The two countries are home to roughly 20 per cent of the world's population and are two of the three largest economies in Asia, a region that is poised to grow rapidly in the coming decades. If these immense resources and human capital can be leveraged towards the common and complementary interests of the two countries, there is every reason to believe that they will be able to accomplish a great deal together and for themselves. The avenues for cooperation are numerous and varied, as has been articulated throughout this volume. The policies that have been advocated in this concluding chapter and in preceding chapters are only some of the possibilities that should be explored. Scholarly work on the future of the Japan–India relationship is still limited, and more support for greater dialogue on and study of the partnership within the academic and think-tank community would doubtless constitute a modest but wise investment in its future. We are cautiously optimistic that this central and mutually rewarding relationship deserves much greater attention in both countries. We look forward to revisiting it in an academic context at some point in the future, hoping to find that it has thrived and expanded.

Notes

1. The authors are deeply indebted to David M. Malone for his intellectual and drafting contributions to this chapter.

2. J.P. Sterba and L. Lescaze, 'Ten Years After—Vietnam's Legacy: Of the Asian Dominoes That Haven't Fallen, Several Are Thriving—The War Pumped in Money, and Trade Brings More for the ASEAN Nations—Communists at Loggerheads', *Wall Street Journal*, 14 March 1985, p. 1.

3. K. Campbell and B. Andrews, *Explaining the US 'Pivot' to Asia*, London: Chatham House, 2013, p. 2; Y. Kato, 'Interview/Kurt Campbell: China Should Accept US Enduring Leadership Role in Asia', *Asahi Shimbun*, 9 February 2013.

4. 'Koreans Consider Japan as Second Biggest Military Threat Next to North Korea', *Business Korea*, 11 July 2014.

5. Associated Press, 'South Korea and Japan Put Intelligence Pact on Hold', *Guardian*, 29 June 2012.

6. P. Mishra, *From the Ruins of Empire: The Intellectuals Who Remade Asia*, New York: Farrar, Straus, Giroux, 2012.

7. See, for example, a Pew survey which places Japan with a 43 per cent favourability rating below only the US at 55 per cent in 2014. See Pew Research Center, 'How Asians View Each Other', 14 July 2014, retrieved from http://www.pewglobal.org/2014/07/14/chapter-4-how-asians-view-each-other on 16 September 2015.

8. See S. Basu and R. Yoshida, 'How to Overcome the Cultural Divide? A Study of Japanese Expatriates' Work Experiences in India', *South Asian Journal of Business and Management Cases*, 1(2), 2012, pp. 115–33.

9. There is some reason to be hopeful on this front, as argued in J. Akashi, 'New Aspects of Japan's Immigration Policies: Is Population Decline Opening the Doors?', *Contemporary Japan*, 26(2), 2014, pp. 175–96.

10. K. Kurokawa, K. Ishibashi, K. Oshima, H. Sakiyama, M. Sakurai, K. Tanaka, M. Tanaka, S. Nomura, R. Hachisuka, and Y. Yokoyama, *The Official Report of the Fukushima Nuclear Accident Independent Investigation Commission: Executive Summary*, Tokyo: The National Diet of Japan, 2012, p. 9.

11. Brought to Japan under the government's Technical Intern Training Program, Chinese immigrants comprised almost 80 per cent of the 49,000 agricultural immigrants in Japan in 2012. See M. Ando and K. Horiguchi, 'Big Farms Deeply Depending on the Technical Intern Training Program', 2013, p. 4, retrieved from http://migrationfiles.ucdavis.edu/uploads/rs/files/2012/ciip/ando-horiguchi-japan-ag.pdf on 16 September 2015.

12. A. Gowen and S. Mufson, 'Is the India Nuclear Agreement Really the 'Breakthrough' Obama Promised?', *Washington Post*, 4 February 2015.

13. D.R. Chaudhury, 'For the First Time, Japan May Allow India to Reprocess Spent Nuclear Fuel from Japanese-Made Reactors', *Economic Times*, 19 June 2015.

14. A. Najam, 'Increasing Occurrence of Severe Weather Events', in *Outlook on the Global Agenda 2015*, Geneva: World Economic Forum, 2014, p. 27.

15. S. von Einsiedel, *Major Recent Trends in Violent Conflict*, United Nations University Centre for Policy Research, Tokyo, 2014.

16. MoFA, 'Japan's Security Policy', n.d., retrieved from http://www.mofa. go.jp/policy/security/ on 16 September 2015; Government of Japan, 'Act on Cooperation for United Nations Peacekeeping Operations and Other Operation', Act No. 79, 1992, retrieved from http://www.pko. go.jp/pko_j/data/law/pdf/law_e.pdf on 16 September 2015.

17. Information based on interview with METI officials.

Index

'Abenomics' strategy 36, 239n38, 277

Abe, Shinzo 1, 11–13, 20–2, 25n2, 27n38, 36, 63, 70–1, 106, 116, 125n43, 159, 161, 169, 177n69, 183–4, 188, 193, 199, 201n1, 202n18, 222, 225, 232, 245, 257, 261, 269n66 277–8, 282

Act East policy 228

Afghanistan 8, 24, 153, 158, 163
  India's strategic interests in 165
  JSDF's involvement in 21
  post-conflict aid by India in 159
  reconstruction effort by Japan and India in 165

agglomeration effect 79

Air Defense Identification Zone (ADIZ) 13, 156

Allied powers 4

al-Qaeda 161

Annual Macroeconomic Database (AMECO) 39

anti-piracy forces 156

anti-terrorism 161

Antony, A.K. 160, 194

arc of freedom and prosperity 21, 183

arc of instability 161

Arctic Sea and receding ice 162

Argonne National Laboratory, United States 119

Asian Century 25, 270–1

Asian Development Bank (ADB) 229, 231–3, 246, 273, 284

Asian Economic Community for trade and investment liberalization 227–8

Asian Games (1951), New Delhi 4

Asian Infrastructure Investment Bank (AIIB) 230, 284
  China's voting rights in 233

Asian NATO 194

Asian power 168

Asian Relations Conference 180
  Japan in 180

Asia-Pacific Economic Cooperation (APEC) 227, 250

Asia, towards strategic coordination in 193–7 (*see also* India–Japan strategic partnership)

Aso, Taro 12, 14, 21, 30n88–9

Association of Southeast Asian Nations (ASEAN) 10, 16–18, 41, 64, 73, 157, 168, 171, 176n53, 178n75, 227, 255, 287n2
  ASEAN6 49–50
  bilateral security cooperation with 16
  Defence Ministers Meeting Plus (ADMM Plus) 168
  Maritime Forum 168

Regional Forum (ARF) 17, 166, 247
Look West policy 171

balance of payments crisis (1991) 8–9
ballistic missiles 156
Bangladesh 6, 14
Bangladesh–China–India–Myanmar corridor 189
Bharat Heavy Electricals Limited (BHEL) 142
Bharatiya Janata Party (BJP), India 196, 214
bilateral economic exchanges 62–4
bilateral initiatives between India and Japan, ongoing 136–7
bilateral naval exercises 160
between India and Japan (first) in 2012 12
border conflict in Kargil (1999) 164 (see also Pakistan)
Bose, Subhas Chandra 11, 190
Brazil, Russia, India, and China (BRIC) 36
Brazil, Russia, India, China, and South Africa (BRICS) 26n11, 230–1, 243n75, 249–50, 260, 266n25, 269n76, 284
Brazil, South Africa, India, and China (BASIC) 249–50, 260, 266n25
Bretton Woods system 230, 283–4
Buddhism 2, 69, 273
Bureau of Energy Efficiency (BEE) 113, 138–40, 143
Bush, George W. 16, 182–3, 258

C-130 aircraft 159
capital markets, India 77
capital-poor country, India as 70

capital-rich country, Japan as 69–70, 73
carbon capture and storage (CCS) technologies 108
Central Pollution Control Board 85
certificate of origins (CoOs) 59
Champions for Societal Manufacturing (CSM) project 226
Chennai–Bangalore Industrial Corridor (CBIC) project 60
Chennai–Bengaluru corridor 79, 189
China/Chinese 17, 70
challenge, in India–Japan relations 189–93 (see also India–Japan strategic partnership)
Japan's investment in 75
nuclear test (1964) 163
trade liberalization of 224
voted as permanent member of UNSC 5
Chinese Development Bank 231
Christine Lagarde's candidacy 253
Chubu Electric Power Company, Japan 116
civil nuclear cooperation agreement between India and US 11–12
between Japan and India 118
hurdle in 125n44
clean coal 108–9, 141–2
clean development mechanism (CDM) 107
clean energy 127–30, 144
climate change 24, 102–3, 107–9, 122, 127–9, 278–80
India's approach to 132–5
Clinton, Bill 8, 10, 16, 182
code of conduct (CoC) 166
Cold War 1–2, 5–7, 10, 13–14, 17, 21 (see also India–Japan strategic partnership)

after the 181–2
India's non-aligned foreign
   policy during 16
   years 180–1
Combined Task Force 151, 247
Committee of 34 (C-34) 254
common but differentiated
   responsibilities and respective
   capabilities (CBDRRC)
   principle 133–4
Commonwealth Fund for Technical
   Cooperation 251
complementary economies 71–5
Comprehensive Convention on
   International Terrorism 263
Comprehensive Nuclear-Test-Ban
   Treaty (CTBT) 27n26, 214,
   216, 248, 258, 260
Confederation of Indian Industry
   (CII) 61, 144, 285
Conference of Parties (CoP) 134
Conference on Disarmament 212
Conference on the Humanitarian
   Impact of Nuclear Weapons
   212–13
Contingent Reserve Arrangement
   231
Convention for the Suppression of
   Acts of Nuclear Terrorism
   215
Convention on the Physical
   Protection of Nuclear Material
   (2005) 215
counter-nuclear terrorism 214
cultural differences between India
   and Japan 274–5
cultural divide 274
cultural exchange 285
cyber domain, threats in 162
cyber espionage 162
cyber security 153, 161–2, 186–8

debt situation of developed
   countries, government 39
dedicated freight corridor (DFC)
   81, 90
defence budget of India between
   1991 and 2000 17
defence engagement, of India and
   Japan 184–6 (see also India–
   Japan strategic partnership)
Delhi Investment Summit on
   Afghanistan 165
Delhi Metro Rail Corporation 85,
   163
Delhi–Mumbai Industrial Corridor
   (DMIC) 60, 79–82, 86, 136,
   138, 141, 183
Democratic Party of Japan (DPJ)
   12
democratic quad 183
Department of Atomic Energy
   (DAE) 188
Department of Industrial Policy
   and Promotion (DIPP), India
   86, 92, 144
Development Assistance
   Committee (DAC) countries 60
Development Partnership
   Administration (DPA) 262
Diego Garcia 169
digital connectivity 87
diplomatic relations between India
   and Japan
   historical review of
      Cold War drift 5–7
      initial warmth 3–5
      lost decade 7–10
      newfound intimacy 10–13
disaster management 159, 186, 262

East Asia Summit 11, 168, 247
East Pakistan crisis 6

East–West Freight Corridor 144
economic challenges in Japan 73–5
economic cooperation/relationship
   between India and Japan 17–20,
   59–62, 275–8
business prospects in India for
   Japanese firms 50–2
international production
   networks in East Asia and
   India 47–50
international trade 42–4
Japan's FDI in India 44–7
joint ventures between Indian
   and Japanese firms 93
obstacles to doing business in
   India 52–6
strategic 188–9 (*see also* India–
   Japan strategic partnership)
economic crisis of 1991 16
Economic Survey of India 2012–13
   80
Economist, The 164
economy of Japan
   Abe's return as prime minister
      and its impact on 36
   growth strategy 36
   structural economic problems
      faced by 35, 37–41
employment by sector, share in
   India 84
energy and climate change
   278–80
Energy Charter 120–1
Energy Conservation Act 140
energy cooperation between India
   and Japan 278–80
   current scenario of 105–8
   mid-and long-term policies
      IEA and Energy Charter
         120–1
      nuclear energy 117–20

Regional Energy Security
   Forum 121–2
   near-term policies
      clean coal 108–9
      energy efficiency 111–14
      natural gas prices 114–17
      renewable energy 109–11
energy interests of Japan 104–5
energy needs of India 103–4
energy sector, India 130–2
Enhancement of Cooperation on
   Environmental Protection and
   Energy Security (2007) 136
European Union (EU) 56, 224
Expanded Maritime Forum 168
Export-Import Bank of China 231

Far Eastern Commission 4
Federation of Indian Chambers
   of Commerce and Industry
   (FICCI) 144, 285
financial crises 229
financial flows 90
First World War 271
Fissile Material Cut-off Treaty
   (FMCT) 258
five year plan 109–10
   Twelfth (2012–17) 72–3
food security 24, 223
foreign aid programme of Japan
   4, 69
foreign direct investment (FDI)
   18–20, 23, 37, 44–7, 56, 61–2,
   68, 87, 278
   challenges for improvement of 63
   importance of 41
   inflows to India 78
   by Japan in India 76–7, 139,
      278
   promising destinations for
      Japanese firms 51

fossil fuels 104–5, 120, 129, 131, 134, 279–80
free trade agreements (FTAs) 36–7, 41, 56–7
Free Trade Area of the Asia Pacific (FTAAP) 224
free trade in Japan 222
Fukuda Doctrine 6
Fukushima Daiichi Nuclear Power Plant disaster (2011) 23, 102, 104, 117–18, 122, 128–9, 276, 279–80

G-2 arrangement 198
G-4 (Brazil, Germany, Japan, and India) 249
  members 217
  resolution 219
G-8 9–10, 229
G-20 249
G-77 220–1, 251
Gakushuin University 3
Gandhi, Indira 5, 196, 274
Gandhi, Rajiv 7
Gandhi, Sonia 196
Gas Authority of India Limited (GAIL) 116
General Agreement on Tariffs and Trade (GATT) 56–7, 221
General Agreement on Trade in Services (GATS) 57–8
Generation IV reactor 118–19
geopolitical considerations 94–5
geopolitics 130, 180, 260
Ghauri I missiles 164
Global Competitiveness Report 2014–15 66n26
global free trade regime 154
global governance 282–4
Global Initiative to Combat Nuclear Terrorism 215

globalization 40
Global Trade Analysis Project (GTAP) model 59
Government of India's High Powered Expert Committee Report of 2011 84
Grant Aid for Grassroots Human Security 226
Green Revolution 275–6
grey zone situations 155
gross capital formation 71–3
gross domestic product (GDP) 39–40, 74, 227
Gulf of Aden 157, 255
Gulf War of 1990–1 7–8

Hashimoto, Ryutaro 9
high-level panel (HLP) 217
Hiroshima and Nagasaki tragedies (1945) 211
historical relations of India with Pakistan 272–3
humanitarian assistance and disaster relief (HADR) 24, 153, 158
hydropower 108, 110–11, 129
Hyogo Prefecture 186

IAEA Amended Protocol 215
Ikeda, Hayato 5
import-substitution industrialization (ISI) economic model 69
India
  interest in global governance with Japan
  challenges and opportunities 259–61
  extensive multilateral interests 245–50
  partnering to shape rules 256–9

performance in the
multilateral arena 250–6
policy recommendations
262–4
in UN peacekeeping 170
India–Bangladesh–Myanmar
corridor 80
India, Brazil, and South Africa
(IBSA) 249–50, 257, 266n25
India–Japan Business Cooperation
Committee 5
India–Japan Business Leaders
Forum (BLF) 35, 61, 64
India–Japan Chamber of
Commerce 94
India–Japan Energy Dialogue 142
India–Japan SME Business Council
285
India–Japan Strategic and Global
Partnership in the Next Decade
(2010) 128
India–Japan strategic partnership
179–80
after the cold war 181–2
China challenge 189–93
cold war years 180–1
overcoming the constraints
197–201
towards a strategic partnership
182–9
towards strategic coordination in
Asia 193–7
Indian Foreign Service 259
Indian National Congress (INC)
190
Indian Ocean Naval Symposium
255
Indian Ocean Rim Association
(IORA) 247, 255, 263, 268n48
Indian Ocean tsunami 159, 247
Indian Rare Earths Limited 188

Indian Space Research
Organisation (ISRO) 186
India's nuclear tests (1998) 182
India–US agreement (on food
security in the WTO, 2014) 227
India–US nuclear agreement of
2008 12, 280
Indira Gandhi Centre for Atomic
Research (IGCAR) 142
Indo-Japanese Global Partnership
for the Twenty-First Century 163
Indo-Pakistani nuclear rivalry 164
Indo-US agreement (on military
cooperation) 169
industrial clusters 79–82
information technology (IT) 68,
80, 92
INS Karmukh 185
INS Rana 185
INS Shakti 185
INS Shivalik 185
integral fast reactor (IFR)
technology 119
integrated gasification combined
cycle (IGCC) 108
intellectual property rights (IPR)
107–8
intended nationally determined
contribution (INDC) 134
Intergovernmental Negotiations on
Security Council Reform 263
Intergovernmental Panel on
Climate Change (IPCC) 130
International Atomic Energy
Agency (IAEA) 209–10
International Bank for
Reconstruction and
Development 245
International Convention on the
Suppression of Acts of Nuclear
Terrorism (2005) 215

International Development Association 245, 251
International Disaster Relief Law 159
International Energy Agency (IEA) 115, 120–1
International financial institutions (IFIs) 25, 244, 283
International Institute for Strategic Studies (IISS) 11th Asia Security Summit 160
International Maritime Organization 248, 262
International Military Tribunal for the Far East 4, 181
International Monetary Fund (IMF) 209, 249, 283
international production networks in East Asia and India 47–50
International Seabed Authority 248
international terrorism, threat of 157
international trade
 importance of 40
 of Japan 221–8
International Tribunal for the Law of the Sea 248
investor–state dispute settlement (ISDS) 58

Jaishankar, S. 9, 193
Japan
 creeping realism 20
 in Asian Relations Conference 180
 and India
  bilateral nuclear agreement between 215
  bilateral trade between 225
  fossil fuel consumption 279

in United Nations Peacekeeping Operations 217
 India cooperation in free trade 224–5
 international contributions 158
 international peace cooperation law 258
 international terrorism 157
 national security 155
 nuclear issue in 163
 National Security Strategy (NSS) 154, 158
 pacifist constitution 162
 policy on arms exports 161
 primary security interests and strategies 154–7
 Proliferation Security Initiative (PSI) member 164–5
 technology transfers to India 225
 trade connections 272
 US alliance 155
Japan Aerospace Exploration Agency (JAXA) 186
Japan Agricultural Cooperatives 222
Japan Air Self-Defense Force (JASDF) 161
Japan–Australia–India trilateral cooperation 170
Japan Bank for International Cooperation (JBIC) 50, 52, 60–1, 70, 76, 80, 136, 142
Japan Chamber of Commerce and Industry in India (JCCII) 19, 30n78, 59
Japan Coal Energy Centre (JCOAL) 136, 142
Japan Defense White Paper (2014) 170
Japanese Defense Agency (JDA) 16

Japanese firms in Asia 49–50
Japanese hostages killing, in Syria
157
Japanese manufacturing companies,
promising countries for overseas
business for 71
Japanese rice agriculture 223
Japan–EU FTA 41
Japan External Trade Organization
(JETRO) 45, 47, 52, 56, 65n9,
136
Japan Foundation 9
Japan Ground Self-Defense Force
(JGSDF) 161
Japan–India Comprehensive
Economic Partnership
Agreement (CEPA) 6–9, 12, 18,
28n43, 35, 37, 56, 61, 66n28,
225
Japan–India Foreign Ministers'
Strategic Dialogue 188
Japan–India FTA 58–9, 64,
66n28
Japan–India relations in global
governance and international
institutions 209–10
bilateral cooperation 209–10
international financial
institutions 228–34
international trade 221–8
nuclear non-proliferation and
international peace and
security 210–16
United Nations 216–21
Japan–India security cooperation
14–17, 153–4, 280–2
expanding opportunities for
cooperation 158–63
growing challenges 163–6
Japan's primary security interests
and strategies 154–7

Joint Declaration on Security
Cooperation (2008) 128,
184
policy recommendations
166–72
Japan International Cooperation
Agency (JICA) 80, 85, 136, 262
Japan Maritime Self-Defense Force
(JMSDF) 156, 185, 160–1, 261
'Japan Month' 7
Japan Peacekeeping Training and
Research Center (JPC) 263
Japan Plus 70, 91–4
Japan Self-Defense Forces (JSDF)
15, 21, 158–9, 170–2, 177n74,
217, 260, 263, 282
Japan Strategic Energy Plan 2030
104
Japan Student Service Organization
64
Japan–US–India trilateral security
mechanism 168–9
Jawaharlal Nehru National Solar
Mission 140
Jihadi terrorism 161
JIMEX12 185
Jinping, Xi 189, 191
Joint Crediting Mechanism (JCM)
107–10, 112–14, 138, 279, 285

kaketsuke-keigo (protection of non-
Japanese peacekeepers) 159
Kargil War (1999) 9
Kawano, Katsutoshi 261
Keio University 1
Khaan Quest peacekeeping exercise
171
Koizumi, Junichiro 10–11, 16,
20–1, 27n38, 29n58, 31n90,
183, 218
Korean War 272

Krishna, S.M. 169, 188
Kyoto Protocol 107, 134

L-69 249
Ladwig III, Walter C. 169–70
League of Democracies 220
League of Nations Council 217
Liberal Democratic Party (LDP),
  Japan 12, 223
liberalization, of beef and oranges
  223
light water reactor (LWR) 118–19
Line of Control 10
liquefied natural gas (LNG) 114,
  116
localization economies 79
Look East policy 9, 128, 168, 171,
  178n75, 227, 241n58, 241n60

'Made in Japan' 276
'Make in India' initiative 63, 186
maritime cooperation, in the
  Indian Ocean 261
maritime security
  cooperation 184
  importance of 160
  ways of ensuring India's 160
maritime terrorism 255
Maruti 800 car 7
Maruti Suzuki 7, 69, 76, 93
McKinsey Global Institute 84–5
Meiji restoration 69
Milan programme 255
Military First policy 156
military isolationism in India 179
Ministry of Coal, India 142–3
Ministry of Commerce and
  Industry (MoCI), India 80,
  91–2
Ministry of Defense (MoD), Japan
  161

Ministry of Economy, Trade and
  Industry (METI), Japan 80, 92,
  106, 108, 114, 136, 138, 186,
  285
Ministry of External Affairs (MEA),
  India 194, 252
Ministry of Foreign Affairs
  (MoFA), Japan 217
Ministry of New and Renewable
  Energy, India 110
Ministry of Power, India 139, 143
Ministry of Urban Development,
  India 84
missed opportunities in trade and
  investment 75
  FDI by Japan 77
  in India 78
  investment in Suzuki in 1980s
    76
  Japan share in total trade 76
Missile Technology Control Regime
  (MTCR) 187, 215, 254
mitigation strategies 279
Modi, Narendra 2, 13, 22, 28n44,
  36, 63, 70, 91, 103, 116, 123n1,
  124n19, 128, 144, 154, 157,
  169, 180, 183–6, 188, 192–4,
  196, 198–200, 205n55, 214,
  225, 228, 236n11, 245, 257,
  261, 269n66, 275, 278, 280
monetary stability 90
Mori, Yoshiro 10, 16, 106, 163,
  182
Mukherjee, Pranab 184
Mumbai–Ahmedabad corridor 90
Mumbai–Pune corridor 79

Nakasone, Yasuhiro 7
Narayanan, K.R. 6, 14
National Action Plan for Climate
  Change (NAPCC), India 134–5

National Capital Region (NCR),
India 79
National Defense Program
Guidelines (NDPG), Japan 154
National Democratic Alliance
(NDA) 194
National Institute of Population
and Social Security Research 38,
64n1
National Institution for
Transforming India (NITI)
Aayog 106
National Security Council, Japan
154
National Security Strategy (NSS)
154, 158
National Skill Development
Corporation (NSDC), India
91
National Thermal Power
Corporation (NTPC), India
142, 144
Nehru, Jawaharlal 4, 180, 273
Cold War years 180–1
New Development Bank (NDB)
230, 260, 284
New Energy and Industrial
Technology Development
Organization (NEDO), Japan
136, 141–2
Newly Industrialized Economies
(NIEs3) 49–50
New Silk Road 165
Nippon Export and Investment
Insurance (NEXI) 60
Nixon, Richard 211
no-first-use policy 164
Non-Aligned Movement (NAM)
5, 247
non-FTA members 36, 57
non-nuclear powers 212

non-nuclear principles of Japan
164, 172, 211
non-proliferation activism 182
Non-Proliferation and
Disarmament Initiative meeting
(2014) 212
Non-Proliferation Treaty (NPT) 209
'no nuclear test' clause 258
North Korea 8–9, 14
nuclear programme 163
nuclear armament agenda of India
254
nuclear disarmament 212–13
nuclear disruption 181–2
nuclear energy 117–20
nuclear issue in Japan 163
nuclear non-proliferation and
international peace and security
210–16
nuclear powers 102, 104–5, 109,
118, 129, 131, 145n4, 210,
213, 215–16, 254, 279–80
Nuclear Security Summit 212
Nuclear Suppliers Group (NSG)
11–12, 187, 215, 254
nuclear terrorism 24
nuclear tests
in India (1998) 1, 8–9, 181–2
by North Korea in 2005 and
2013 11, 13
at Pokhran 254
nuclear weapons
of India 153
Japan's position on 211

Obama, Barack 13, 162, 168–9,
176n62, 177n64, 196, 212,
253, 280, 288n12
official development assistance
(ODA) 19–20, 60–1, 69, 90,
128, 181, 226

Okinawa, nuclear weapons in 211
'one belt, one road' initiatives 189
opportunities for partnership for
    India and Japan
    clean coal 141–2
    energy efficiency 138–40
    solar energy 140–1
Organisation for Economic
    Co-operation and Development
    (OECD) 67n38, 120
outer space and cyber security
    186–8 (see also India–Japan
    strategic partnership)
    overarching issues 284–6
    Japan–India relationship 284

P5 220
Padukone, Neil 163
Pakistan 6, 14
    attention towards Kashmir
        valley 8
    border conflict in Kargil (1999)
        164
    external threat from China 17
    nuclear capabilities 164
    nuclear tests conducted by 8
    violation of de facto border
        9–10
Paracel Islands 166
Parrikar, Manohar 186
peace and stability 193
Peacebuilding Commission 258
peaceful nuclear explosion 181
peaceful, stable, and free of conflict
    162
peacekeeping operations (PKO)
    153, 216
Pearl Harbor attack (1941) 271
Perform, Achieve and Trade scheme
    140
Persian Gulf 160

Petroleum Conservation Research
    Association (PCRA), India 138
Planning Commission of India
    72–3, 106, 110, 128
Pokhran-II nuclear tests (1998) by
    India 8–9
population of Japan 38
Prakash, Arun 160
'proactive contribution to peace'
    153–4, 173n1, 282
Proliferation Security Initiative
    (PSI) 164
public debt of Japan, increase in
    73–5
public–private partnerships (PPPs)
    82, 84, 162
Putin, Vladimir 213, 236n9

railway system
    capacity addition in India and
        China 88
    Indian 88
    Japanese investments in 90
    investment in 88
    modal share of freight 89
Rajinikanth 69
Rao, Narasimha 9
Regional Comprehensive Economic
    Partnership (RCEP) 37, 41,
    64, 227–8, 241n56, 241n57,
    241n61, 278
Regional Cooperation Agreement
    on Combating Piracy and
    Armed Robbery 256
Research Institute of Economy,
    Trade and Industry (RIETI),
    Japan 42
Reserve Bank of India (RBI) 18–19
'responsibility to protect' (R2P) 246
'responsibility while protecting'
    (RWP) 263

Russian–American rivalry 210

Sagami Bay 160
Saiki, Akitaka 193
salami-slicing tactic 156
San Francisco Peace Treaty (1951)
    216
sanitary and phytosanitary (SPS)
    measures 57
Sato, Eisaku 211
    Nobel Peace Prize (1974) 211
Scarborough Shoal 166
sea lines of communication
    (SLOC) 159, 185
    protection of 159–60
    India's effort 160
    Japan's effort 160
    secure in the Asia Pacific 160
Second World War 2–3, 11, 16,
    70–1, 155, 271–2
    Tokyo's relationships with China
    and South Korea 272
security bills of Japan 217
security cooperation 280–2
security cooperation/relationship
    between India and Japan 14–17,
    280–2
Security Council Working Group
    on Peacekeeping Operations 258
Senkaku/Diaoyu Islands dispute
    13–15, 156, 166, 188
Shanghai Cooperation
    Organization (SCO) 247
Shared Awareness and
    De-confliction mechanism 256
ShinMaywa Industries Ltd 186
Silk Road Fund 231
silk roads 189
Singapore 12, 17
Singh, Manmohan 11, 106, 183–5,
    191–2, 195–6, 227, 255

Sino-American detente (1972) 181
Sino-centric Asia 192
Sino-Indian trade hit 260
Sino-Indian War of 1962 14
Sino-Japanese relations 218
Sino-Japanese tensions 192
small and medium-sized enterprises
    (SMEs) 48, 92, 285
Small Five Group (S5) 219–20
smart cities programme by India 84
smart city bonds 86
societal exchanges 284–5
solar energy 24, 127, 129, 131,
    135, 138, 140–1, 143
Solar Energy Corporation of India
    141, 143
solar mission, India 134–5
solar power 110–11, 134–6,
    140–1, 144
South Asian Association for
    Regional Cooperation (SAARC)
    194
South Korea 12, 17, 70, 272, 277
Soviet Union 16, 120
space security 162
Special Commonwealth Assistance
    for Africa Programme 251
Special Strategic and Global
    Partnership 13, 154, 171, 180
Spratly Islands 166
Stages of Economic Growth, The
    (W.W. Rostow) 87
Stockholm International Peace
    Research Institute (SIPRI)
    28n53
Strait of Hormuz 161
Strait of Malacca 161, 247
Strategic Arms Reduction Treaty
    (START) 213
Strategic Energy Plan (2014), Japan
    105, 110, 140

string of pearls policy 156
Summer Olympics (1948), London 4
supply chains 79–82
Swaraj, Sushma 171, 228

Taepodong ballistic missile, North Korea 8, 11
Tagore, Rabindranath 1
Taiwan Strait 8
Taliban regime, fall of (2001) 165
technical barriers to trade (TBT) 57
Teng-hui, Lee 8
9/11 terrorist attacks 161, 210, 260, 264
Third World countries 4
Tokyo Conference (Afghanistan) 165
Tokyo Declaration (2014) 70–1, 116, 185, 186, 193, 195
'Top Runner' programme, Japan 112–13, 139
Toshin fund exposure to overseas assets, Japan 78
Trade Facilitation Agreement 226
Transatlantic Trade and Investment Partnership (TTIP) 94–5
Trans-Pacific Partnership (TPP) 37, 41, 94–5, 221
Japan and 224
Treaty of Peace (1952) 128
Treaty of San Francisco 4
trunk infrastructure 81, 96n10
tsunami (2004) 159
HADR missions and 159
'two plus two' dialogue 184
Typhoon Haiyan 157

Ukraine, crisis in 213

UN Framework Convention on Climate Change (UNFCCC) 133–5
United Arab Emirates 161
United Nations (UN) 216–21
(see also Japan–India relations in global governance and international institutions)
United Nations Conference on Trade and Development (UNCTAD) 29n73, 65n13, 251
United Nations Convention on the Law of the Sea (UNCLOS) 248
United Nations General Assembly (UNGA) 5, 212, 249, 283
United Nations Industrial Development Organization 251
United Nations Operation in the Congo (UNOC) 254
United Nations Peacekeeping Operations (UNPKOs) 158, 172, 217, 244, 247, 257, 282
United Nations Security Council (UNSC) 5, 9, 24–5, 106, 172, 182, 209, 244, 246, 283
Resolution 1540 214
United Progressive Alliance (UPA), India 192
United States of America 3, 5, 77
disapproval of chequebook diplomacy 8
H1-B visa programme 91
and India relationship 16, 20
and Japan relationship
investment in US 75
reliance in mutual defence agreement 4, 6

security alliance 15
newfound hegemony 17
Uniting for Consensus (UFC)
   217–18
University of Delhi 5
UN Military Units Manuals project
   258
urban challenge in India 82–7
urban spaces in India 84
US-2 amphibious aircraft 186
US Energy Information
   Administration 108
US–Japan alliance 191, 261
US–Japan security treaty 211

Vajpayee, Atal Bihari 8, 10, 106,
   183, 214
value-oriented diplomacy 1, 20–2
Varghese, Peter 193
Vietnam 17

Visionary Leaders for Manufacturing
   (VLFM) project 226

Wassenaar Arrangement 187, 215,
   254
White House's National Strategy
   for the Arctic Region 162
World Bank 209, 229, 245
   Ease of Doing Business Index
      53
   Global Logistics Performance
      Index 56
World Trade Organization (WTO)
   56, 58
   Doha round 226
   establishment of 221

Yoshida Doctrine 4

zone of peace 248

Editors and Contributors

Mitsuyo Ando is Associate Professor, Faculty of Business and Commerce, Keio University, where she specializes in international trade. She holds an MA and PhD in economics from Keio University. She previously served as Assistant Professor at Keio University and Hitotsubashi University, Research Analyst at the World Bank Institute, and Research Associate at Keio University. Her publications include *International Production/Distribution Networks in East Asia: Machinery Industries* (2006), 'Evolution of Machinery Production Networks: Linkage of North America with East Asia' (*Asian Economic Papers*, 2014, co-authored), and 'Production Linkage of Asia and Europe via Central and Eastern Europe' (*Journal of Economic Integration*, 2013).

Rishika Chauhan is a doctoral candidate at the Centre for International Politics, Organization and Disarmament, School of International Studies, Jawaharlal Nehru University, New Delhi. Previously, she has worked with the Observer Research Foundation as a Junior Fellow, and as an Assistant Professor at the University of Delhi. Her research interests include Indian and Chinese foreign policy, international sanctions, and nuclear politics.

Devesh Kapur is Professor of Political Science, Director of the Center for the Advanced Study of India (CASI), and Madan Lal Sobti Professor for the Study of Contemporary India at the University of Pennsylvania. He is also a non-resident fellow at the Center for Global Development, Washington, D.C., and a member of the Brookings Institution–National Council of Applied Economic Research (New Delhi) India Panel.

Radhika Khosla is a Fellow at the Centre for Policy Research, New Delhi. Her research interests are in energy efficiency with a focus on the buildings sector and the broader linkages between energy and climate change in India. She is also a fellow at the India Centre for Sustainable Development at Somerville College, Oxford. Previously, she led the work on building energy efficiency at the Natural Resources Defense Council's India Initiative. She holds a PhD in geophysical sciences from the University of Chicago and undergraduate and master's degrees in Physics from the University of Oxford.

Shinichi Kitaoka is President, the International University of Japan; Senior Professor, National Graduate Institute for Policy Studies; Executive Director of Research, Institute for International Policy Studies; and Emeritus Professor, University of Tokyo. He was the Japanese ambassador to the United Nations (2004–6) and has served on advisory panels for foreign ministers and prime ministers. He is the acting chair of the Advisory Panel on the History of the 20th Century and on Japan's Role and the World Order in the 21st Century. He has published numerous books and was the recipient of the Imperial Medal with Purple Ribbon in 2011.

Naoko Kumagai is Associate Professor at the International University of Japan, where she teaches international politics, international organization, and conflict resolution. She earned a PhD in political science at the Graduate Center of the City University of New York. In her current research on reconciliation, she compares the Asian Women's Fund, the Japanese government–initiated moral atonement project for former comfort women, and the German Fund of Remembrance, Responsibility, and Future for moral compensation for East European slave and forced labourers in the Nazi era. She published a book, *Ianfu Mondai* (The Issue of Comfort Women), in June 2014.

Rohit Lamba is Assistant Professor of Economics at Pennsylvania State University. He received his PhD in Economics at Princeton University, following which he was a postdoctoral fellow at the University of Cambridge. He has also served twice as an economist at the Office of the Chief Economic Adviser to the Government of

India, and helped draft the *Economic Survey of India* 2012–13 and 2014–15. He was also a visiting research scholar at CAFRAL, the research wing of the Reserve Bank of India. His research focuses on mechanism design, finance, development, and Indian economic policy.

C. Raja Mohan is a Distinguished Fellow at the Observer Research Foundation and heads its strategic studies programme. He is a non-resident Senior Associate at the Carnegie Endowment for International Peace in Washington, D.C., and Adjunct Professor of South Asian Studies at the Rajaratnam School of International Studies, Singapore. He has served on India's National Security Advisory Board. Mohan has published widely on India's foreign and security policies. His recent books include *Samudra Manthan: Sino-Indian Rivalry in the Indo-Pacific* (2013) and *Modi's World: Expanding India's Sphere of Influence* (2015).

Rohan Mukherjee is a Stanton Nuclear Security Fellow at the Massachusetts Institute of Technology; a doctoral candidate in politics at Princeton University; and a non-resident Visiting Fellow at the United Nations University in Tokyo. His work on Indian security and foreign policy has been published in edited volumes from Stanford University Press, the Brookings Institution Press, and Oxford University Press, as well as in journals such as *Survival, International Affairs, Global Governance,* and *International Journal.* He holds a master's in public affairs from Princeton University and a BA in philosophy, politics, and economics from the University of Oxford.

Karthik Nachiappan is a PhD candidate at the India Institute, King's College London. His research focuses on how state capacity and domestic interests influence India's multilateral behaviour. Previously, he has worked in the International Institutions team at UNDP China and the Centre on Asia and Globalization at the National University of Singapore, where he researched the policy implications of the rise of China and India in the international order. His writings have been published in various journals, including *Global Policy, Global Health Governance,* and *Policy and Society.*

Shutaro Sano is Deputy Director, Professor at the Center for International Exchange, the National Defense Academy of Japan (NDA). His previous posts include researcher at the Office of the Commanding General, JGSDF Research and Development Command. He graduated from NDA (1989), and received an MA (2007) and PhD (2013) in international security from NDA. He also has an MA in public policy from the John F. Kennedy School of Government, Harvard University (1995). His recent publications include one on private military and security companies, in Japanese (Strategic Significance of Private Military and Security Companies: US Pursuit of a 21st Century-Type Military Force).

Shyam Saran is a former Foreign Secretary of India and has served as the prime minister's special envoy for nuclear affairs and climate change. He is former Chairman of the National Security Advisory Board and current Chairman of the Research and Information System for Developing Countries. He is a Senior Fellow at the Centre for Policy Research, New Delhi. Saran was awarded the Padma Bhushan, the third highest national award, in January 2011 for his contributions to civil service. He writes and speaks regularly on foreign policy, climate change, energy security, and national and international security-related issues.

Waheguru Pal Singh Sidhu is Senior Fellow for Foreign Policy at the Brookings Institution and at the Brookings India Centre. He is also a non-resident Senior Fellow at the Center on International Cooperation, New York University. Prior to that he was President of Programs at the EastWest Institute, New York. His research focuses on India's role in the global order and addressing nuclear weapons challenges. He is a co-editor of *Shaping the Emerging World: India and the Multilateral Order* (Brookings Institution Press, 2013). He is also a regular columnist for the *Mint* newspaper on international, regional, and strategic issues.

Nobuo Tanaka is currently President of the Sasakawa Peace Foundation and a Visiting Professor at the University of Tokyo, where he teaches energy security. He is a Distinguished Fellow at the Institute of Energy Economics, Japan, and the Center on Global

Energy Policy at Columbia University. As Executive Director of the International Energy Agency from 2007 to 2011, he was responsible for pioneering the concept of 'comprehensive energy security' while also expanding the agency's focus on climate change, renewable energy, and the transition to a low-carbon energy economy.

Shujiro Urata is Professor of Economics at the Graduate School of Asia-Pacific Studies, Waseda University; Faculty Fellow at the Research Institute of Economy, Trade and Industry; Research Fellow at the Japanese Centre for Economic Research; and Senior Research Advisor, Economic Research Institute for ASEAN and East Asia. He received his PhD in economics from Stanford University. He specializes in international economics and has published a number of books and articles on international economic issues, including *Free Trade Agreements in the Asia-Pacific* (World Scientific, 2010) and *Economic Consequences of Globalization: Evidence from East Asia* (Routledge, 2012).

Noboru Yamaguchi (Lieutenant General, Retired) is Professor at the International University of Japan. A graduate of the National Defense Academy of Japan (NDA), he originally trained as an army aviator. His assignments in uniform include Senior Defense Attaché at the Japanese embassy in Washington and Commanding General of the Ground Self-Defense Force Research and Development Command. After retiring from active duty in 2008, he served at the NDA as professor of military history and strategy. After the Great East Japan Earthquake in 2011, Yamaguchi served at the Prime Minister's Office as special adviser for crisis management.

Anthony Yazaki is a Research Fellow at the United Nations University Centre for Policy Research, Tokyo, where he works on UN policies in the fields of international development and peace and security. He previously worked as a producer at NHK News' Washington bureau, where he covered the State Department and US foreign policy. He holds an MSc in sustainability, development, and peace from the United Nations University, and a BA in journalism and mass communications from the George Washington University.